All Things Strings

An Illustrated Dictionary

Jo Nardolillo

Illustrations by T. M. Larsen

ROWMAN & LITTLEFIELD
Lanham • Boulder • New York • Toronto • Plymouth, UK

Published by Rowman & Littlefield
4501 Forbes Boulevard, Suite 200, Lanham, Maryland 20706
www.rowman.com

10 Thornbury Road, Plymouth PL6 7PP, United Kingdom

British Library Cataloguing in Publication Information Available

Library of Congress Cataloging-in-Publication Data
Nardolillo, Jo, 1972– author.
  All things strings : an illustrated dictionary / Jo Nardolillo ; illustrations by T. M. Larsen.
    pages ; cm
  Includes bibliographical references.
  ISBN 978-0-8108-8443-4 (cloth : alk. paper) – ISBN 978-0-8108-8444-1 (ebook) 1. Bowed
stringed instruments–Dictionaries. I. Larsen, T. M., illustrator. II. Title.
  ML108.N373 2013
  787.03–dc23   2013007904

To Christophe Chagnard

Contents

Foreword

Jo Nardolillo has done it again. Her 2011 book, *The Canon of Violin Literature*, was hailed as "a well-researched and comprehensive resource for the performer, teacher and advanced student-violinist . . . a valuable and broad resource of the violin literature."

Now this brilliant author and violinist writes for all string players—violin, viola, cello, and double bass—and all styles, from jazz to bluegrass to country-western fiddle music to early music. Her range is the whole world of string playing. *All Things Strings: An Illustrated Dictionary* will find its place at the side of the veteran performer, the experienced teacher, the avid student, and even the curious intermediate player.

David Daniels, editor

Acknowledgments

David Daniels, author of the conductor's bible *Orchestral Music* and my editor, whose insightful suggestions and lively challenges provided the greatest source of pleasure in researching and writing this book. It is a far better resource for the tireless work he put into every entry.

T. M. Larsen, one of the Pacific Northwest's finest double bassists and creator of the beautiful illustrations found throughout this book, who effortlessly captured the essence of each concept with elegant simplicity.

Sarah Mattox and **Cordelia Wikarski-Miedel**, two of Seattle's preeminent musicians and my dearest friends, whose incredible generosity made this project possible.

Christophe Chagnard, composer and conductor, my esteemed colleague and my treasured husband, who has been solidly behind me with unwavering enthusiasm from the very beginning.

Introduction

String players face a bewildering mass of vocabulary relating to our instruments and techniques. Because string playing is a living art form passed directly from a master of the instrument to the student, the words used to convey complex concepts such as bow technique or fingering systems have developed into an extensive vocabulary that is complicated, often vague, and even contradictory. Most of these terms are in French, Italian, or German, and few of them are included in any standard music dictionary. In addition, the gulf separating classical playing from other genres of music, including fiddle, bluegrass, and jazz, has led to the development of style-specific terminology that has not previously been codified into any reference.

All Things Strings: An Illustrated Dictionary offers a comprehensive guide to the terminology used by violin, viola, cello, and double bass, inclusive of all genres and playing styles. Entries cover techniques from shifting to fingerboard mapping to thumb position; the entire gamut of bowstrokes; terms found in orchestral parts; instrument structure and repair; accessories and equipment; ornaments including those used in jazz and bluegrass; explanation of various bow holds; conventions of orchestral playing; and types of strings. Organized alphabetically, the terms are defined in dictionary style with an emphasis on the relevance for string players. Every term is formatted according to current academic standards, indicating the correct use of italics and capitalization as well as the spellings appropriate for program notes, papers, and other musicological writing.

In addition, *All Things Strings* includes short biographies for a select number of famous luthiers, influential pedagogues, and legendary performers. These luminaries have been chosen because they have made a major contribution to the development of their instrument that extends well beyond their career and lifetime. I offer my apologies to the many greats who are not found within these pages (in particular my favorite, the incomparable David Oistrakh). Referenced in the Further Reading section at the end of this volume are several excellent books featuring full biographies of an extensive list of superstar virtuosos and beloved teachers of string instruments.

The elegant illustrations found throughout *All Things Strings* were created by T. M. Larsen, a highly accomplished double bass player whose personal experience as a musician provided unique insight into the nature of each term. All musical examples have been drawn from the standard literature.

All Things Strings is designed to be used in several ways. Like any dictionary, it is a resource for looking up the meanings of words found in music and the various terms used by fellow musicians, teachers, and conductors. By using the book in this way, the reader may learn the meaning of new words, gain a deeper insight into terms that are already familiar, and be able to look up the particular vocabulary used by musicians working in other genres. In addition, *All Things Strings* offers two paths for exploring the extensive terminology specific to playing string instruments. By following the "see also" recommendations at the end of many entries, the reader may follow a map from term to term, exploring the intricate relationships between ideas and discovering new concepts in the process. And with its large page size and beautiful illustrations by T. M. Larsen, *All Things Strings* is a pleasure to simply open and browse.

Jo Nardolillo

Pitch Chart

All Things Strings uses the Acoustical Society of America (ASA) system of pitch notation. This chart is a guide to understanding the ASA system in relation to the grand staff, the piano keyboard, and the range of each instrument in the modern string family.

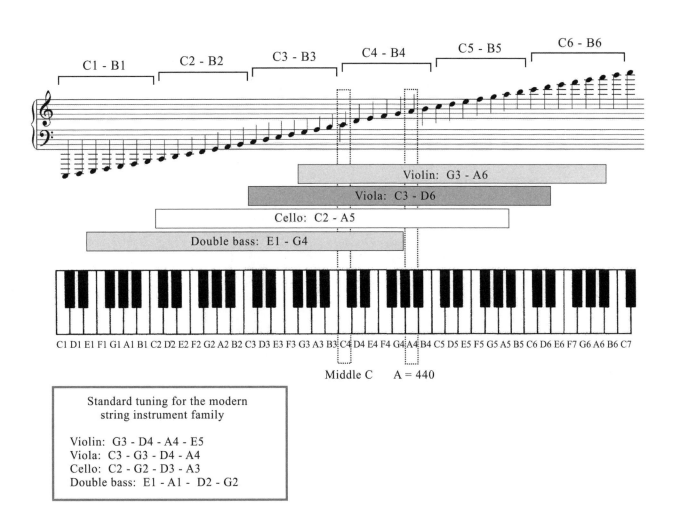

The Dictionary

8va. (It.) *Ottava alta.* Play an octave higher than notated. 8va may also be notated simply 8. 8va *bassa* means **8vb,** or play an octave lower.

8vb. (It.) *Ottava bassa.* Play an octave lower than notated. 8vb may also be notated 8va *bassa* or 8va *sotto.*

~ A ~

a due. (It.) Play in two parts. See **divisi.**

à la corda. (Fr.) Play on one **string.**

a piacere. (It.) Play freely, as you like.

a punta d'arco. (It.) Play at the **tip** of the **bow.**

a una corda. (It.) Play on a single **string.** The indication *a una corda* may be followed by a roman numeral indicating which string is desired: IV. for the lowest string to I. for the highest string.

abdämpfen. (Ger.) Play with a **mute.**

abgesetzt. (Ger.) Separated, *staccato,* or with a **retake.** See *abgestossen,* *détaché,* **lifted bowstroke,** and **articulation.**

abgestossen. (Ger.) *Staccato.*

abgezucht. (Ger.) *Détaché.*

above fingers. A 20th-century technique of bowing the **string** between the fingers and the **nut,** creating a muted sound. Abbreviated AF.

absetzen. (Ger.) To play with separated, *staccato* **bowstrokes** or, when found in the phrase *Dämpfer absetzen,* to remove the **mute.**

absolute pitch. See **perfect pitch.**

abstossen. (Ger.) Play with separation between notes. See *staccato.*

Abstrich. (Ger.) **Down-bow.**

accent. To emphasize a particular note. An accent can be created using **articulation, dynamics,** or **vibrato.** See **articulation** for a list of specific accent markings and their meanings, and **agogic accent** for information about using the broadening of time to emphasize a note.

accidental. An indication to chromatically modify a pitch in relation to the key signature. The sharp raises the pitch a **half-step,** the double sharp raises the pitch a **whole-step,** the flat lowers the pitch a half-step, and the double flat lowers the pitch a whole-step. The natural cancels any other accidentals, even those indicated by the key signature. Accidentals traditionally modify every note of a pitch class for the remainder of the measure, including the same note in a different octave, though this rule may not apply to works by contemporary composers writing outside standard key systems. See also **quarter tone** and **microtone.**

accompagnato. (It.) Play beneath and in support of the primary melody when accompanying a soloist.

accordaura. (It.) Play in **standard tuning,** as opposed to *scordatura.*

Acer. The genus of trees commonly known as **maple.**

acoustic. Without electronic amplification. See also **acoustics.**

acoustic bass. A **bass guitar** with a hollow body. Sometimes the term acoustic bass refers to a **double bass.**

acoustic enhancement. The use of subtle amplification during an **acoustic** performance. See also **amplifier** and **pickup.**

acoustics.
   1. The scientific study of the physics of sound and **sound waves**.
   2. The characteristics of how sound behaves in a particular space.

action. The height of the **strings** over the **fingerboard**. The action is determined by the height and curve of **bridge**, the height of the **nut**, and the amount of concave **scoop** in the fingerboard. An action that is too high will make pressing down the **strings** down difficult and may affect **intonation**, while an action that is too low will cause the strings to **buzz** against the fingerboard. Finding the correct action is part of an instrument **adjustment**.

ad libitum. (Lat.) Freely, at the discretion of the performer; e.g., "**8va** *ad libitum*" means to play up an octave if you wish. *Ad libitum* can also be an indication to **improvise**.

adjustable bridge. See **bridge adjuster**.

adjuster. See **fine tuner**.

adjustment. The precise arranging of the materials and placement of the various pieces of an instrument which have an impact on the **tone**. A **luthier** will perform an instrument adjustment to help find the optimal tone, improve playability, and maintain the overall health of the instrument. Work done during an adjustment includes aligning the **strings**, **bridge**, **neck**, **tailpiece**, **endpin**, and **nut**; repositioning, reshaping, or replacing the **soundpost**; reshaping the contour, height, and fit of the bridge; planing the **fingerboard**; reshaping or replacing the nut; adjusting the **tailgut** and **afterlength**; replacing the tailpiece; **rebushing** or replacing the **pegs**; and cleaning the instrument. Professional players take their instruments to a **luthier** for adjustment at least once a year. An adjustment is also called an instrument adjustment or a tonal adjustment.

affections, doctrine of. The baroque theory of musical aesthetics placing emphasis on the power of music to evoke emotions. Theorists and composers believed that particular techniques in rhythm, melody, and harmony could produce prescribed emotions in the audience. Known as "affections," these were not the personal emotional expressions of the composer but rather universal emotional states. It was thought that each piece or movement should focus on portraying a single affection. Knowing the association between musical techniques and the emotions they are intended to convey can be very useful to a musician in developing a personal interpretation of a baroque piece.

The ideas of the doctrine of affections were codified in 1739 in Johann Mattheson's book *Der vollkommene Capellmeister*. See also **historically informed performance**.

affetuoso. (It.) Play with tenderness and affection.

affrettando. (It.) Hurrying.

afterlength. The section of **string** between the **bridge** and the **tailpiece**. The afterlength is usually tuned in a sympathetic ratio to the string length, enhancing the **resonance** of the instrument. Changing the tailpiece or **tailgut** length to create the ideal afterlength is one element of an instrument **adjustment**. Adding a **fine tuner** can shorten the afterlength, potentially damping resonance.

agitato. (It.) Play with agitation and excitement.

agogic accent. To emphasize a note by delaying it or extending it beyond its normal duration. See also **accent** and **phrasing**.

agréments. (Fr.) **Ornaments**.

air. A melody or a song.

air varié. (Fr.) A set of variations on a song.

ajaeng. (Kor.) A Korean bowed **string instrument** similar to a zither. The *ajaeng* has seven **strings** of twisted silk that run over a large **bridge** on the right across seven small bridges that are moved to adjust **tuning**, to cross a second large bridge on the left. The instrument is played horizontally, propped up on a small stand with the player seated on the floor at the right end. The *ajaeng* player presses on the strings with the left hand and **bows** the far end of the strings with a **rosined** stick. The *ajaeng* has been used in court music **ensembles** for many centuries, often paired with the *haegŭm*, a Koren relative of the *erhu*. The *sanjo ajaeng*, a smaller version of the *ajaeng* with eight strings, is played in a **virtuosic** style, often with a **horsehair** bow in place of the stick.

Alard, Jean-Delphin (1815-1888). French violinist and composer. Alard, considered a child prodigy, was sponsored at age twelve to study at the Paris Conservatoire under Habeneck. As a soloist, Alard garnered praise from **Paganini** and was chosen to perform Mendelssohn's violin **concerto** in the composer's 1848 memorial concert. Alard performed regularly as a member of his own **string quartet** and served as **concertmaster** of King Louis Philippe's

Royal Orchestra and Napoléon III's Imperial Orchestra. Alard succeeded **Baillot** as professor of **violin** at the Paris Conservatoire, where he taught from 1843 to 1875. In this role, Alard wrote his violin treatise *Ecole du violon: méthode complète et progressive* [Studies for the violin: A complete and progressive method] and produced many successful students, including **Pablo de Sarasate**.

Alexander Technique. An educational method of teaching posture, balance, and movement to eliminate unnecessary physical **tension**. Alexander Technique is based on the ideas of Frederick Matthias Alexander, who developed the method in the 1890's to eliminate the hoarseness he experienced as a Shakespearean actor. Musicians who study Alexander Technique are seeking to learn how to stand, sit, and play in a naturally aligned, relaxed posture. See the website of the American Society for the Alexander Technique for more detailed information. See also **ergonomics**, **ergonomic instrument**, **Feldenkrais method**, and **kinesthetic**.

all' ottava. (It.) At the octave, either higher or lower. See also **8va** and **8vb**.

Alle. (Ger.) Tutti, everyone.

allein. (Ger.) Unaccompanied, **solo**.

allemande. (Fr.) A stylized dance in moderate 4/4 time, used as the first movement of a baroque **suite**.

Altgeige. (Ger.) A large **viola** with a fifth string created by Hermann Ritter in the late 19th century, also called *viola alta* or tenor violin.

alto. A term for the **viola**.

alto clef. The C clef which places middle C on the center line of the staff. The alto clef is used almost exclusively for the **viola**.

alto violin. See **vertical viola**.

alzare l'arco. (It.) To lift the **bow**.

am. (Ger.) At, found in bowing directions such as *am Frosch*, meaning at the **frog**, or *am Griffbrett*, meaning at the **fingerboard**.

am Frosch. (Ger.) Play at the **frog**. Also called *au talon* (Fr.).

am Griffbrett. (Ger.) Play over the **fingerboard**. See *sul tasto*.

am Steg. (Ger.) Play near the **bridge**. See *ponticello*.

Amati family. A family of celebrated **luthiers** in Cremona during the 16th and 17th centuries. Andrea Amati (ca. 1505-1578) founded the Cremonese school of violin making, creating the modern **violin family**. His instruments are the earliest surviving violins. Andrea Amati was succeeded by his sons Antonio Amati (ca. 1537-1607) and Girolamo Amati (ca. 1551-1630), who are known as the brothers Amati. The most famous of the dynasty is Andrea's grandson Nicolò Amati (1596-1684), whose pupils included **Antonio Stradivari** and **Andrea Guarneri**. Antoni's son Girolamo Amati (1649-1740), known as Hieronymus II, was the last of the family line, making instruments considered inferior to those of his predecessors.

amp, amplifier. An electronic device that converts an electric signal from an instrument into a signal strong enough to be broadcast through a loudspeaker, commonly called an amp. An amplifier requires use of a **pickup** or microphone to capture the sound and convert it into an electric signal. Amplifiers designed specifically for **string instruments** are called **acoustic** amps, and may include **feedback** reduction, additional reverb, and **tone** controls. The use of an amplifier is extremely rare in **art music** but quite common in the other **genres**. See also **acoustic enhancement**.

amplitude. The height of a **sound wave**, indicating volume. The taller the amplitude of the sound wave, the louder the sound.

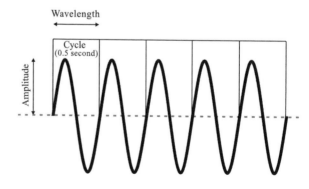

Figure 1. **Amplitude** as measured on the sound wave.

annular rings. Growth lines in wood. Close annular rings indicate a dense piece of wood, which is believed to produce a more beautiful **tone**. See also **flaming** and **bearclaw**.

anreissen. (Ger.) Play with a forceful attack. See also **accent** and **articulation**.

Anstrich. (Ger.) **Up-bow**.

antinode. The point where the **amplitude** of a **sound wave** is at maximum. See **sound wave** for an illustration.

antiquing. The technique of making a new instrument look old by creating chips, scratches, wear marks, and cracks in the **varnish**.

aperto. (It.) Open and clear.

apoyando. (Sp.) A *pizzicato* technique in which the plucking finger finishes by coming to rest on a neighboring **string**, creating a deliberate, controlled movement. *Apoyando* is frequently used by **jazz double bass** players when plucking the string with the sides of the fingers. On **violin** and **viola**, *apoyando* usually produces a more articulated, less resonant **tone** than standard *pizzicato* technique.

appoggiatura. (It.) A type of **ornament**, named for the verb *appoggiare*, meaning "to lean on." The *appoggiatura* has appeared with many different names, notations, and meanings, and it continues to be the subject of musicological debate. In essence, the *appoggiatura* is a non-harmonic pitch played on a strong beat and resolved stepwise to the principal note.

The *appoggiatura* may be notated in small font as a type of **grace note** which shares the value with the note it ornaments. For example, if the *appoggiatura* is notated as a tiny note attached to an eighth note, both notes would become equal 16th notes, with the *appoggiatura* occurring on the beat. If this type of *appoggiatura* is attached to a dotted note, making an equal division impossible, the ornament receives the first two-thirds of the principal note's value. If there are two such grace notes, they are a double *appoggiatura*, with the first of the ornamental notes played on the beat. *Appoggiaturas* are notated in this manner to make the basic harmony visually clear, information which players may be using to guide their own improvisation and ornamentation. The use of stems, flags, and slashed stems on grace note *appoggiaturas* is inconsistent, varies widely, and is often not the mark of the composer but rather the result of a particular engraver's style of shorthand. Additionally, *appoggiaturas* are not always notated as grace notes. Often they are already written into the rhythm of the

bar, or they may remain completely unnotated, being simply implied by the style of the piece.

Figure 2a. *Appoggiaturas* and double *appoggiaturas* from W.A. Mozart's ***Rondo: Alla Turca***, K 311, mm 1-7.

Figure 2b. The realization of the ***appoggiaturas*** and double *appoggiaturas* from W.A. Mozart's ***Rondo: Alla Turca***, K 311, mm 1-7.

Arányi, Jelly d' (1893-1966). Hungarian violinist whose flashy **technique** and gypsy **bravura** inspired important compositions including Bartók's two **violin sonatas** and Ravel's *Tzigane*. Arányi studied in Budapest with Jenõ Hubay, toured Europe and America as a soloist often in concert with her sister Adila Fachiri, and performed **recitals** with Béla Bartók.

arcata. (It.) **Bowstroke**, often followed by the words *in giù*, for **down-bow**, or *in su*, for **up-bow**.

arcato. (It.) Played with the **bow**. See *arco*.

archet. (Fr.) The **bow**, commonly used in the phrases *au milieu de l'archet*, in the middle of the bow; *tout l'archet*, with the whole bow; *bout d'archet*, tip of the bow; and *coup d'archet*, **bowstroke**.

archetier. (Fr.) **Bow** maker.

arching. The hand-carved, convex curve of the front and back **plates** of an instrument, designed to provide structural support under the weight of the **strings** on the **bridge**.

arco. (It.) Play with the **bow**. *Arco* usually appears in music to indicate the end of a *pizzicato* passage.

arm vibrato. A vibrato technique on **string instruments** in which the pitch oscillation is created by forearm movement using the elbow as the pivot point. On the **cello** and **double bass**, arm vibrato is used exclusively. See **hand vibrato** and **finger vibrato** for other vibrato techniques used on **violin** and **viola**. See also **vibrato**.

armonici. (It.) See **harmonics**.

arpeggiando. (It.) To play a chord in **arpeggiation** at the performer's discretion. The most famous *arpeggiando* passage is found in J. S. Bach's **Chaconne** from the **Partita** no. 2 for solo violin.

arpeggiation. The technique of playing the notes of a **chord** in rapid succession rather than simultaneously. Also called a rolled chord, the term arpeggiation is derived from the Italian *arpeggiare*, meaning "to play on a harp." Arpeggiation can be notated by a wavy vertical line adjacent to the chord, though most often it is simply implied, since an unbroken four-note chord is impossible on bowed **string instruments**. Depending on personal interpretive style, a performer may choose to break the chord rather than arpeggiate it, and convention dictates that the notes of arpeggiated or broken chords be played from low to high. See also **chord**, **broken chord**, and **voiceleading**.

arpeggio. The notes of a **chord** played in succession rather than simultaneously. Practicing arpeggios is one of the foundational **technique** exercises for all string players. See also **springing arpeggio**.

arpeggione. An unusual bowed **string instrument** designed by guitar **luthier** Johann Staufer in 1823. Also called a bowed guitar, or guitar **cello**, the arpeggione has six **strings** which are tuned E2 – A2 – D3 – G3 – B3 – E4 like a classical guitar, a guitar-shaped body, and a **fretted fingerboard**. The instrument is held vertically between the knees and bowed like a **viol**. Although the arpeggione was not well received in a time when the viol was already going out of fashion in favor of the brighter, louder instruments of the **violin family**, Franz Schubert's celebrated *Sonata for Arpeggione and Fortepiano*, D. 821, has remained in the repertoire in adaptations for **viola** and **cello**. Recently the arpeggione has enjoyed a revival through the **historically informed performance** movement of the late 20th century. The arpeggione is also called the *guitarre d'amour* (Fr.), and the *Sentiment, Bogenguitar*, or *Violoncellguitarre* (Ger.).

Figure 3. The **arpeggione**.

arraché. (Fr.) Forceful **pizzicato**, from the French word for "torn."

arrangement. The adaptation of a composition into a new form, usually to accommodate performance by instruments for which the piece was not originally intended, or as a simplification to allow the work to be accessible to more players. Unlike a **transcription** or an **orchestration** which remain as true to the original composition as possible, an arrangement may include reworked melodic material, reharmonization, or structural changes. Portions of the original composition may be omitted and substantial new materials may be added when creating the arrangement. See also **transcription**, **orchestration**, and **reduction**.

art music. The music of the Western classical tradition, intended as serious art and distinguished from folk music or popular music. Often referred to as "classical music," art music is characterized by complexity of thematic development, **phrasing**, harmonization, modulation, texture, and a highly sophisticated use of form. Art music is also distinguished by an expectation of focused attention from the listener. Unlike popular or folk music, a work of art music is defined by the notated version rather than a particular performance. This practice of using a notated score enables the composer to create intricate works on a large scale and to preserve and communicate these works in great detail.

Although **jazz** is usually categorized as a type of popular music, it has been argued that some forms of jazz could be considered art music.

The term "art music" is preferable to "classical music," as it distinguishes it from music from the Classical Era (generally 1750-1820).

articulation. The amount and type of definition given to a note. On **string instruments**, articulation is achieved mainly by the bow. In general, *staccato* bow strokes give notes a clear articulation, especially when accented, while **legato** bowstrokes provide a gentler articulation. Various combinations of **bow speed**, **contact point**, and **bowstrokes** can create a large variety of articulations. The degree of articulation for notes connected under slurs can also be affected by the **finger angle** and force of impact from the left hand.

Like many aspects of written music, articulation markings have evolved over time to have a variety of meanings depending on the era in which the music was written and the particular design of instrument or equipment being used. String players wishing to thoroughly understand a composer's intentions behind articulation markings should consult books specific to the era or composer of any given piece of music. (See the bibliography at the back of this text for books of particular value to string players.)

The general, modern interpretation of articulation symbols includes two kinds of information: how a note should begin, indicated by a variety of accents, and how a note should end, indicated by dots or dashes.

Markings for **accents** include symbols placed over the note-head, such as any of these:

Accents can also be indicated by directions placed below the staff, such as:

sfz   *rfz*   *sf*

Depending on the era and composer, even the *f* usually interpreted as a *forte* dynamic or the *staccato* dot over a note-head can be indications of accents.

A dot over the note-head indicates that the note should be played *staccato*, that is, detached from the note that follows. (The common interpretation of a dot as a direction to play the note "short" is an oversimplification because the exact length of any detached note is an interpretive choice that depends on tempo, style, dynamics, and many other considerations.) String players achieve this detached articulation either by stopping the bow on the string or by removing the bow from the string altogether. At a slower tempo, this may be accomplished by using an **on-the-string** bowstroke such as *détaché lancé*, or *martelé*. In fast passage work, dots over notes are usually achieved with an **off-the-string** bowstroke such as *spiccato* or *sautillé*. Dots in combination with a **slur** mean to detach the notes without changing the direction of the bow, accomplished by bowstrokes including a **hooked bow**, **flying** *staccato*, or *jeté*.

A dash or *tenuto* line over a note-head has two somewhat contradictory meanings. The dash may indicate that the note should be played *legato*, that is, smoothly connected to the note that follows. Depending on the context, the dash may even mean that the note should be played with an **agogic accent**, lasting slightly longer than its portion of the rhythm. Contrary to that, the dash may also indicate that the note should be played *portato*, with a leaning into the note and a slight detachment from the note that follows. When combined with a slur, the dash means to make a slight, pulsed separation between notes without changing bow.

artificial harmonics. High overtones created by stopping the **string** with one finger and lightly touching the string at a precise spot with another finger. The most common artificial harmonic is at the interval of the fourth, created by touching the string a perfect fourth above the **fundamental**, producing a pitch two octaves higher than the stopped note. An artificial harmonic can also be created by lightly touching a perfect fifth above the stopped note, producing a pitch one octave and a fifth above the stopped note. It is also possible to play an artificial harmonic at the major third above the stopped note, producing a pitch two octaves above the touched note, but these are rare.

On **violin** and **viola**, artificial harmonics are played with the first finger stopping the **string** at any point and the fourth finger touching lightly a perfect fourth or fifth higher. On **cello** the string is stopped with the thumb and the harmonic is activated with the third finger. False harmonics, particularly those at the third, are possible but very rare on **double bass.**

Artificial harmonics are notated with a solid note-head for the stopped pitch and a **diamond note-head** for the harmonic. Artificial harmonics are sometimes called false harmonics or stopped harmonics. See also **harmonics** and **natural harmonics.**

Figure 4. **Artificial harmonics** from **Pablo de Sarasate**'s *Navarra* op. 33, solo violin 1, mm 298-301.

assai. (It.) Very, used to intensify the term it modifies, e.g., *allegro assai,* meaning "very fast."

Atempause. (Ger.) See *Luftpause.*

atonal. Using a system of musical composition that is independent of the rules of functional harmony.

attaca. (It.) Continue immediately without pause.

au chevalet. (Fr.) To **bow** on or near the **bridge.** See **ponticello.**

au talon. (Fr.) **Bow** at the **frog.**

Auer, Leopold (1845-1930). Hungarian-American violinist renowned for his legacy of star students. After studying **violin** with Jakob Dont and **Joseph Joachim,** Auer's performance career centered on his **concertmaster** position at the St. Petersburg Imperial Theatrers, where noted composers including Tchaikovsky and Glazunov created **solo** parts in their ballets just for Auer. Both composers also dedicated their violin **concertos** to Auer, who premiered the Glazunov concerto in 1905, but famously refused to premiere the Tchaikovsky concerto, claiming it was unviolinistic. Auer's **pedagogical** work began at the St. Petersburg **Conservatory** in 1868, and then continued in the United States in 1918, where he taught in New York and eventually joined the faculty of the Curtis Institute of Music. His legacy of students includes Mischa Elman, **Jascha Heifetz,** Nathan Milstein, and Efrem Zimbalist. Auer's book *Violin Playing as I Teach It* (1920) remains an important treatise, and numerous editions of the great violin works are still published with Auer's **fingerings, bowings,** and **cadenzas,** including his own revised version of the Tchaikovsky concerto.

auf dem Steg. (Ger.) Play on or near the **bridge.** See *ponticello.*

aufheben. (Ger.) To lift, as in to lift the **bow** from the **string.** See **lifted bowstroke** and **retake.**

Aufstrich. (Ger.) **Up-bow.**

ausdrucksvoll. (Ger.) Expressively, with feeling.

authentic performance. See **historically informed performance.**

axe. A term of endearment for one's instrument. Also spelled ax.

~ B ~

B extension. An extra length of **fingerboard** added to the E string of a **double bass,** built over the **pegbox.** The B extension extends the lower range of the instrument by five pitches, allowing for a low B. See also **C extension.**

baby bass. A design of **electric upright bass** with a full-sized wooden **neck** paired with a **cello**-sized plastic body.

Bach bow. A modern **bow** innovation featuring a highly curved **stick** and a **lever** mechanism on the **frog,** allowing the hair **tension** to be loosened while playing to engage all four **strings** simultaneously. Also called a polyphonic bow, various Bach bow designs include Albert Schweitzer's Curved Bow, **luthier** Knud Vestergaard's Vega Bach Bow, and cellist Michael Bach's BACH.Bogen.

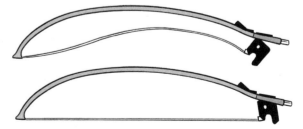

Figure 5. A **Bach bow** with released and tightened **hair tension.**

Bach, Carl Philipp Emanuel (1714-1788). German composer and clavier player, second son of **Johann Sebastian Bach,** and important figure in the transition from Baroque to Classical styles. C. P. E. Bach studied at St. Thomas in Leipzig, where his father was cantor, then enjoyed a successful career as one of the foremost clavier players in Europe and as a prolific composer employed in the court of Frederick the Great of Prussia. For string players wanting to understand how to perform music of the late Baroque and early Classical eras, C. P. E. Bach's systematic treatise *An Essay on the True Art of Playing Keyboard Instruments* offers a particularly helpful chapter explaining the execution of **trills**, **turns**, **mordents**, and other **ornaments**.

Bach, Johann Sebastian (1685-1750). German composer, organist, and instrumentalist whose works for **solo violin** and solo **cello** have become the foundational core of the standard **repertoire**. As the central figure in a family of musicians, Bach probably learned to play **string instruments** from his father. Bach's first employment was as a violinist in the court at Weimar, an **orchestra** where he eventually served as **concertmaster** from 1714 to 1717. Though his career was centered around the organ and he was known in his own time primarily as a keyboard **virtuoso**, Bach's duties always included playing and teaching string instruments. According to his son **C. P. E. Bach**, J. S. Bach loved to play the **viola** in **chamber music** and usually directed the orchestra not from the keyboard but from his violin as concertmaster.

Bach's great contribution to string playing is his compositions. His Brandenburg concertos, violin **concertos** in A minor and E major, and double concerto for two violins are standards in the **repertoire**, but it is his music for unaccompanied violin and cello, works of such complexity and virtuosity that they could only have been crafted by a master of the instrument, that has fascinated and inspired generations of artists.

The six **sonatas** and **partitas** for solo violin encompass a wide spectrum of **polyphonic** playing, including three fugues and the monumental **chaconne**. The pieces were completed by 1720 but not published until 1802, and they were only brought to the concert stage when the celebrated violinist **Joachim** started performing them at the end of the 19th century. Requiring the highest level of skill in left-hand **technique**, bow work, and personal artistry, Bach's violin solos have become the benchmark of violin mastery and are required pieces to audition for and graduate from any major **conservatory** or school of music.

The six **suites** for solo cello are the heart of the standard repertoire for cello and **viola**, and they are increasingly played on **double bass**. Like the violin solos, the cello suites were brought to the concert repertoire long after their composition when **Casals** made the first recording of the works in 1925. The

suites have since become the measure of cellists and violists for conservatory and professional auditions. Unlike the violin, the cello was a relatively new instrument during Bach's life, and he was the first to write unaccompanied virtuosic music for it. Musicologists believe that some or all of the cello suites may have been intended for *viola da spalla*, *violoncello piccolo*, or *viola pomposa*, particularly the sixth suite which included a **tuning** indication for five **strings**.

Bach's six violin solos and six cello suites are beloved favorites widely studied, performed, and recorded by generations of artists, and have inspired many new solo works including those by Bartók, Britten, and **Ysaÿe**.

back plate. The thin piece of carved wood that is the underside of the instrument. The back plate is hand carved from either a single slab or two matching halves of **maple** or another hardwood, and includes the **button** which attaches to the **heel** of the **neck**. On the **violin**, **viola**, and **cello**, the back plate is shaped into a convex arch to add strength to the structure of the instrument. The **double bass** may also have an arched back plate, or it may have a **viol**-like flat back plate with an upper **break** and three to six reinforcing **braces** inside for support. See also **top plate** and **plate** for an illustration.

backup. Playing accompaniment to the lead instrument or singer, particularly in the **genres** of rock, country, **jazz**, **bluegrass**, and folk. An **ensemble** of musicians playing backup is called a backing band or backup band, which can either be an established band or a **pickup** group of **session** musicians.

Baillot, Pierre (1771-1842). French violinist, pedagogue, and composer best known for his treatise on **violin** playing. Baillot was a student of **Viotti** and launched his career with a well-received public performance of one of Viotti's **concertos**. As an orchestral musician, Baillot served as **principal** second in Napoleon's private **orchestra** and was **concertmaster** of the Paris Opéra and the Chapelle Royale. Baillot had great success in one of the first **chamber music** groups of all professional musicians, touring extensively throughout Europe, England, and Russia, performing the **quartets** and **quintets** of **Boccherini**, Haydn, Mozart, and Beethoven. As a soloist, Baillot often performed his own works and those of his contemporaries, which he paired with rediscovered music of old masters, including **J. S. Bach**, **Corelli**, and **Tartini**.

A prolific composer, Baillot wrote largely for violin, including nine concertos, as well as many **duets**, **string quartets**, **études**, and various pieces for violin and piano, none of which remain in the standard **repertoire**.

The great legacy of Baillot is in his work as a **pedagogue**. Along with **Kreutzer** and **Rode**, Baillot created the violin method for the newly opened Paris Conservatoire, where he served as a professor of violin beginning in 1795. Among his many students were Mazas, Dancla, and Habeneck, who went on to be master teachers themselves, creating a lineage through **Flesch** and Galamian to many of the 20th century's virtuoso players, and making Baillot a crucial link between Viotti and numerous great violinists to follow. In his treatise, *L'art du violon* [The Art of the Violin], Baillot documented the 19th-century conventions of **fingering**, **bowing**, **ornamentation**, and expression, complete with a comparison between what he called the "old" and "modern" styles of violin playing. Baillot's book, still published and recently translated into English, stands as one of the most significant documents for understanding the development of violin **technique** and is a vital guide for anyone involved in **historically informed performance**.

balance point. The place on a **bow** at which the weight is equal on both sides. The balance point of a **bow** can be found by setting the **stick** on a finger and then moving it until it balances evenly. On a modern bow, the balance point, as measured from the end of the wood where the stick meets the **screw button**, is usually about 9.5 inches for a **violin** or **viola** bow, about 8.5 inches for a **cello** bow, about 8 inches for a **French bass bow**, and about 7.5 inches for a **German bass bow**. Knowing the balance point is crucial to executing rapid string crossings and mastering bowstrokes such as **bariolage**, **spiccato**, *sautillé*, and *ricochet*.

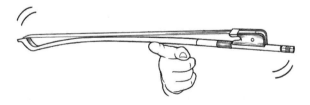

Figure 6. Finding the **balance point** of a **bow**.

balancement. (Fr.) **Tremolo** or **vibrato**.

ball end. The small metal ball at the end of a **string**, used to anchor it into the slotted hole of the **tailpiece**. For use with **fine tuners**, the ball can usually be pried out, leaving just a loop at the end of the string. See also **string**.

ballad. A slow, sentimental song.

bariolage. A technique of rapid alternation between a moving line and a static note, often an **open string**, creating a dazzling virtuosic effect. Bariolage was particularly popular in the Baroque era.

Figure 7. **Bariolage** from J. S. Bach's Partita no. 3 for **solo violin**, **BWV** 1006, Preludio, mm 13-14.

baroque bow. A **bow** with the design that was used in the Baroque era (1600-1750). The baroque bow is shorter than the modern **Tourte** design, and is characterized by a **snakewood** stick with a straight or even slightly convex **cambre**, an elongated **tip**, and an open **frog**. Historically, baroque bows had **clip-in frogs**, though many of those made today use a more modern **screw** mechanism for adjusting the hair **tension**. Baroque bows are used in **historically informed performance**. See also **baroque instrument**, **bow**, and **gamba bow**.

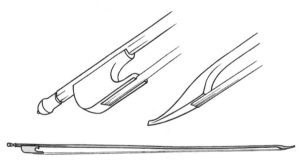

Figure 8: A **baroque bow** with a detail of the **tip** and **frog**.

baroque cello. A **cello** with the same structure as was used in the Baroque era (1600-1750). See **baroque instrument**.

baroque instrument. An instrument with the same structure and materials as were used in the Baroque era (1600-1750). A baroque instrument can be an original instrument that has not been converted to modern, a new instrument made to baroque specifications, or even an old instrument which has been reconverted back to the earlier model. Using baroque instruments to perform music of their era has grown increasingly popular as part of the **historically informed performance** or HIP movement.

Baroque **string instruments** have a number of characteristics that distinguish them from modern instruments. They use a **bridge** that is lower, thicker, and more open, and inside the **bass bar** is smaller. The **neck** is generally parallel to the **plate**, not tilted back like a modern instrument, and the veneered **fingerboard** is wider at the **nut** and does not extend as far over the **belly**. The **tailpiece** is flatter, has no **saddle**, and its string holes are not keyed with slits. Baroque instruments use **gut strings** and are played without modern inventions such as **fine tuners**, **chin rests**, **shoulder rests**, and **endpins**.

Violas and **cellos** built during the Baroque era were larger than their modern counterparts, and many surviving instruments have been cut down as part of their modernization. The baroque **double bass** was made in a wide array of sizes and shapes, with varying numbers of strings and tunings, and was called by many different names. See the bibliography at the end of this text for recommended resources exploring the complex history of baroque string instruments and their performance.

See also **baroque bow**, **historically informed performance**, and **gamba bow**.

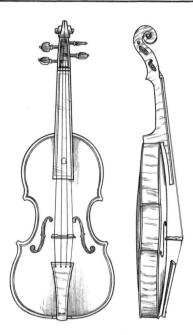

Figure 9b. A **baroque violin**.

baroque pitch. The system of tuning used in **historically informed performance**, centering around A4 = 415 Hz, a **half-step** lower than modern **standard tuning** of A4 = 440 Hz. This generally accepted baroque pitch is only one of many possibilities, as tuning varied widely depending on the particular time and location, until it was standardized in 1859.

baroque violin. A **violin** with the same structure as was used in the Baroque era (1600-1750). See **baroque instrument**.

Bartók *pizzicato*. To pluck the **string** in such a way that it snaps back against the **fingerboard**, producing a percussive pop. Bartók *pizzicato* is indicated by this symbol:

baryton. A bowed **string instrument** of the **viol family**, with six or seven **gut strings** over a **fretted fingerboard** and as many as twenty metal strings lying behind the **neck**. These metal strings resonate sympathetically while the baryton is being played and can be plucked or strummed by the thumb. Like a bass **viol**, the baryton is held vertically, supported by the player's legs.

The best known repertoire for the baryton includes the more than 170 compositions written by Franz Joseph Haydn for his patron, Prince Nikolaus Esterházy, who played the instrument. Although the baryton lost

Figure 9a. A **baroque cello** held without an **endpin**.

popularity during the 19th century, the **historically informed performance** movement of the late 20th century has brought a revival to the instrument.

bass. See **double bass**.

bass bib. See **bib**.

bass fiddle. See **double bass**.

bass guitar. A guitar with four low **strings** tuned like a **double bass** (E1 – A1 – D2 – G2). The bass guitar is most often a solid-bodied **electric instrument**, though **acoustic** bass guitars are made with heavy bass strings stretched over a hollow guitar resonator. The electric bass guitar was invented by Fender in 1951 to offer a louder, more portable instrument to double bass players in dance bands. With a solid wood body, **fretted fingerboard**, and **magnetic pickup**, the electric bass is shaped and held like an electric guitar. Easier to play and transport than a large acoustic double bass and capable of a huge sound to match the electric guitar, the bass guitar immediately gained popularity in the **genres** of **jazz**, **blues**, and rock. Because the strings of the double bass and bass guitar have the same **tunings** and relative note placements, many musicians play both, though the specific **techniques** of playing each instrument well are significantly different. Electric bass guitars often include a lower fifth string, and some have six strings. Fretless electric bass designs are popular in jazz and R&B because they feel and sound similar to an acoustic double bass.

bass violin.
1. A bass instrument of the **violin family** used primarily in 16th- and 17th-century French operatic music. The early bass violin has three strings tuned F2 – C3 – G3 with a low Bb1 string added to later instruments. The bass violin is slightly larger than a cello and may also be called a *basse de violon* (Fr.).
2. A term for the **double bass**.

bass walkup. A bass line that leads into a **chord** change by moving up stepwise or chromatically, used mainly in **genres** such as **jazz**, country, and **bluegrass**. See also **walking bass**.

bass wheel. A wheel attached to the **endpin** of a **double bass** allowing the player to transport the instrument by rolling rather than carrying. The wheel has a metal shaft that is fitted into the **endpin** socket for moving, and then is removed and replaced by the endpin while playing. The bass wheel is also called an endpin wheel.

Figure 10. A **bass wheel**.

bass-bar. A tapered piece of spruce glued lengthwise inside the **top plate** of bowed **string instruments**, just beneath the left foot of the **bridge** and opposite the **sound post**. The bass-bar transmits the vibrations of the lower pitches across the surface of the plate and strengthens the top beneath the weight of the bridge.

bass-bar crack. A split running along the **top plate** of an instrument where the **bass-bar** is located beneath the left foot of the **bridge**. One of the more serious types of damage a **string instrument** may sustain, a bass-bar crack is difficult to repair and usually lowers the value of the instrument.

basse de violon. (Fr.) A bass member of the **violin family**, slightly larger than the **cello** and usually tuned Bb1 – F2 – C3 – G3. The *basse de violon* was used primarily as a **continuo** instrument in early 18th-century French operatic music. Also called a **bass violin**.

bassetto. A small chamber **double bass**, slightly larger than a **cello**. The bassetto has the same string length as a cello and is tuned G1 – D2 – A2 – E3, two octaves below the **violin** and a fourth below the cello. Modern bassetto double basses are shaped like a violin and are made as part of the **New Violin Family** of instruments.

bassetto di viola. (It.) One of many early names for the **cello**.

basso continuo. (It.) A fundamental bass line common in the Baroque era intended for a **cello** or *viola da gamba* player and a choral instrument. The *basso continuo* may be in the form of a **figured bass** with numeric shorthand indicating **chords** for a keyboard player. See **continuo**.

basso da brazzo. (It.) An early name for the **cello**.

basso viola da brazzo. (It.) One of many early names for the **cello**.

battuto. (It.) Beaten, meaning to beat the **string** with the **bow**, usually by swatting at the string with an entirely vertical stroke. *Battuto* is often used in tandem with **left-hand pizzicato**. See *col legno battuto* for the stroke which involves beating the string with the wood of the bow. See **Table 1: Bowstrokes** for a list of strokes and their notation.

bearbeitet. (Ger.) **Arranged** or **transcribed**.

bearclaw. A curl in the grain of wood, also called hazelficte. Bearclaws are an indicator of a high quality **tonewood**.

beats. See **Tartini tones**.

bebend. (Ger.) Trembling, used as an indication for **tremolo** or possibly **vibrato**.

bebop. A style of **jazz** characterized by fast tempos, **improvisation**, and instrumental virtuosity. The most celebrated bebop musicians include saxophonist Charlie Parker and trumpet player Dizzy Gillespie, who worked with **ensembles** of saxophone, trumpet, **bass**, drums, and piano, performing in small clubs where the audience was listening rather than dancing. See also **jazz**.

bee-sting. The point where the **purfling** meets at the corners of the instrument.

Figure 11. **Bee-sting** at the corner of an instrument.

behind the bridge. To bow the **strings** on the **afterlength** between the **bridge** and **tailpiece**. Used primarily in 20th-century music, playing behind the bridge produces a scratchy, high-pitched **tone**. There is no standardized notation for this technique. See also *ponticello* and **scratch tone**.

belly. The top of an instrument. See **top plate**.

bend. A **jazz** term for pulling the pitch down a **half-step** and returning, all within the rhythmic value of

the note. On **string instruments**, a bend can be produced either by rolling the tip of the finger along the string or by sliding the fingertip up and down the string. See also **fall off, plop, scoop, drop, doit**, and *glissando*.

Figure 12. **Bend** notation.

bent note. Pulling the **string** to the side while playing to raise the **pitch**, used as an expressive tool primarily in **jazz** and **blues**. The technique can also be called note bending or string bending. See also **bend, fall off, plop, scoop, drop, doit**, and *glissando*.

Bergonzi, Carlos (1683-1747). Italian **luthier** of the Cremona school held as high in esteem as **Stradivari** and **Guarneri** "del Gesù." Although Bergonzi's training is not firmly documented, it is known that he had close ties to both Guarneri and Stradivari. Bergonzi began labeling his **violins** around 1720 and enjoyed a golden period of particularly fine instruments from 1730 to 1740. His work is characterized by finely crafted, delicate **scrolls**, pointed **sound holes**, beautifully figured wood, and rich **varnish**. There is no evidence that Bergonzi made **violas, cellos**, or **double basses**.

Bériot, Charles Auguste de (1802-1870). Belgian violinist, composer, and founder of the **Franco-Belgian school of violin playing**. Bériot studied **violin** with **Viotti's** student Robberechts, and had a highly successful 1826 solo début in Paris, launching a career of touring across Europe, England, and Russia. In 1843 Bériot refused a position at the Paris Conservatoire, taking instead a post as violin professor at the Brussels Conservatoire, where he taught until 1852 when blindness forced him to retire. As director of the Brussels violin program, Bériot was able to develop a new school of playing, one that combined the Classical elegance of Viotti's **French school of violin playing** with the flashy virtuosity of **Paganini** and the Romantics. From among Bériot's many students, **Vieuxtemps** became the most famous. Bériot documented his approach in two books: *Méthode de violon* and *Ecole transcendante de violon*.

Composing mainly for his own instrument, Bériot wrote ten violin **concertos** as well as many **etudes**, two-violin duets, and pieces for violin and piano. Because his works use many of the same virtuosic techniques as Paganini, including **harmonics, left-hand** *pizzicato*, and *ricochet*, yet are shorter and easier, they remain in the **repertoire** as training pieces for students.

bib. A soft cloth placed between the back of a **double bass** or **cello** and the player, protecting the instrument from scratches. Some bibs include a pocket.

Biber, Heinrich Ignaz Franz von (1644-1704). Bohemian composer and celebrated **virtuoso** violinist of the Baroque era. Biber is best known for his *Passacaglia* for **solo violin** and his *Mystery Sonatas* (also called the *Rosary Sonatas*) for violin and **continuo**. His music is characterized by brilliant virtuosity, programmatic symbolism, and use of *scordatura*.

Bindung. (Ger.) **Slur**.

bisbigliando. (It.) A rapid *pizzicato tremolo*, usually played *sotto voce*. *Bisbigliando* is Italian for "whispering."

bitonal. The simultaneous use of two tonal centers in a composition.

blanketing. A **jazz improvisation** technique in which a single **scale** is used over an entire chord progression.

Blanton, Jimmy (1918-1942). American **jazz double bass** player who was the first to **improvise** full **solos** on the instrument. As a member of Duke Ellington's orchestra, Blanton's large range, contrapuntal bass lines, and melodic approach to playing made the double bass a prominent member of the band.

block chord. A chord in which all the notes are played simultaneously, rather than being **broken** or **arpeggiated**.

blocks. Pieces of softwood holding the instrument together inside where the ends of the **ribs** meet. The **top-block** strengthens the **neck**, the **bottom-block** reinforces the **belly** against **string** tension, and the **corner-blocks** hold the ribs in place where the **C bouts** meet at the corners.

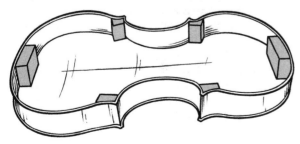

Figure 13. **Blocks** inside an instrument.

blowing changes. The chord progression of a **jazz** tune over which **solos** are **improvised**. See also **lead sheet** and **improvise**.

blue note. A flatted third or seventh **scale** degree characteristically used in **blues** melodies. The blue note is often lowered by bending the **pitch**. See also **blues** and **bent note**.

bluegrass. An American traditional music that developed from the mountain music of Appalachia. Bluegrass is characterized by stacked vocal harmonies, virtuosic instrumental **improvisations,** and **ensembles** of **acoustic** instruments including banjo, **fiddle**, guitar, **mandolin**, **double bass**, and dobro.

Showy fiddle solos are a centerpiece of bluegrass music, particularly in up-tempo **breakdowns**. These displays of virtuosity are often improvised and include fiddle techniques such as **slides**, **fall offs**, **drone strings**, and **double-stops**. When playing **backup**, fiddle players may use rhythmic **chops** or strum the **violin** like a guitar. Famous bluegrass fiddle players include Kenny Baker, Sam Bush, Mark O'Connor, and Vassar Clements.

Traditional bluegrass uses upright acoustic double bass, sometimes called a doghouse bass, rather than the electric bass guitar preferred by rock and other **genres**. Progressive bluegrass, known as **newgrass**, blends **electric instruments** and rock elements into the traditional sound.

blues.
1. A **genre** of music originating in the folk songs, spirituals, work songs, and chants of African Americans living in the South. Blues melodies, **scales**, and style have had a strong influence on the development of **jazz**, rock, and classical music in the 20th century.
2. A musical form using a twelve-bar structure that is characterized by a strong 4/4 rhythm, melancholy lyrics, and improvisation, often using **blue notes** and other scale modifications. The blues form is used in **jazz**, blues, and rock music.

Boccherini, Luigi (1743-1805). Italian composer and cellist. As chamber composer in the service of Prince Friedrich Wilhelm of Prussia (crowned King Friedrich Wilhelm II), who was an amateur cellist himself, Boccherini composed over three hundred **chamber music** works and greatly developed the role of the **cello** in the chamber **genre**. Most notable are his string **quintets** requiring two cellos in which the high cello part plays a role almost equal to that of the **first violin**.

body mapping. A technique of exploring how the body works to cultivate an accurate understanding of how to use and control movement. Based on the idea of William Conable that his cello students moved according to how they perceived their bodies rather than how their bodies actually worked, body mapping uses kinesthetic exploration of weight and balance to readjust one's concept of the body. Body mapping is one of the basic tenets of **Alexander Technique** and **Feldenkrais**. See also **ergonomics**.

Bogen. (Ger.) **Bow**. Phrases commonly found in music include *ganzer Bogen*: the whole bow; *in der Mitte des Bogens*: in the middle of the bow; *langer Bogen*: long bowstrokes; *mit dem Bogen schlagen*: to strike with the bow; *springender Bogen*: **off the string**; *viel Bogen*: lots of bow; *viel Bogenwechsel*: with many bow changes.

Bogenguitar. (Ger.) See **arpeggione**.

Bogenwechsel. (Ger.) Changes of **bow** direction. *Viel Bogenwechsel* means to play many bow changes, usually on a long note. *Kein Bogenwechsel* means to play without changing bow direction.

bois. (Fr.) Wood, stick of the **bow**.

bombi. (It.) **Tremolo** (archaic).

book match. The technique of cutting both halves of an instrument's **plates** from the same piece of wood then opening them like the pages of a book to create symmetry in the figure and grain of the wood. See also **annular rings** and **curl**.

Bottesini bow. A **double bass** bow design named after **Giovanni Bottesini**, commonly known as the **French bow**. See **French bow** and **French bow hold** for illustrations.

Bottesini, Giovanni (1821-1889). Italian **double bass** player, composer, and conductor, nicknamed the "**Paganini** of the double bass," who made great contributions to the popularity and technique of his instrument. Bottesini toured Europe and America, playing **solos** and performing the **cello** part in **chamber music** on a three-string *basso da camera* tuned a whole-step higher than standard and using a bow that resembles a cello bow. Even today the **French bass bow** is often referred to as a Bottesini bow. Bottesini expanded the range and technical capabilities of the double bass and his virtuosic compositions for the instrument are still considered among the most difficult.

bottom block. See **blocks**.

bourée. A French dance form popular in the Baroque era, in quick duple meter with an upbeat.

bouts. The curved portions of the **ribs** of an instrument. The upper bouts are at the shoulders, the **C bouts** are at the waist, and the lower bouts curve around the bottom of the instrument. The rounded shape of a **string instrument** creates clearance for the **bow** while maximizing air space in the **resonance chamber**.

Figure 14. The **bouts** of a **violin**.

bow. A long curved rod with a flat span of **horsehair** stretched between either end, used to play **string instruments** including those of the **violin** and **viol** families. The bow works when the coarse horsehair is dragged along the **string**, pulling it and causing it to vibrate.

Most string players use a modern bow as designed by **François Tourte**, which is the model discussed here. Bass players choose between two distinctly different types of bow: a **French bow** in the modern Tourte design, or a **German bow**, descended from the **viol family**. These bass bow designs and the many other specialized types of bow are discussed in their own entries.

The **stick** of a bow is most often made of wood, usually **pernambuco** or **brazilwood**, though inexpensive student bows can be made from **fiberglass**, and recently developed **carbon fiber** bow designs rival the performance of fine wood bows. A wood bow is

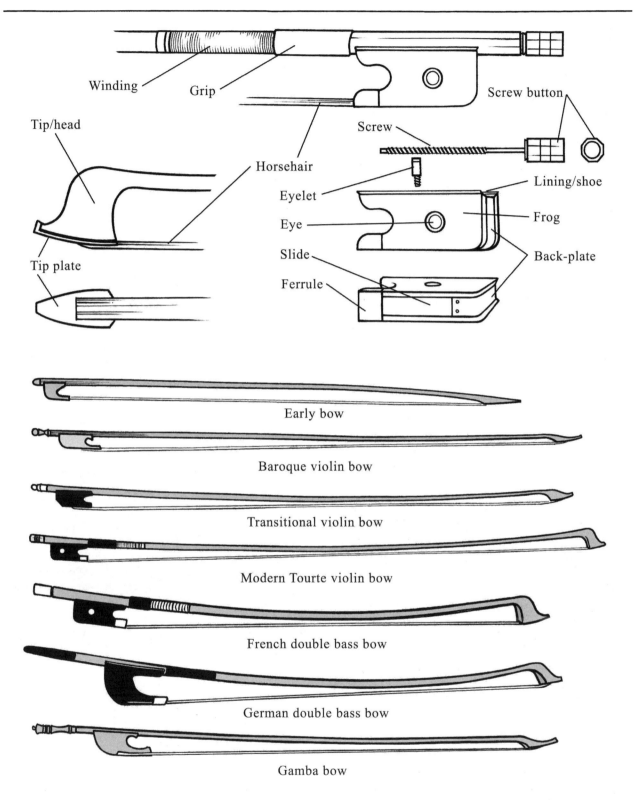

Figure 15. The **bow**, including details of the modern **Tourte frog** and **tip**   as well as a comparison of various **stick** designs.

carved into a round or octagonal rod with a form that tapers towards the **tip**. Initially the stick is carved straight, and then is bent into the ideal **cambre** using water and heat to produce a permanent concave curve that bends inward towards the hair.

Each end of the bow has a piece that holds the hair away from the stick, allowing **tension** to be put on the hair. At the top end is the **tip**, a hatchet-shaped piece of wood carved from the same block as the stick. The point of the tip is protected by a plate of ivory, metal, or other material. Attached to the lower end of the bow is the **frog**, a separate piece of wood that houses the **screw** mechanism for adjusting the tension on the hair. The frog is typically made of **ebony**, though it can be made from a variety of hardwoods or even tortoiseshell or ivory. The corner of the frog of a **viola** or **cello** bow is usually rounded, distinguishing it from the square-cornered **violin** bow. Metal **mountings** on the frog include the **screw button**, the **ferrule**, the **slide**, the **back-plate**, and the **lining** between the frog and stick. The bow maker will often indicate his opinion of the quality of the stick by his choice of metal for the mountings, using nickel for the most ordinary bows, silver for finer bows, and gold mountings only for a stick of which the maker is most proud. The frog is often decorated with abalone in an **eye** on either side of the frog, a slide inlay on the bottom of the frog, and a **pearl dot** on the end of the screw button.

The stick is covered by a protective **winding** and **grip** where the bow is held near the frog. The winding, which is used to prevent wear and tear on the stick, is traditionally whalebone **lapping**, though modern bows more often use plastic or metal threads instead. At the base of the winding is the grip, a piece of leather glued around the stick to cushion and protect the contact point between the thumb and frog. A bow typically has 150-200 hairs from the tail of a horse. White hair is used most for violin, viola, and cello, though some musicians, especially **double bass** players, use black hair for its additional coarseness. **Rosin**, a sticky resin, is applied to the hair to improve its grip on the string.

Caring for a bow includes loosening the hair whenever not in use, keeping the stick clean of **rosin dust** and oils from the hand, replacing the hair as it becomes smooth (see **rehair**), replacing the winding and grip as they become worn, and occasionally replacing the screw or eyelet within the frog. The bow is the primary expressive tool of a string player.

See also **bow angle**, **bow tilt**, **articulation**, **phrasing**, and **Table 1: Bowstrokes** for a list of strokes and their notation. For information about **bow holds**, see **Russian bow hold**, **Franco-Belgian bow hold**, **German bow hold**, and **French bow hold**. Entries on specific types of bow include **crémaillère bow**, **baroque bow**, **Bach bow**, **German bow**, **French bow**, and **Tourte bow**.

bow angle. How the **bow** moves in relation to the **bridge**. In general, string players use a straight bow angle, with the **stick** running exactly parallel to the line of the bridge. Changing the angle of the bow facilitates changing the **contact point**, which is used to create dynamics, **tone colors**, and phrasings. "Angled in" means the bow is positioned so the **frog** end is closer to the bridge, moving the contact point away from the bridge on a **down-bow**. "Angled out" means the bow is positioned so the frog end is farther from the bridge, moving the contact point closer to the bridge on a down-bow. Some players "play into the curve" by using a rounded, continuously changing bow angle that brings the **hair** closer to the bridge at all times. See also **sounding point**.

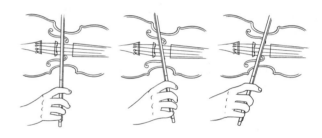

Figure 16. **Bow angles** shown on the violin or viola: straight, angled out, and angled in.

bow case. A case designed to hold just the **bow**. Bow cases are made from wood or another hard material to protect the delicate stick from damage while transporting. **Double bass** players and cellists who keep their instruments in **soft cases** use a bow case for extra protection. A **luthier** may carry a case designed to hold as many as twenty bows.

bow change. The moment when the movement of the **bow** reverses direction, either from an **up-bow** to a **down-bow** or vice versa.

bow distribution. The amount of **bow** used on a particular note in proportion to the entire length of the stick. For example, in a sustained melodic line, two slurred quarter notes would logically use a bow distribution of half the bow each, while four slurred eighth notes would receive a quarter of the bow each. A dotted-quarter hooked to an eighth note would mean a distribution of three quarters of the bow on the first note and the remaining quarter bow on the second. This system of measuring bow usage in relation to the rhythm can be expanded to apply to endless combinations of patterns at any tempo.

Understanding and controlling bow distribution is fundamental to expressive lyrical lines, rhythmic work, and even brilliant technical passages. Distributing notes evenly along the bow as described above presumes constant bow speed. Combining a varying **bow speed** with an uneven bow distribution can be one of the primary tools used to create phrasing, dynamics, and emphasis within music. For example, eight slurred sixteenth notes might usually be evenly distributed with an eighth of the bow each; however, if the first note has an **accent**, playing a whipped bow using half the length of the stick on the first note alone, followed by a slow bow distributing the other seven notes along the remaining length can make for a very exciting **articulation**.

Combinations of bow speed and bow distribution can be used to create a swell within a phrase, highlight a particular melodic note, build an exciting crescendo, taper the end of a melodic line, change tone color, and create countless other expressive effects.

bow grip. See **bow hold**.

bow hand. The hand in which the **bow** is held while playing, usually the right. See **bow hold**.

bow hold. The placement of the fingers on the **stick** of the **bow**, also called the bow grip. The specific way the fingers interact with the bow is foundational to **tone** production and mastery of every type of **bowstroke**.

Because it is held at one end, the bow must be operated as a **lever** in order for the **hair** to grip the **string** along the entire length of the stick. The fingers manipulate the rotation of the stick across the thumb, which serves as the lever's **fulcrum**. Whether this is accomplished by **weight** or **pressure**, using primarily the fingers or the arm, and with an interface that is constant or flexible are some of the fundamental factors determined by the type of bow hold a player uses.

As the techniques of playing and the physics of bow design have developed through history, ideas of how to hold the bow have evolved as well. Two main schools of technique are used by modern **violin** and **viola** players: the **Franco-Belgian bow hold**, which uses flexible, rounded fingers and an active wrist to operate the bow, and the **Russian bow hold**, which relies on **pronation** of the arm and a strong index finger pivot point. Both schools have produced great **virtuoso** players. The Franco-Belgian hold is exemplified by Itzhak Perlman; **Jascha Heifetz** was a master of the Russian hold.

Double bass players also use one of two distinctly different methods of bow hold, depending on the design of the bow: the **French bow hold**, an overhand

approach similar to a cello bow hold, or the **German bow hold**, a side grip developed from **viol** technique.

Musicians involved in **historically informed performance** will often use bow holds appropriate to the era of music they are playing.

For specifics, see also **bow, Franco-Belgian bow hold, French bow hold, German bow hold, lever**, and **Russian bow hold**.

bow quiver. A leather pouch tied to a **double bass tailpiece**, designed to hold the **bow** while playing **pizzicato**.

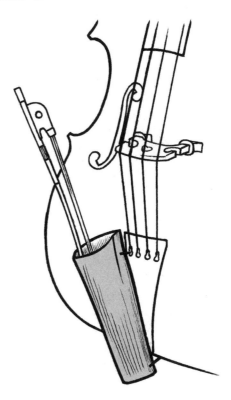

Figure 17. A **bow quiver**.

bow rocking. Rapid alternation between two or more **strings**, creating a rhythmic effect characteristic of Appalachian fiddling. The bow rocking movement is usually generated from the shoulder of the bow arm, and works best at the **balance point**. Some fiddle players choke up on the **stick** to facilitate bow rocking. See also *bariolage*.

bow speed. How fast the **bow hair** moves as it pulls the **string**. Bow speed is a crucial factor in producing a clear sound, changing **tone** colors, creating accents, playing **harmonics**, and achieving bowstrokes such as *sautillé* and *ricochet*. Bow speed is also a potent tool for shaping expressive **phrasing**, particularly when a combination of speeds is used within a single **bowstroke**.

bow tilt. The relationship between the **stick** and the **hair** of the **bow** as it sits on the **string**. A flat bow is held with no tilt, the stick sitting directly atop the hair. The bow can be tilted away from the **bridge**, placing more weight on the hair closest to the **fingerboard**, or towards the bridge, leaning more weight on the hair closest to the bridge.

The frequency and degree of bow tilt is one of the primary components of various schools of **bow hold**, and the effect achieved by tilting the bow varies based on the amount of **tension** on the hair as well as the player's specific **technique** of using weight or pressure to grip the string.

All schools of bow technique include tilting the weight of the bow as one way to create **tone colors** and change **dynamics**. Leaning the stick far enough to raise some hair from the string will produce a quieter, more translucent **tone**, while playing heavily on a completely flat ribbon of hair will create a denser, bolder tone. Tilting the stick can also facilitate changing the **contact point** by using the uneven weight to push the hair closer to or further from the bridge.

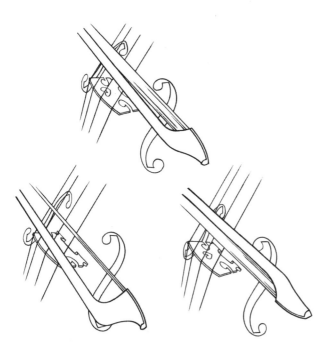

Figure 18. **Bow tilt** shown on a **cello** or **double bass**. A flat bow tilt is shown above with a tilt towards the **bridge** below left and a tilt away from the bridge below right.

bow treble. An **ornament** common in **Irish fiddle** music. A bow treble is a quick, flicking bow change that creates a stutter in the sound. The bow treble is usually down-up-down, though it can also be done up-down-up.

bowed guitar. See **arpeggione**.

bowed psaltery. A medieval string instrument, also called a violin zither or ukelin. The traditional bowed psaltery is a triangular wooden resonator with unstopped **strings** stretched across it, and is played with a simple **fixed-frog bow**.

bowings. The combination of **bowstrokes** used for a particular phrase or piece. The term bowings broadly includes all choices made regarding the use of the bow, including bow direction for each note, the use of **slurs** or **hooked bows**, playing the note **on the string** or **off the string**, and any specific bowstroke being used. The choice of bowings is one of the primary tools a string player has for artistic expression.

In chamber music and orchestral playing, string players usually coordinate bowings to unify their sound and facilitate good **ensemble**.

See also **conventions of orchestral playing** and **Table 1: Bowstrokes**.

bowstroke. The specific manner in which the **bow** interacts with the **string** when playing. A bowstroke may be as basic as a back-and-forth *détaché*, or may involve a combination of **articulation**, **bow speeds**, weight, and attack, as found in the complex *fouetté* stroke. Bowstrokes can be divided into two types: those in which the hair remains **on the string** and those that involve the hair bouncing **off the string**. The terms naming individual bowstrokes are usually in French and have generally agreed-upon meanings, though the specific definitions and the **technique** of exactly how to achieve each stroke varies depending on **bow hold**, era, and legacy of teaching lineage.

In a living art form such as string playing, when bow techniques are learned directly from another person and passed down from generation to generation, it is hardly surprising that differing meanings for the same term have arisen over time. In this text, an effort has been made to offer clear definitions of bowstrokes according to modern conventions. In addition, **Table 1: Bowstrokes** is a compilation of bowstrokes, with their various names and notations, and a brief explanation to aid in understanding the often subtle differences between them.

boxwood. A light-colored wood of the Buxus genus, often chosen for **string instrument fittings** because its high density makes it smooth and sturdy.

bracing. The wooden bars glued to the inside of a **flat-back double bass**, supporting the **plate** against cracking. Bracing usually consists of one bar running vertically beneath the center joint and three or more bars spread horizontally along back plate, one of which reinforces the joint at the **break**. Some **luthiers** prefer a less standard diagonal bracing.

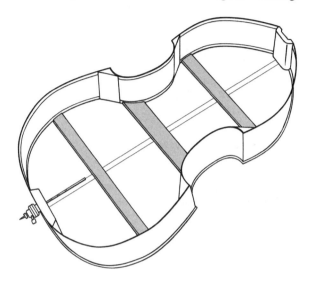

Figure 19. **Bracing** inside a **double bass**.

brand. A bow maker's name or mark, usually stamped into the stick just above the **frog**. See also **label**.

Bratsche. (Ger.) **Viola**.

bravura. Play with boldness, showmanship, and panache.

brazilwood. A reddish wood of the Caesalpinia genus, also called pernambuco, used to make **bows** for string instruments. Brazilwood, currently a protected flora species, is becoming so scarce that bowmakers have formed the International Pernambuco Conservation Initiative (IPCI) to rescue the tree.

break.
1. To play a chord by dividing it into two parts. See **broken chord**.
2. An instrumental interlude between verses of a song, used mostly in **bluegrass** and popular music.
3. In jazz, the moment when the rhythm section stops playing for several bars, often used to prepare the return of the head or to lead into an instrumental solo. Also called a **solo break**.
4. The angled top portion of the back **plate** on a **flat-back double bass**. The break is supported inside by **bracing**.

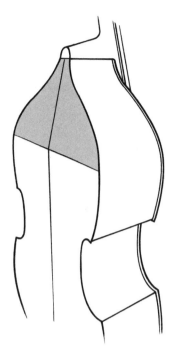

Figure 20. The **break** at the top of a **double bass** back **plate**.

breakdown. An instrumental form in **bluegrass** that features virtuosic solos. A breakdown can be a fast showpiece, such as "Foggy Mountain Breakdown" or "Orange Blossom Special," or it may follow a song, with the instrumentalists bursting into an up-tempo **break**.

breit. (Ger.) Broad.

breit gestrichen. (Ger.) Broadly bowed.

breit gezogen. (Ger.) Broadly bowed.

bridge.
1. The thin piece of **maple** wedged between the **strings** and the **top plate** of the instrument, used to transmit vibrations from the strings to the body of the instrument. The bridge is custom cut to fit an instrument, with feet sitting flush on the top plate and an arched top edge that matches the curve of the **fingerboard** to maintain consistent string height. Small notches are cut into the top of the bridge to guide each string in the correct spacing, often with the highest string notch reinforced by a piece of plastic or **ebony inlay** to prevent the string from cutting into the wood of the bridge. Held in place only by the **tension** of the strings, the proper placement of the bridge in relation to the **soundpost**, **bass-bar**, and fingerboard is crucial to the sound of the instrument. Moving, reshap-

ing, and even replacing the bridge are components of instrument **adjustment**. See also **bridge adjuster**.

2. The contrasting section of a song, usually the B phrase in a standard AABA verse-chorus form.

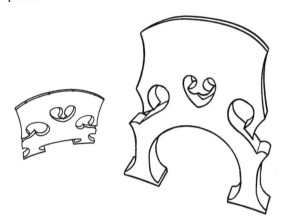

Figure 21. A **violin bridge** on the left and a **cello** bridge on the right.

bridge adjuster. A wheel threaded onto a post imbedded into each leg of the **bridge**, rotated up or down to precisely set the height of the bridge. Bridge adjusters are typically made of aluminum, brass, **ebony**, or **boxwood**, and are used primarily by **double bass** players. Occasionally a cellist will use a bridge adjuster.

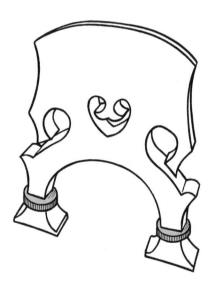

Figure 22. **Bridge adjusters** on a **double bass bridge**.

bridge protector. A tiny piece of plastic encasing a steel string where it passes across the **bridge**, preventing the string from cutting into the wood. Bridge protectors may **buzz**, especially if they are not placed correctly, and may be unnecessary if the bridge al-ready has an **inlay** or protective plastic piece. Most bridge protectors can be removed by sliding them off the straight end of the **string**.

brisé. (Fr.) **Staccato**.

brisure. (Fr.) A **bowstroke** used for passages with notes that alternate on nonadjacent **strings**, requiring a jump over the strings in between.

Figure 23. *Brisure* from **David Popper's** *High School of Cello Playing*, no. 25, mm 6-7.

broken chord. A chord that is divided into two double-stops, played in rapid succession. A broken chord is used for playing a **triple-** or **quadruple-stop** when using a **block chord** is not possible. As an alternative to a **rolled chord**, the broken chord may produce a stronger, more brilliant effect. See also **block chord**, **rolled chord**, and **arpeggiation**.

broken consort. A **consort** comprised of instruments of different families. See **consort**.

broken time. Rhythm played in such a way that the beat is not explicit, used mainly by **double bass** in the **jazz genre**.

brush stroke, brushed. A broad *spiccato* bowstroke in which the **bow** approaches the **string** with wide, horizontal movements, creating a longer **articulation** than regular *spiccato*. The brush stroke is commonly referred to as playing "on-ish" or "off-ish," depending on the degree of bounce. With no standard notation, the brush stroke may be an interpretation of **dots**, lines, the combination of lines and dots, or it may simply be stylistically understood. See also **on the string**, **off the string**, and *spiccato*, as well as **Table 1: Bowstrokes** for a list of strokes and their notation.

bull fiddle. See **double bass**.

Butler bow. See **German bow**.

bumpers. Leather or rubber pads attached to the **ribs** of a **double bass**, used to protect the edges when setting the instrument on its side.

Figure 24. **Bumpers** protecting the edges of a **double bass**.

busetto. A design for **double bass** in which the lower corners of the **C bouts** are curved.

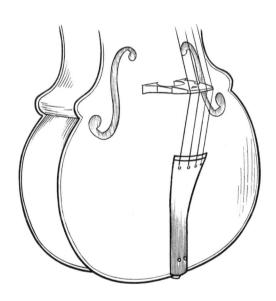

Figure 25. **Busetto** corners.

bushing. A repair to the **pegbox** of an instrument in which the peg holes are completely filled in with wood and new holes are drilled. Bushing becomes necessary when friction from turning the **pegs** wears down the wood of the pegbox so much that the pegs no longer fit or the pegbox cracks.

button.
1. The rounded piece at the top of the back **plate** of an instrument, to which the **neck** is glued.
2. The small wooden peg sticking through the bottom **bout** of the instrument around which the **tailgut** is looped, securing the **tailpiece**. Also called the end button. On **cello** and **double bass**, the end button is usually replaced by the **endpin**.

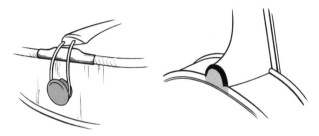

Figure 26. An **end button** on the left and the **button** of a **back plate** on the right.

buzz. Unwanted noise caused by an extraneous vibration when an instrument is played. A buzz can indicate serious damage to the instrument, such as an open seam or a crack in one of the **plates**. More often, the buzz is caused by a loose accessory, such as a **fine tuner** screw, a **chin rest** bracket, a **shoulder rest** foot, a **mute**, or a plastic **bridge protector**. A buzz may also be the result of a player's button or piece of jewelry touching the surface of the instrument.

buzz *pizzicato*. An **extended technique** of holding the left hand so that the **string** vibrates against a fingernail when plucked.

BWV. Abbreviation for *Bach-Werke-Verzeichnes*, the system for cataloging the music of **J. S. Bach** in lieu of opus numbers. See also **thematic index**.

~ C ~

C bouts. The curve in the **ribs** of an instrument at the waist, providing clearance for the **bow**. To create the C bouts, the ribs are shaped into a concave curve with a hot iron, and then glued to the top and back **plates** of the instrument. The C bouts are reinforced inside by the **corner blocks**.

On **violin**, **viola**, and **cello**, the C bouts meet the ribs in sharp points, known as the instrument's corners. On rare occasions, an instrument may be **cornerless** with a gently curved guitar shape. **Double** basses have three distinct designs for the corners of C bouts: pointed like those of a violin, C-shaped like those of a *viola da gamba*, or outwardly rounded **busetto** corners.

Figure 27. The **C bouts** on a **violin** or **viola**.

C extension. An extra length of **fingerboard** added to the E string of a **double bass**, built over the **pegbox**. The C extension extends the lower range of the instrument by four pitches, allowing for a low C. C extensions are made in several designs, the simplest of which is the **fingered extension**, which has only a locking stop at the **nut**, allowing the bassist to engage the addition string length, then reach back to finger pitches. The advantage of this design is that it allows the player to adjust pitch and play **vibrato**. The disadvantage is that the extended hand position makes it difficult to integrate the lowest pitches into passagework on the regular fingerboard. A variety of other designs aim to improve playability of the C extension, from the **chromatic extension**, a set of wooden fingers or capos that can be engaged to **stop** each pitch, to a **machine extension**, a set of levers mounted next to the regular fingerboard which function similar to keys on a bassoon. See also **B extension, chromatic extension, fingered extension,** and **machine extension**.

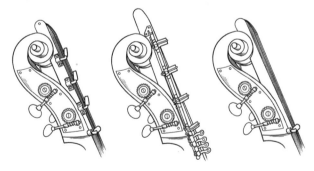

Figure 28. Three types of **C extensions** for **double bass: chromatic extension** on the left, **machine extension** in the center, and **fingered extension** on the right.

C hole. A **sound-hole** carved in the shape of a C, commonly found on **viols**. See **sound-hole**.

c.a. (It.) Abbreviation for *coll'arco*, meaning with the bow. See **arco**.

cadenza. A brilliant **solo** passage in the style of an **improvisation**, most often included in a concerto. The cadenza grew from a tradition of adding a flourish of **ornamentation** on the dominant chord of a final cadence. Early **concertos** indicate the opportunity for a cadenza by placing a fermata over the dominant chord with the expectation that the soloist will improvise passage work as a display of technical **virtuosity** and musical understanding. The soloist will traditionally end the cadenza with a **trill** on the dominant, signaling to the **orchestra** that the improvisation is finished.

As the skill of improvisation has faded from the **art music** tradition, string players have ceased creating their own cadenzas, choosing instead to perform those written by great performers such as **Joseph Joachim, Leopold Auer,** and **Janos Starker**. Most of these performer-written cadenzas for the standard literature are in a newer style than the original composition, though the **historically informed performance** movement of the late 20th century is producing historically appropriate cadenzas and has brought a return to performer improvisations.

Beethoven, unhappy with the quality of improvisation by other pianists in his concertos, was the first composer to notate a cadenza as part of the score. Many composers since have followed suit, and most Romantic and 20th-century concertos include fully composed cadenzas or cadenzas integrated into the orchestral texture of the piece. Some of the most virtuosic cadenzas are the product of collaboration between the composer and a famous performer, as was the case with Mendelssohn and violinist **Ferdinand David** in the creation of the brilliant cadenza to Mendelssohn's violin concerto.

See also **improvisation** and **concerto**.

cambre. The concave curve of the stick of a **bow**. The cambre is created by using heat to shape the carved stick to a precise curve using a wooden or metal template. The cambre is a feature of the modern **Tourte** bow and is not found on **baroque bows**, which are straight or even slightly convex.

camerata. (It.) A small **chamber ensemble** or **orchestra**. The term *camerata* derives from 16th-century groups of intellectuals and artists who gathered to discuss and further the arts.

canon.

1. A musical form created by strict imitation in which all voices perform the same material, entering one after the other in succession to create layers of counterpoint. One particularly famous example of this technique is Johann Pachelbel's *Canon in D*, which is a three-voice canon built over a repeated **ground bass**.
2. A foundational collection of work.

cantabile. (It.) Play in a singing style.

canzona, canzonetta. (It.) A piece written in a singing style. For example, the lyrical second movement of Tchaikovsky's **violin concerto** is titled *Canzonetta*.

Capet, Lucien (1873-1928). French violinist and **pedagogue** known for his contributions to the art of **bow technique**. After completing studies at the Paris Conservatoire where he was awarded a *premier prix,* Capet had a successful career as a soloist and member of the Capet Quartet. His interest in the art of bowing led him to write the treatise *La technique supérieure de l'archet*, a book that remains one of the foremost explorations of **bowstrokes**. In 1924 Capet became the director of the Paris *Institut de Violon*, and his pedagogical legacy extends through his two most notable students: Jascha Brodsky and **Ivan Galamian**, who were to become among the most influential teachers of the 20th century, producing violin superstars including Hilary Hahn, Itzhak Perlman, and Pinchas Zukerman.

capriccioso. (It.) Having a lighthearted, whimsical character.

caprice. A short composition with a playful, flashy character. In string playing, a caprice is often a virtuosic **etude**, as in **Paganini's** *24 Caprices for Solo Violin* or Piatti's *12 Caprices for Solo Cello*.

carbon fiber. An extremely strong thin strand of pure carbon created through pyrolyzation. Carbon fibers are used in composites to create sturdy, flexible, lightweight materials with many uses for musicians, including **cases**, **endpins**, **shoulder rests**, **bows**, and even entire instruments. Also called graphite fiber. See **carbon fiber bow** and **carbon fiber instrument**.

carbon fiber bow. A synthetic **bow** made from woven **carbon fiber**, designed to imitate the shape, weight, and flexibility of the finest **pernambuco** sticks. Bows made of carbon fiber are an inexpensive, durable alternative to a traditional wood bow and are often chosen for use on outdoor stages, in schools, clubs, and other risky environments. Recent technology and de-

sign have produced carbon fiber bows that perform at a high standard, and many professionals use them.

carbon fiber instrument. An instrument with a body made from woven **carbon fiber**. Carbon fiber instruments are highly durable and immune to damage from changes in humidity, temperature, direct sunlight, and water. Since the technology of carbon fiber design has evolved to produce instruments that perform well enough to be played professionally, a carbon fiber instrument can be an inexpensive, indestructible alternative to a traditional wood instrument, particularly for outdoor stages, in nightclubs, at schools, and on tour.

carpal tunnel syndrome. An injury commonly suffered by string players. Carpal tunnel syndrome is caused by pressure on the median nerve of the wrist, producing numbness, tingling, and weakness of the hand and fingers. Repetitive movements of the hand and wrist such as the motions of playing a **string instrument** may cause swelling that pinches the median nerve as it passes through the narrow carpal tunnel. Symptoms of carpal tunnel syndrome include numbness or tingling of the palm, thumb, or first three fingers, pain in the wrist extending to the elbow, difficulty with finger coordination, and weakness in the hand.

Treatment of carpal tunnel syndrome may entail the use of a splint to immobilize the hand, changes to playing and other activities to reduce stress on the wrist, and use of an **ergonomic instrument** and accessories. Anti-inflammatory medications may provide temporary relief, and severe cases can be treated with surgery. Carpal tunnel syndrome should be taken seriously, as an untreated condition can damage the median nerve, causing permanent weakness, numbness, and tingling.

See also **Alexander Technique, ergonomics, ergonomic instrument, Feldenkrais Method,** and **tendonitis.**

Casals, Pablo (1876-1973). Spanish cellist, pianist, conductor, and composer beloved for his view of music as a powerful force uniting people and his serious, intellectual approach to the **cello**. One of the earliest cellists to make recordings, Casals' artistry fostered a new appreciation for the cello and its repertoire, especially the six unaccompanied **suites** by **J. S. Bach**. Casals dedicated his life to activism for peace and humanity, work which earned him international recognition including the United Nations Peace Prize and the U.S. Presidential Medal of Freedom. "My first obligation is to the welfare of my fellow man. I will endeavour to meet this obligation through music, since it transcends language, politics and national boundaries."

case. A protective trunk for storing and transporting an instrument. Most **violin, viola,** and **cello** players keep their fragile instruments in a hard case with a shell built from **fiberglass**, plastic, foam, wood, or **carbon fiber** and made in a large variety of designs ranging from cheap shaped foam to pricey, lightweight carbon fiber.

Many string-instrument cases feature a suspension system which holds the instrument by the top and bottom **blocks** and **neck**, placing no weight on the delicate back or **bridge**. Usually cases are able to hold several **bows** and have pockets for storing pencils, **rosin, mutes, endpin stops,** and other accessories. Cases may also include a **hygrometer** for monitoring humidity levels, a built-in **humidifier**, a **string tube**, backpack straps, and a waterproof rain cover. Many cello cases are fitted with wheels for ease of transportation. Because of the size and weight of the instrument, **double bass** players primarily use padded soft cases made of reinforced nylon, with a separate hard **bow case**.

Air travel with **string instruments** can be challenging. Violins and violas can usually be carried on and stored in the overhead bin, and cellists often purchase a second seat to hold their instrument during the flight. Special heavy-duty flight cases offer extra protection for double bass players and cellists who need to check their instruments as luggage. (See also **collapsible upright bass**.)

For musicians traveling with more than one instrument, double cases are designed to hold two violins, or a violin and a viola. Some cases are made to hold as many as four violins, though all these cases are large and may prove more difficult to transport.

See also **bow case** and **gig bag**.

cat gut. A cord of stretched animal intestines traditionally used to make the **strings** of **string instruments**. Cat gut is made from sheep, goats, or cattle; the name is probably shortened from "cattle gut." While most modern string players use **synthetic** or **steel strings**, **gut strings** are still popular, particularly on **baroque instruments** and in **historically informed performance**. See **gut string**.

cédez. (Fr.) Slow down.

cello. The second-lowest instrument in the **modern string family**, formally called the violoncello. The cello measures twice the size of the **violin** and is tuned C2 – G2 – D3 – A3, an octave and a fifth lower. The cello is held vertically between the knees, usually supported on the floor by an **endpin**, and is played with a horsehair **bow**.

The cello was developed in the early 16th century along with the **violin** and **viola**. The earliest surviving cello is an **Amati**, made between 1560 and 1570. Initially the cello was used in an accompanimental role, gradually replacing the bass **viola da gamba** in an ensemble's **continuo**. The cello has always been an essential member of string **chamber music** groups and **orchestras**: it is the lowest instrument of the **string quartet**, a member of the **piano trio**, and the modern orchestra includes a section of six to fourteen cellists. The cello began being used as an unaccompanied solo instrument at the end of the 17th century, most famously in **J. S. Bach**'s six unaccompanied cello **suites**.

The cello is constructed of a top and back **plate**, each hand carved into an arched shape to support the weight from the **bridge**. The sides of the instrument are the **ribs**, made from six thin strips of maple that have been bent using heat and water to match the shape of the plates. The ribs and plates are held together with **hide glue** and reinforced at the joints by **linings** and **blocks**. Inside the body, the **soundpost** and **bass-bar** sit beneath the bridge, supporting the structure of the instrument against the tension of the **strings** and helping to transfer sound waves across the surfaces of the plates. **F-holes** cut into the top plate are shaped to maximize the **acoustic resonance** of the sounding chamber. The **fingerboard**, usually made of **ebony** for its smooth texture, is glued to a **neck** of maple, which is carved in a single piece from the **heel** to the **scroll**. The four strings are stretched taut between a **tailpiece** tied to the **end button** on the lower **bouts** and the **pegs** wedged into holes in the **pegbox** on the instrument's **head**. The strings pass over a high bridge, carved from a thin wedge of maple, that transfers the vibrations of the strings into the **resonance chamber** of the body. The strings are held slightly above the surface of the fingerboard by the raised ebony **nut** at the top of the fingerboard. An endpin, usually metal, extends from the end button to support the cello on the floor while playing.

cello chair. A seat designed specifically for cellists. The ideal **cello** chair provides a flat, forward-leaning seat, adjustable height, and good stability. Several companies manufacture cello chairs, including designs that are lightweight and portable. See also **ergonomics**.

cellone. A type of **cello** that is tuned G1 – D2 – A2 – E3, two octaves lower than the standard **violin**. Along with the *violetta*, the *cellone* was designed by German violinist, mathematician, and physicist Dr. Alfred

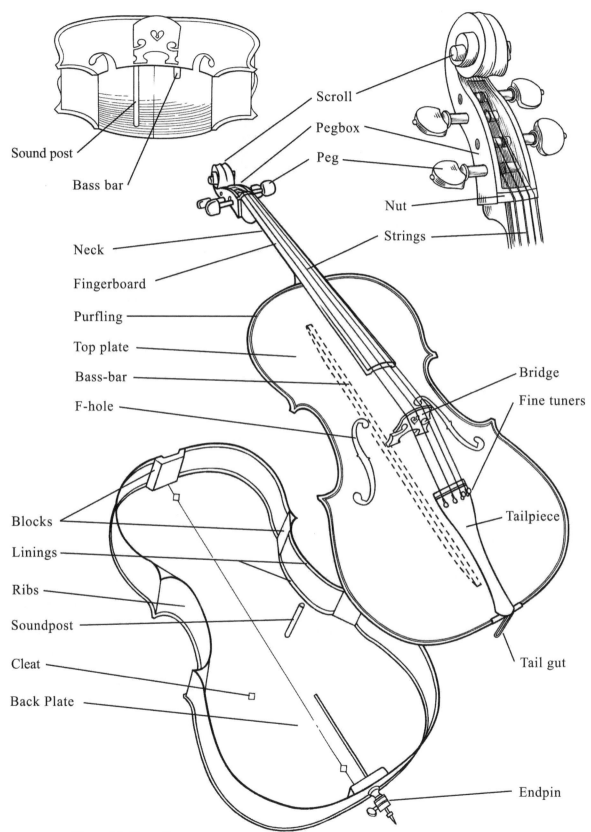

Sound post

Bass bar

Scroll

Pegbox

Peg

Nut

Strings

Neck

Fingerboard

Purfling

Top plate

Bass-bar

F-hole

Bridge

Fine tuners

Blocks

Linings

Ribs

Soundpost

Cleat

Back Plate

Tailpiece

Tail gut

Endpin

Figure 29. The **cello**.

Stelzner (1852-1906). **Luthiers** Richard Wiedemann and Augustus Paulus made the instrument based on Stelzner's ideas of elliptical curves and elongated **sound holes**.

Celtic fiddle. See **Irish fiddle**.

chaconne. (Fr.) A baroque dance form composed of variations on a repeated harmonic progression, also found with the Italian spelling *ciaccona*. The most famous string chaconne is by **J. S. Bach**, found at the end of his second **Partita** for Solo Violin BWV 1004.

chair. An indication of seating placement within a string section of an **orchestra**. First chair means being placed at the head of the section next to the conductor in the chair that is closest to the edge of the stage, also called the outside chair. The first chair first violin holds the position of **concertmaster**, and the first chair second violin, viola, cello, and double bass are the **principal**s, or leaders, of their sections. Second chair, or **assistant principal**, is the inside chair on the front stand or desk. This numbering system typically continues through the stands, moving front to back, with the outside player receiving an odd number and the inside player receiving an even number. A chair assignment has many purposes, including organization of players, indication of leadership positions, assignment of page-turning duties, and distribution of **divisi** parts. See **conventions of orchestra playing**, **principal**, and **concertmaster** for more details.

chamber bass. A small **double bass** intended for **chamber music** or **solo** performance.

chamber music. A form of **art music** written for a small instrumental **ensemble** with one player to a part and no conductor. Called "chamber music" because it is intended for performance in an intimate space such as a private home or small recital hall, the art form is considered music among friends, enjoyed by amateur and professional musicians alike.

Chamber music is classified according to the number of players. The **duet** is the smallest chamber group, with just two players. For string players, **sonatas** are the most common duets, usually combining a **string instrument** with the piano. To be considered chamber music, the piano part must be the equal partner of the string part, not merely accompaniment. The **trio** has three players, most often a **string trio** of **violin**, **viola**, and **cello**, or a **piano trio** of violin, cello, and piano. **Quartets**, particularly **string quartets** with two violins, viola, and cello, are the most popular chamber group, and many celebrated composers have written for this instrumentation. The **quintet** of-

ten adds an instrument such as piano, **double bass**, or a second cello to the string quartet. With almost any combination of instruments possible, chamber music is written for **septet**, **octet**, and even **nonet**, though a groups larger than this is considered a **chamber orchestra**. Works that combine strings with other types of instruments are usually named for the non-string instrument: a piano trio is strings and piano, and an oboe quartet is most often violin, viola, cello, and oboe.

chamber orchestra. A small **orchestra** usually composed of twenty to thirty players. Some chamber orchestras perform without a conductor. See also **full orchestra** and **symphony**.

chamfer. A bevel cut along the corner of two surfaces where they meet at a 90-degree angle, creating a third surface at a 45-degree angle to soften the edge. On **string instruments**, a **luthier** may cut a chamfer along the back of the **head** on the **tip** of the **bow** or along the sides of the **scroll** where they meet the **peg-box**.

changes. The chord progression of a **jazz** tune. Changes are found notated as chord symbols on a **lead sheet**.

channel. The upward curve at the edge of the **plates** of an instrument where the arch reverses to meet the **purfling** at the outer edge. A deeper channel makes the plates more responsive but less powerful.

chapeau. (Fr.) **Slur** sign.

character piece. A short piece intended to convey a single emotion or programmatic idea.

chart.
1. A type of minimal musical notation of a piece used by **jazz** musicians. See also **lead sheet**.
2. An informal term for any **ensemble** piece or musical **arrangement**.

chase. A **jazz** term for two **soloists** taking turns **improvising** in alternating **phrases** or half-phrases.

chevalet. (Fr.) **Bridge**.

chin rest. The carved piece of wood or other material attached to the lower **bouts** of a **violin** or **viola**, used to balance the instrument under the jawbone. The chin rest is usually made of wood to match the other fittings, and is clamped onto the instrument near or over the **tailpiece**. Violinist **Louis Spohr** is credited with having invented the chin rest around 1820, allowing the player to balance the instrument under the jaw as increasing technical demands of music required greater freedom of the left hand. Because the chin rest is clamped only to the edges of the instrument, it provides the player with a contact that does not dampen the instrument's vibrations.

Modern players have a choice of over fifty chin rest designs, from the standard left-mounted Guarneri model or the centered Flesch model, to customizable designs with adjustable heights and angles. Some **luthiers** even carve custom chin rests to fit the exact needs of a client. Choosing the right chin rest is a highly personalized decision based on the individual player's jaw shape, neck length, and placement of the instrument on the shoulder.

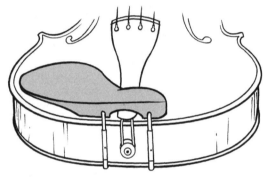

Figure 30. A **Guarneri**-style **chin rest**.

chops.
1. Technical skill on the instrument. Someone who plays with highly developed virtuosity is said to have great chops.
2. Rhythmic **bow** technique of striking the **string** near the **frog** to make a percussive sound of indeterminate **pitch**, frequently used in **jazz** and **bluegrass**.

chord. Three or more notes played simultaneously. String players have three techniques for playing chords: the **block chord**, in which all notes are played at once, which is only possible with three-note chords; the **broken chord**, in which two sets of **double-stops** are played in rapid succession; and the **rolled chord**, in which the notes are quickly **arpeggiated**.

chordophone. Any musical instrument that produces sound through the vibration of **strings**.

chromatic extension. A mechanized **C extension** for the **double bass** using a set of wooden fingers or capos which can be engaged to **stop** each **pitch**. See also **C extension**, **machine extension**, and **fingered extension**.

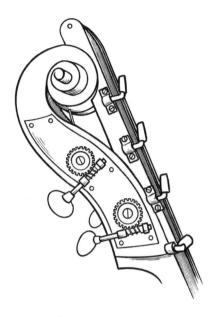

Figure 31. A **chromatic extension** for **double bass**.

chromatic *glissando*. See *glissando*.

chromatic scale. Every possible pitch played consecutively. The chromatic scale divides the octave into twelve notes, each a **half-step** apart.

chûte. (Fr.) A **grace note** that serves as an anticipation and is approached by a descending **slur** from the preceding note.

ciaccona. (It.) See **chaconne**.

circular bowing. A 20th-century **bowstroke** in which the bow travels in a light glide away from the **bridge** to the **fingerboard** on a **down-bow**, then circles to glide lightly back towards the bridge on an **up-bow**, creating a continuous, sighing sound.

circular temperament. A system of **tempered tuning** based on the circle of fifths.

Clarke, Rebecca (1886-1979). English **viola** player and composer who was a trailblazer for women's place in **art music**. In 1908 Clarke was the first woman to be accepted to study composition at the Royal College of Music, and in 1912 became one of the first female professional orchestral musicians by joining the all-male Queen's Hall Orchestra. Two of Clarke's compositions, the viola **sonata** and the **piano trio**, were runner-up in the Berkshire Festival of Chamber Music competition, sponsored by Elizabeth Sprague Coolidge, who then commissioned the Rhapsody for **Cello** and Piano, making Clarke the only woman recipient of Coolidge's patronage. In spite of these achievements, Clarke's work was often discouraged, and most of her music has never been published. In 2000 the Rebecca Clarke Society was established to promote performance, scholarship, and awareness of the works of Rebecca Clarke.

classical bow. A bow with a design that was used in the Classical era (1750-1820). See **transitional bow**.

cleat. Small pieces of wood glued to the inside of a **plate**, used to hold together a repaired crack.

clef. The symbol on the far left of printed music indicating the exact pitches assigned to the lines and spaces of the staff. **Violin** reads exclusively in treble clef, **viola** reads in alto clef with occasional treble clef, **cello** reads primarily in bass clef with high passages in tenor or treble clef, and **double bass** reads in bass clef, sounding an octave lower than written.

click track. A **metronome** designed to help musicians coordinate laying tracks for a recording or synchronize the music when playing the soundtrack with a film. In a recording **session**, the click track is played through headphones, allowing the players to hear the track without the microphones picking up the clicks. Digital click tracks can be programmed to match even the most complex timing of the action on screen. See also **metronome**.

clicks.
1. The crisp **articulation** created with the change of bow direction when playing a solid *détaché* bowstroke. Clicks mean the passage will sound clean and clearly articulated in a hall.
2. The ticking sound produced by a metronome. To play something "a few clicks faster" means at a tempo that is several beats per minute faster. See **metronome** and **click track**.

clip-in frog. A type of **bow** design used prior to 1725 when the modern **screw adjuster** was developed. The clip-in-frog allows the hair to be released by unclipping the frog when the bow is not in use, extending the life of the stick and the horse hair. The clip-in-frog bow is still used with **baroque instruments** and **viols**. See also **bow** and **historically informed performance**.

close shake. A two-fingered **vibrato** technique used on the **viol** and other **fretted** instruments, in which one finger holds down the string while the next finger flutters in a **trill**-like movement. A close shake is also called two-finger vibrato, vibrato trill, or *langueur*.

closed position. A **finger pattern** on the **cello** in which each finger measures a consecutive **half-step**. See also **extended position** and **finger pattern**.

co-principal. A shared leadership position within an **orchestra**. See also **principal** and **conventions of orchestral playing**.

coffin case. An old style of wooden instrument **case**, usually painted black, thought of as resembling a coffin.

col, coll', colla, colle. (It.) With.

col arco. (It.) With the **bow**, usually indicating the end of a *pizzicato* passage.

col legno. (It.) Play with the wood of the **bow**. *Col Legno* is usually short for *col legno battuto*, meaning to strike the **string** with the **stick** in a percussive manner. Much less common are *col legno tratto*, to bow the string with the wood of the stick rather than the hair, and *col legno frotté*, to rub the string with the stick. Other terms meaning *col legno* include *coll' arco al roverscio*, *geschlagen*, and *frappez avec le bois de l'archet*.
There is concern that playing *col legno* can cause damage to the stick of the bow, leading some players to choose a **carbon fiber bow** or cheap wood bow for this technique.

col legno frotté. (Fr.) Rub the **strings** with the wood of the **bow**. See also *col legno*.

coll' arco al roverscio. (It.) With the bow reversed, meaning to play with the wood of the **bow**. See also *col legno*.

colla parte. (It.) Play accompaniment to the other part.

colla punto. (It.) With the **tip** of the **bow**.

colla voce. (It.) With the voice. *Colla voce* is usually found in opera, indicating that the singer will treat the passage with freedom and the **orchestra** should follow.

collapsible upright bass. A **double bass** modified to fold or disassemble into a small size to facilitate travel. Designs for collapsible basses include instruments with removable necks, instruments in which the neck folds into a slot cut into the back of the body, and instruments with reduced, compact bodies. See also **electric upright bass** and **travel bass**.

collar. A decorative ring around the shaft of a tuning **peg** just at the base of the head. A loose collar may be the source of an instrument **buzz**.

collé. (Fr.) A **bow technique** executed entirely with the fingers. *Collé* can be used in a **legato** stroke to smooth the moment of a change in direction, or it can be used to create a biting *staccato* stroke near the **frog** in which the bow pinches the **string** then is picked off by pulling the fingers sharply into the hand. Instruction on exactly how *collé* is executed and when it should be used varies widely depending on the pedagogue and the era. See **Table 1: Bowstrokes** for a list of strokes and their notation.

colophony. See **rosin**.

colpo d'arco. (It.) **Bowstroke**.

combination tones. See **Tartini tones**.

con. (It.) With.

con sordino. (It.) With the **mute**.

concert pitch. The actual sounding **pitch** played by an instrument, usually used in reference to **transposing instruments** such as clarinet or trumpet. The only transposing **string instrument** is the **double bass**, which has a concert pitch one octave lower than is indicated by printed music. On occasion a string instrument playing *scordatura* will read from standard notation but play on strings with unusual tunings, in which case the notated pitch will differ from the concert pitch. See also **standard pitch**.

concertino. (It.) The **solo** player(s) in a *concerto grosso*, as opposed to the *ripieno*, or full **section**.

concertmaster. The **principal** first violin player and representative of all the musicians in an **orchestra**. In addition to leading the first violin **section**, the concertmaster's responsibilities include overseeing the tuning of the orchestra, creating the coordinated **bowings** for the strings, leading the quartet of principal string players, making artistic decisions for the string sections, assigning *divisi* parts, playing all first violin **solos**, and cueing entrances. The concertmaster also leads the orchestra in standing for bows and is involved as a representative of the orchestra in serving on committees, attending fundraising events, and making personnel decisions. The concertmaster may be called the **super soloist** in some European orchestras and **leader** in the UK.
    See also **conventions of orchestral playing**.

concerto. A large-scale composition for **solo** instrument and **orchestra**, often serving as a showcase for the technical brilliance and musical artistry of the soloist. Traditionally, a concerto consists of three contrasting movements and at least one **cadenza**.

concerto grosso. A composition for a group of **solo** instruments and **orchestra**, most popular in the Baroque era. The concerto grosso contrasts the soloists, called the *concertino* with the orchestra, called the *ripieno*, and usually includes a **continuo**.

conservatory. A college specializing in musical training.

consort. An instrumental **chamber music** ensemble popular during the Renaissance. A **whole consort** plays instruments of the same family, as with a **viol** consort, while a **broken consort** mixes instruments of different families. See also **historically informed performance** and **viol family**.

contact point. The exact place where the **hair** of the **bow** meets the **string** while playing, also called the **sounding point**. A contact point closer to the **bridge** will produce a denser, more penetrating sound; a contact point closer to the **fingerboard** will produce a lighter, more translucent sound. Manipulation of the contact point is one of a string player's most potent tools for changing **tone color** and creating **phrasing**. See **sounding point** for an illustration.

continuo. The group of musicians playing the **basso continuo** line, usually comprised of a **cello** or *viola da gamba* player and a keyboard player, typically harpsichord or organ. Continuo is most commonly found in music from the Baroque era. See also **historically informed performance** and **viol family**.

contra bass. See **double bass**.

contralto viola. A **viola** with an enlarged **resonance chamber**. Various **luthiers** have designed contralto violas in an attempt to improve the **acoustic** qualities of the instrument. One characteristic example, made in 1855 by Vuillaume in collaboration with acoustician Felix Savart, maintains the body length while widening the bouts significantly, thus creating an air capacity that is large enough to match the proportions of the acoustically ideal **violin**. Like most attempts at enlarging a shoulder-held viola, Vuillaume's contralto proved too cumbersome to play. Other makers of contralto violas include **Maggini, Stradivari**, and **Amati**. See also *Altgeige*, **tenor viola**, *viola pomposa*, *viola da spalla*, *violetta*, **Tertis viola**, and **vertical viola**.

conventions of orchestral playing. The standard procedures and traditions associated with playing a
string instrument in an **orchestra**. The string choir
is the foundation of any **symphony** orchestra or
chamber orchestra, with as many as eighty string
players in an orchestra. These musicians are divided
into five sections: **first violin, second violin, viola,
cello,** and **double bass,** with everyone in a section
usually playing in exact unison. Orchestras have developed conventions of section playing that are invaluable in organizing such a large group and facilitate
the difficult skill of playing in unison.

I. Leadership. An orchestra is a highly structured
hierarchy of leadership roles with the **concertmaster**
at the helm and specific responsibilities reaching to
the very last **chair** player. The leader of the string
choir and the representative of all the musicians in the
orchestra is the concertmaster, who is ultimately re-
sponsible for all **bowings**, musical interpretations,
and technical decisions of an orchestra's mass of
string players. The concertmaster is also the **principal**
of the first violin section and works closely with the
principal players of each string section, forming a
string quartet circled around the conductor, plus the
principal bassist who usually stands behind the cello
section. Principals follow the lead of the concertmaster, making all the musical and technical decisions for
their respective sections, unifying their timing, bow
work, phrasing, and musicality with each other just as
a string quartet would. Bowings are determined by the
principals and should match those chosen by the concertmaster. Often principals meet as a quartet prior to
the first rehearsal to coordinate bowings and musical
ideas. Principals lead their section in making entrances, playing the right dynamics, and interpreting the
gestures of the conductor by cueing with large physical gestures that enable their section players to anticipate and synchronize. The stand partner of each
principal is the assistant principal, who helps in
communication with the section and is prepared to sit
principal should the need arise. In a professional orchestra, the concertmaster and other principal players
receive a higher salary than section players as a reflection of these additional responsibilities.

II. Section playing. Many orchestral conventions
facilitate the section player, whose job is to follow
their principal, aid the work of all players seated behind, and blend seamlessly into the unison sound of
the section. Each section player is expected to watch
the principal carefully, matching every detail of timing, bowing, and musicality. The bow work of the
section players is exactly synchronized, imitating the
**bowstroke, contact point, bow speed, articulation,
dynamic, bow distribution, phrasing,** and **tone col-
or** of the principal. Players towards the back of the
section who may not have a clear view of the princi-

pal's bow watch the player as close to the front as
possible, relying on that player to match the principal.

III. Communication. Orchestras have guidelines for
communicating within the section to prevent comments from the principals and questions from the section from disrupting a rehearsal. When decisions are
made by the principal players or dictated from the po-
dium, a network of message passing is activated. The
assistant principal of each section turns and quietly
passes the information to the stand directly behind
them, allowing the principal to continue playing and
attend to the rehearsal. Because it can be difficult or
impossible for players in the rear of the section to see
and hear what happens at the front of the section, it is
imperative that each member of a section pass any information from their principals to the stand behind
them, who will then pass it to the stand behind them,
and so on until every member of the section has received the message. Similarly, if a member of the section has a question, the inside player of each stand
passes it quietly forward until it has reached the assistant principal, who will consult the principal then pass
the answer back through this chain until the entire
section knows the answer. If a question requires con-
sultation with another principal or the conductor, only
the principal can pose the question. Any missed questions, bowings, or other concerns of a section player
are addressed directly to the principal during break or
after the rehearsal.

IV. Sharing sheet music. Most orchestral string
players share music with one other player, called their
stand partner, and orchestral players have adopted
an understood set of etiquette for dealing with a
common stand and shared parts. The **outside player**,
that is the one closer to the edge of the stage, is re-
sponsible for the printed parts, including bringing the
music to each rehearsal and performance. The **inside
player** is provided with a practice part, usually photo-
copied from the principal's part, which is intended for
that player's practice only and is never used in rehearsal or performance. The inside player has the duty
of keeping the shared parts correctly marked during
rehearsals. If writing in the music is needed to correct
a bowing or change a dynamic, the outside player will
continue playing while the inside player stops to write
the new marking into the part. This rule applies to
page turns as well, with the inside stopping to turn the
page while the outside continues playing. For personal markings on the music such as fingerings or position indications, the outside player places their
markings above the notes and the inside player writes
theirs below the notes.

corda. (It.) **String.** Common phrases found in music
include *a una corda*: to play on a single string; *à la
corda* or *alla corda*: to play **on the string**, signaling

the end of **spiccato**; *tres a la corda*: very **legato**; *corda vuota*: **open string**.

Corelli, Arcangelo (1653-1713). Italian violinist and composer whose playing, directing, composing, and teaching had a tremendous influence on string playing. As a favorite of powerful Roman patrons, Corelli enjoyed an active career as a high-profile **violin virtuoso**, composer, and director of **ensembles**. His compositions for the violin demand a balance of technical brilliance and melodic elegance, and he is credited with popularizing the **walking bass**. Corelli's insistence that his string players be utterly synchronized in their **bowings** began a standard still practiced by **orchestras** today, and his teaching legacy was so influential that almost every great violinist can trace their **pedagogical** lineage back to him.

corner blocks. The pieces of wood inside the instrument securing the **ribs** at the **bouts**. See **blocks**.

cornerless instrument. An instrument with the gently rounded body shape of a guitar. Cornerless instruments are often conceived as a means of simplifying the manufacture of the instrument. In addition to the missing **corners**, these instrument designs may have **plates** that do not overhang the **ribs**, with the edges secured by bindings rather than reinforced by **purfling**. Many cornerless instruments also have modified or simplified **sound hole** shapes and may even have a flat back. **Luthiers** have made cornerless **violins**, **violas**, **cellos**, and **double basses** for hundreds of years, including **Stradivarius'** 1718 "Chanot-Chardon" violin played by a young Joshua Bell. Many modern **carbon fiber instruments** are made in the cornerless shape. Cornerless instruments are also called guitar-shaped.

corners. The points where the **C bouts** join to the **ribs** of an instrument. On **violin**, **viola**, and **cello**, the corners are sharply pointed, a shape mirrored by the outline of the top and back **plates** and emphasized by the **bee-sting** in the **purfling**. **Double basses** have three distinct designs for the corners of C bouts: pointed like those of a **violin**, C-shaped like those of a *viola da gamba*, or outwardly rounded **busetto** corners. On rare occasions, an instrument of the **modern string family** may be **cornerless**. See also **busetto**, **C bouts**, **cornerless instrument**, and **gamba shape**.

cornet violin. See stroh viol.

corrente. (It.) See *courante*.

counterpoint. The compositional technique of creating **polyphony** by combining two or more independent melodies in harmonically linked horizontal layers. Counterpoint is one of the fundamental building blocks of **art music**.

coup d'archet. (Fr.) **Bowstroke**.

courante. (Fr.) A lively baroque dance in triple time, also spelled *corrente* (It.) to distinguish the French and Italian styles.

Cramer bow. A **transitional bow** design popular among major soloists during the Classical era, characterized by a tall hatchet-shaped **tip**, a sturdy, concave stick, and a **clip-in frog**.

craquer l'archet. (Fr.) Two successive **up-bows** with a stop between them, notated by **dots** under a **slur**, used to reposition the bow correctly to follow the **rule of down-bow**. See **hooked bow**.

crawling fingering. A technique of using **finger extensions** rather than **shifts** to move through positions. Crawling fingerings are popular among modern players as a way of playing very cleanly, particularly in orchestral work. Also called creeping fingering.

creeping fingering. See **crawling fingering**.

crémaillère bow. An early design for adjusting the **hair tension** on a **bow**. The **frog** of a crémaillère bow has a metal loop that hooks over a row of notches atop the end of the **stick**, allowing the player to tighten or release **tension** on the hair.

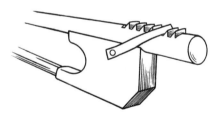

Figure 32. The mechanism for adjusting the **hair tension** on a **crémaillère bow**.

critical edition. Sheet music based on historical research that seeks to present the score as faithfully as possible to the composer's intentions, free of interpretive markings and modernization added by editors. Critical editions, also called historical editions, usually include scholarly commentary about the work. See also **historically informed performance** and *Urtext*.

cross shuffle. A fiddle **shuffle** bowing pattern played across two or more strings. See also **double shuffle** and **shuffle**.

crwth. (Wel.) An ancient bowed lyre of Welsh origin, characterized by a U-shaped yoke, a flat, fretless **fingerboard**, and six **strings**. Crwth is pronounced "krooth."

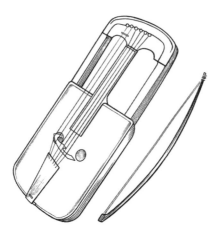

Figure 33. A **crwth**.

cue.
1. A physical gesture anticipating and signaling a musical event. String player cues include **bow** movement, raising and lowering the **scroll**, nodding the head, leaning forward or back, and breathing audibly.
2. The notes of another instrument indicated in small print and intended to aid the player in making an entrance after a rest.

curl. See **flaming**.

cut. An **ornament** common in **Irish fiddle** music. A cut is a **grace note** placed between two notes of the same pitch in a melody, played by lightly tapping a second or third above the melody note, making more of an interruption than a clear pitch. A double cut uses two grace notes, the first of which is the same note as the melody.

cutaway instrument. An instrument with the right upper **bout** shaped into an indentation to facilitate reaching notes in high **positions**. **Violas** are the most common instruments of the **modern string family** to be given a cutaway form, though **violins, cellos,** and **double basses** are also occasionally made with this modification. See also **ergonomic instrument.**

Figure 34. A **five-string double bass** with a **cutaway** left shoulder.

~ D ~

D. Abbreviation for Deutsch, the system for cataloging the music of Franz Schubert in lieu of opus numbers, created by Otto Erich Deutsch. See also **thematic index.**

da camera. (It.) Music intended for intimate spaces. See **chamber music.**

da chiesa. (It.) Music intended for performance in church.

Dalcroze Eurhythmics. A method of using **kinesthetic** sense and physical movement to understand rhythm, meter, structure, and **phrasing** in music. Dalcroze Eurhythmics, also known as the Dalcroze Method or simply Eurhythmics, was developed in the early 20th century by Émile Jaques-Dalcroze to enhance musicianship by focusing on the physical experience of artistic performance.

damp, dampen. To stop a **string** from vibrating, usually by touching it with the left hand.

Dämpfer. (Ger.) **Mute**. The phrase *mit Dämpfer* means to play with the mute. *Ohne Dämpfer* means without the mute, and *Dämpfer weg* means to remove the mute.

dampit. A **humidifier** made of a rubber tube filled with sponge. A moistened dampit is snaked into the instrument through the **f-hole**, where it slowly releases moisture to prevent the instrument from cracking. The brand name dampit, written lowercase by the designer, has become a general-use term for any humidifier of this type.

dance master's fiddle/violin. See *pochette*.

David, Ferdinand (1810-1873). German violinist, composer, and **pedagogue** best known for his close collaboration with Mendelssohn. David was considered a prodigy and studied **violin** with **Spohr**. In 1835, after two years of touring with his pianist sister and ten years of **orchestra** and **quartet** work, David was offered the **concertmaster** position of the Leipzig Gewandhaus orchestra under the baton of Mendelssohn, a post he held for the rest of his life

David gave many recitals and **chamber music** concerts in Leipzig with Mendelssohn at the keyboard and the two worked together on the **solo** part for Mendelssohn's violin **concerto**, leaving two manuscripts: the composer's initial version and a second version with extensive revisions made by David. The second version is the one premiered in 1845 by David and still performed today, including the single, integrated **cadenza** largely created by David.

In 1843 David became head of the violin faculty of the newly opened Leipzig **conservatory**, where his students included **Joachim** and Wilhelmj. As part of his pedagogical work, David created editions of studies by **Kreutzer**, **Rode**, Fiorillo, Gaviniés, and **Paganini**, as well as a new edition of **J. S. Bach's** six **sonatas** and **partitas** for solo violin, and many chamber works. His *Violinschule* and **etudes** were widely used until the end of the 19th century.

As a composer, David produced forty works including five violin concertos, an opera, two **symphonies**, and a variety of chamber works. Of these, only the concertino for trombone has entered the standard **repertoire**.

démancher. (Fr.) **Shifting** the left hand from one **position** to another.

desk. A shared music stand, typically in an orchestra. The desk can refer literally to the **music stand** or generally to the musicians sharing the music on the stand. The front desk refers to the first stand of **principal** players. See also **principal** and **conventions of orchestral playing**.

détaché. (Fr.) The most basic **bowstroke** with one *legato* bow per note. In general, all notes written with no **articulation** markings or **slurs** are considered *détaché*. See **Table 1: Bowstrokes** for a list of strokes and their notation.

détaché lancé. (Fr.) A *legato* **bowstroke** with one note per **bow** in which the beginning of each note is given a sharp **accent**. See **Table 1: Bowstrokes** for a list of strokes and their notation.

détaché porté. (Fr.) A *legato* **bowstroke** with one note per **bow** in which the beginning of each note is leaned on for emphasis. See **Table 1: Bowstrokes** for a list of strokes and their notation.

deutlich. (Ger.) Clearly, distinctly, articulated.

Deutsch number. The system for cataloging the music of Franz Schubert in lieu of opus numbers, abbreviated D. and created by Otto Erich Deutsch. See also **thematic index**.

diamond note, diamond note-head. A square note-head turned on its point to have a diamond shape, indicating a **harmonic**. The diamond note-head is placed to show where the harmonic can be found on the **fingerboard**, with the resulting pitch sounding much higher than indicated. When combined on a single stem above a regular note-head, the diamond note indicates an **artificial harmonic**, in which the regular note is played solidly and the diamond note is touched lightly. The head of a diamond note is always open regardless of the rhythm.

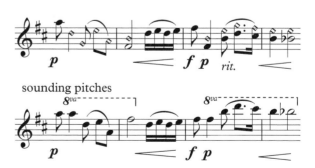

Figure 35. **Diamond note-heads** from **Henryk Wieniawski's** *Concert Polonaise* no. 2, op. 4 mm 19-22, and the sounding pitches actually produced.

dietro il ponticello. (It.) Play by bowing **behind the bridge**.

difference tones, differential tones. See **Tartini tones**.

digital music stand. An electronic device that displays sheet music on a screen. Digital **music stands** can be hardware and software in a single designated device, or may be just software that runs on any computer system. These programs are designed to display pages of music digitally, replacing paper music. Many digital music stands also allow a musician to scan, play back, and edit scores, and they may be capable of displaying either a **part** or the entire score. With the ability to digitally store an entire library of sheet music, these devices offer great convenience for traveling musicians. Other advantages include adjustable back lighting, eliminating the need for a **stand light**, and automated page-turns using an attached pedal.

div., divisi. (It.) Divided, to separate the notes into two or more parts, usually found in **orchestra** music. The *divisi* can be arranged by player or by **stand**, as decided by the **concertmaster** or other **principal**, and depending on how many parts need to be covered. Unless otherwise instructed, it is assumed that a two-part *divisi* is split between each pair of players sharing a stand, with the **outside players** taking the upper line and the **inside players** covering the lower line. A *divisi* of three or more parts can be split by player in order of seating, or by stand, with both players sharing a stand covering the same part. It is traditional in some orchestras to play all double, triple, and quadruple **stops** *divisi* even when not specifically indicated in the music, in order to create a clean **articulation** and improve **intonation**. Some composers specify *non divisi* to ensure the section plays a **block chord**.

division viol. The middle of three sizes of bass **viol** used during the 17th century for **improvising** highly **ornamented** variations on a melody. With a **tuning** of D2 – G2 – C3 – E3 – A3 – D4, the division viol has a large range, and players read from staff notation rather than the **tablature** used by the smaller **lyra viol**. See also **viol family**.

Dodd family. An English family of bowmakers whose shop was begun in London by Edward Dodd (1705-1810). While little is known about the work of Edward, his son John Dodd (1752-1839) was considered the greatest English bowmaker before **Tubbs**. John Dodd made **transitional bows** with either the high, hammer-style **head** or the long, graceful swan head. By the end of his career Dodd had incorporated all of the modern developments, including a **ferrule** to

spread the **horsehair**, a **Tourte** head design, and an octagonal **stick**. His **cello** bows are particularly valued. The Dodd family business was continued by Edward's sons and grandsons until it entered bankruptcy in 1838.

doghouse bass. A term for the **double bass**.

doit. A **jazz** term (pronounced "doyt") for ending a note with an upward slide. The technique can be notated by an upward sloping line following the notehead. See also **bend, drop, fall off, plop, scoop**, and *glissando*.

Figure 36. **Doit** notation.

dolce. (It.) Sweet.

Doppelgriff. (Ger.) **Double-stop**.

doppio. (It.) See **double**.

dot.
1. A dot over the note-head indicates that the note should be played *staccato*, that is, detached from the note that follows. (The common interpretation of a dot as a direction to play the note "short" is an oversimplification because the exact length of any detached note is an interpretive choice that depends on tempo, style, dynamics, and many other considerations.) String players achieve this detached articulation either by stopping the bow on the string or by removing the bow from the string altogether. At a slower tempo, this may be accomplished by using an **on-the-string** bowstroke such as *détaché lancé* or *martelé*. In fast passage work, dots over notes are usually achieved with an **off-the-string** bowstroke such as *spiccato* or *sautillé*. Dots in combination with a **slur** means to detach the notes without changing the direction of the bow, accomplished by bowstrokes including a **hooked bow, flying *staccato***, or *jeté*. See also **articulation**.
2. A dot following the note-head indicates the added duration of half the value of the note. See also **double dotting**.

double.
1. A variation on a dance in which the original melody is ornamented, for example the first **Partita** for Solo Violin BWV 1002 by **J. S. Bach**.
2. A repair to the **button** on the **back plate** of an instrument, made by grafting a new layer of wood onto

the existing button.

double appoggiatura. See **appoggiatura**.

double bass. The largest and lowest-pitched instrument of the **modern string family**, which also includes the **violin, viola,** and **cello**. The double bass measures about three times the size of the violin and is standardly tuned in fourths, E1 – A1 – D2 – G2 (orchestral tuning). The double bass is held vertically, supported on the floor by an **endpin**, and turned in slightly to lean against the player's body. Depending on the **genre** of music, the double bass is played *arco* with a horsehair bow or plucked *pizzicato* with the fingers.

The heritage of the double bass can be traced back to both the **viol family** and the **violin family** of instruments, with the modern bass showing characteristics of both. Traditionally described as a bass violin, the double bass was developed in Europe in the early 16th century along with the violin, viola, and cello. The double bass was made in a large variety of sizes and shapes, with as few as three and as many as six **strings**, and numerous **tuning** systems.

By the 20th century, the double bass was somewhat standardized to a three-quarter size body with four strings tuned in fourths, though most modern orchestral basses include either a **C extension** or a fifth B string to extend the lower range. Solo double bass players often use *scordatura*, the most common of which is F#1 – B1 – E2 – A2, called **solo tuning**. The double bass is a **transposing instrument**, sounding one octave lower than notated.

The modern double bass can be hand-carved from wood with techniques similar to those used for violins and cellos, or built from layers of laminated wood. Some instruments combine both, pairing carved plates with laminated ribs. Classical bassists tend to prefer hand-carved instruments for their richness and beauty of sound, while players in many other genres like the durability of a laminated bass. The double bass is constructed of a top and back **plate**, the top formed into an arched shape to support the weight from the **bridge**. The back plate may also be arched, or it may be made flat with interior **bracing** for support. The sides of the instrument are the **ribs**, made from six thin strips of wood that have been bent using heat and water to match the shape of the plates. The ribs and plates are held together with **hide glue** and reinforced at the joints by **linings** and **blocks**. Inside the body, the **soundpost** and **bass-bar** sit beneath the bridge, supporting the structure of the instrument against the tension of the **strings** and helping to transfer **sound waves** across the surfaces of the plates. **F-holes** cut into the top plate are shaped to maximize the **acoustic resonance** of the sounding chamber. The **fingerboard**, usually made of **ebony** for its smooth texture, is glued to a **neck** of **maple**, which is carved in a single piece from the **heel** to the **scroll**. The strings are stretched taut between a **tailpiece** tied to the **end button** on the lower **bouts**, and **mechanical peg** tuners built into the sides of the **pegbox** on the instrument's **head**. The strings pass over a high bridge, carved from a wedge of maple, which transfers the vibrations of the strings to the **resonance chamber** of the body. The strings are held slightly above the surface of the fingerboard by the raised ebony **nut** at the top of the fingerboard. An endpin, usually metal, extends from the end button to support the bass on the floor while playing.

Double bass players use one of two distinctly different types of **bow**: the **French bow**, which looks like a cello bow and is held overhand, or the **German bow**, which has a tall, slender **frog** and is grasped endwise.

The double bass provides the lowest voice in the string choir of the modern **orchestra**, which has a **section** of three to ten bass players, and it plays a central role in the rhythm sections of **ensembles** playing in every genre of music, including **jazz, blues,** country, **bluegrass,** folk, and rock, where it is called an upright bass or an acoustic bass to distinguish it from the electric bass guitar. Other names for the instrument include string bass, bass fiddle, bass violin, doghouse bass, contrabass, bass viol, and stand-up bass.

See Figure 37 on the following page.

double case. A case designed to hold two instruments, usually two violins or a **violin** and a **viola**.

double concerto. A large-scale orchestral work featuring two soloists, such as the **concerto** for two violins by **J. S. Bach**, *Sinfonia Concertante* for **violin** and **viola** by W. A. Mozart, and the concerto for violin and **cello** by Johannes Brahms.

double cut. See **cut**.

double dot, double dotting. Two dots following the note-head, indicating an added duration of three-quarters the note value. The practice of interpreting dotted rhythms as double-dotted rhythms is common in the performance of baroque music. See also **historically informed performance** and **dot**.

double shift. An archaic term indicating a **shift** the distance of two thirds, or two **whole shifts**.

double shuffle. A rhythmic **bowing** pattern of rapid double-stop string crossings, as in the "Orange Blossom Special." See also **shuffle, Nashville shuffle,** and **Georgia shuffle**.

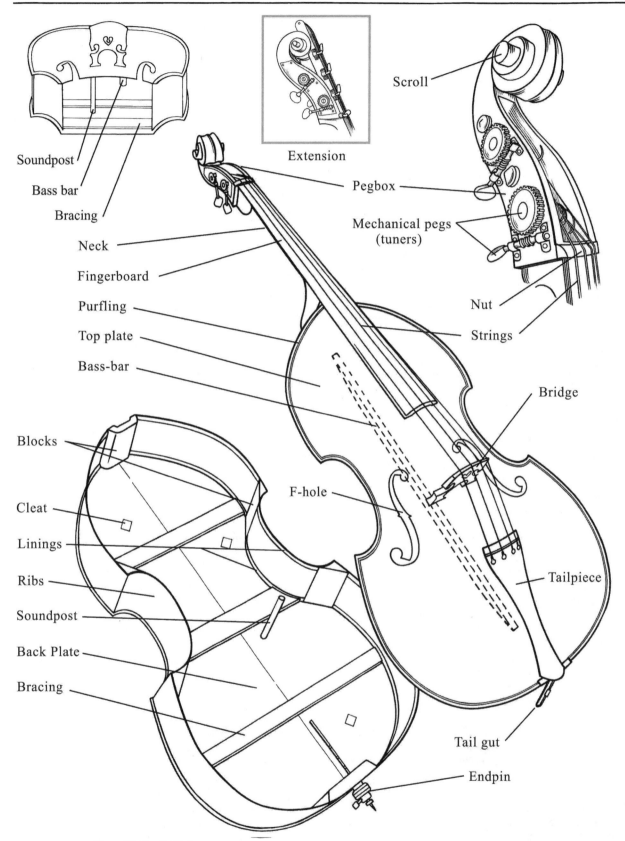

Soundpost

Bass bar

Bracing

Neck

Fingerboard

Purfling

Top plate

Bass-bar

Blocks

Cleat

Linings

Ribs

Soundpost

Back Plate

Bracing

Extension

Scroll

Pegbox

Mechanical pegs
(tuners)

Nut

Strings

Bridge

F-hole

Tailpiece

Tail gut

Endpin

Figure 37. The **double bass**.

double stop. Two notes sounding simultaneously. Double stops are notated by two vertically aligned note-heads, often sharing a single stem.

Andante religioso

Figure 38. Melodic **double stops** from **Alfredo Piatti's Caprice** no. 2, op. 25, mm 1-4.

double string violin. A **violin** with the middle two **strings** placed close to the outer strings, often tuned *scordatura*. The double string violin, also called a **klezmer fiddle**, is used in Middle-Eastern music.

double trill. A **double stop** in which both notes are trilled simultaneously. The double trill is notated with a *tr* mark over or under each of the two notes.

Figure 39. **Double trills** from **Nicolò Paganini's Caprice** no. 2, op. 1, mm 21-24.

double-note. See **double stop**.

dovetail. See **mortice**.

down-bow. A **bowstroke** that is pulled away from the **frog** and towards the **tip**, indicated by the symbol ⊓ placed above the note. Because down-bow is generally considered a stronger movement than **up-bow**, it is conventionally chosen for notes played on strong beats. Also called *Abstrich* in German, *arcata in giù,* in Italian, and *tiré,* or "pull" in French. See also **rule of down-bow** and **Table 1: Bowstrokes** for a list of strokes and their notation.

down-bow rule. See **rule of down-bow**.

Dragonetti bow. A **double bass bow** designed by bass virtuoso **Domenico Dragonetti** in the early 19th century. The Dragonetti bow is characterized by a convex stick and is held endwise with a **German bow hold**.

Dragonetti, Domenico (1763-1846). Italian **double bass virtuoso** and composer whose brilliant playing changed perceptions about the capabilities of the in-

strument. Dragonetti had a successful career as an orchestral musician in England and composed numerous works featuring double bass for his **solo** performances, which were very popular. His concerts were most often given on a three-string double bass tuned in fourths and played with a convex **bow**, which is still sometimes referred to as a **Dragonetti bow**.

Historians often credit Dragonetti with inspiring Beethoven to write challenging bass parts in his **symphonies** that are a significant voice independent of the **cello** line. Dragonetti is even sometimes depicted as premiering the recitative in Beethoven's ninth symphony as a double bass solo, though evidence shows that Dragonetti did not perform in the Vienna **premiere**, nor did he participate in the London premiere, as the London Philharmonic Society was unwilling to pay the exorbitant fee he requested.

dress. To **plane** a **fingerboard** smooth of grooves.

drone. A note or **chord** that is sustained throughout a large section or an entire piece. On **string instruments**, a drone is usually created by playing an **open string** in **double stop** with a melody on an adjacent string.

drone string. An **open string** used to play a sustained tone throughout a piece, often specially tuned to suit the key of the piece. See also **drone** and *scordatura*.

drop. A **jazz** term for ending a note with a downward slide. The technique can be notated by a downward sloping line following the note-head. See also **fall off, bend, doit, plop, scoop,** and *glissando*.

Figure 40. **Drop** notation.

drop D tuning. A *scordatura* **double bass tuning** of D1 – A1 – D2 – G2 borrowed from electric **bass guitar**.

drum stroke. A thrown *ricochet* **bowstroke** with two rapidly bounced notes per bow on alternating bows. The drum stroke is notated by a combination of **slurs** and dots over consecutive pairs of notes. Drum stroke is also called feather bowing. See **Table 1: Bowstrokes** for a list of strokes and their notation.

Du Pré, Jacqueline (1945-1987). English **virtuoso** cellist beloved for her charismatic stage presence and her interpretation of Elgar's cello **concerto**. Du Pré was the first woman to achieve fame as an international **cello** soloist, ranked alongside Itzhak Perlman, **Yehudi Menuhin**, Pinchas Zukerman, and Daniel Barenboim, with whom she frequently collaborated. Although Jacqueline du Pré's concert career lasted little more than a decade, cut short by multiple sclerosis, she was able to record much of the cello literature, and she served as a great inspiration to a new generation of aspiring cellists.

due corde. (It.) Playing the same pitch simultaneously on two **strings**, creating a unison **double stop**.

duet.
1. An **ensemble** of two players.
2. The music composed for an ensemble of two players.

duo. See **duet**.

duo concertante. See **concerto**.

Duport, Jean-Louis (1749-1819). French cellist and composer whose systemization of sequential **finger patterns** in all **positions** for every key in his 1806 **cello** treatise *Essai sur le doigté du violoncelle et sur la conduite de l'archet* [Essay on the fingering of the violoncello and on the conduct of the bow] is one of the most influential pedagogical contributions to the development of cello **technique**. Duport frequently performed with **Viotti**, and Beethoven wrote his two op. 5 cello **sonatas** for himself and Duport. As an early advocate for the **Tourte bow**, Duport's playing was known for its clear **tone** and light, elegant approach.

dynamic accent. Emphasizing a note by increasing volume or adding **articulation**, as opposed to an **agogic accent** which emphasizes a note using the broadening of time. See **articulation** for a list of specific accent markings and their meanings.

~ E ~

E bevel. See **Romberg bevel**.

ears. The flared edges of the **scroll** that protrude as the curl tightens into the center. See **scroll**.

ebony. A dark hardwood of the Diospyros genus, often chosen for **string instrument fingerboards** because its high density makes it smooth and resistant to the grooves and troughs caused by the wear and tear of playing. Ebony may be used for other **fittings** as well, including the **tailpiece**, **chin rest**, **pegs**, and **end button**.

edge bumpers. See **bumpers**.

effleurant, effleurant la corde. (Fr.) Grazing the **string** lightly with the **bow**. See *flautando*.

effleuré pizzicato. (Fr.) Touching the **string** lightly with the left hand when plucking. *Effleuré pizzicato* usually produces only a soft thump, though if it is done touching one of the **nodes**, a resonant **pizzicato harmonic** is produced.

egg pin. A **double bass endpin** design intended to redistribute the weight of the instrument for ease of left hand work. The egg pin is made of two interlocking metal rods attached to the standard endpin **button** that can be adjusted to any angle and height. See also **endpin**, **tilt-block**, and **Laborie endpin**.

electric bass guitar. See **bass guitar** and **electric instrument**.

electric instrument. An instrument designed to produce sound through electric amplification rather than **acoustic resonance**. An electric **string instrument** usually has a **piezo pickup** built into a solid body, allowing the player to generate and control the **tone** through an **amplifier** or **synthesizer** without any additional acoustic sound. The signal from the pickup can be processed for effects such as delay, reverb, looping, distortion, and chorus.

Figure 41. A solid-bodied electric **violin** or **viola**.

The solid body is designed to avoid the **feedback** caused by the vibrations of a **resonance chamber**, and is often made of synthetic materials such as plastic, **carbon fiber**, or acrylic.

Electric string instruments frequently feature modifications such as the addition of extra strings for greater range, *scordatura* tunings, **fretted fingerboards**, and **mechanical pegs**.

Rarely used in **art music**, electric string instruments are the choice of players in **jazz**, rock, and even hip-hop. In the country, folk, **bluegrass**, and Celtic **genres**, players often prefer to amplify traditional instruments with a microphone or by fitting them with a piezo pickup.

See **MIDI instrument** for information about using a string instrument as the controller for a synthesizer.

electric stand-up bass. See **electric upright bass**.

electric upright bass. An amplified, portable **double bass**, often referred to as an EUB. A variety of electric upright bass designs are available, all using a minimal body and electric amplification to create a small, lightweight instrument. There are two distinct types of EUB: those with a curved **bridge** and **fingerboard** like an **acoustic** double bass, and those with a flat bridge and fingerboard like a bass guitar. The difference is significant, as the flat design cannot be played with a **bow**.

Figure 42. Playing an **electric upright bass**, or EUB.

Some EUBs have a small **resonance chamber** for an element of acoustic tone, while others are completely solid-bodied to eliminate the feedback common with hollow basses. Designs that are geared towards the traditional double bass player include reference points that correspond to features on the acoustic double bass. Some EUB designs have as many eight **strings**. EUBs are also called stick bass, electric stand-up bass, silent upright bass, and travel bass.

electronic music stand. See **digital music stand**.

embellishment. See **ornament** and **ornamentation**.

encore. A piece performed as a bonus at the discretion of the performer, drawn from the French word for "again." Traditionally an encore is to be played in response to a sustained standing ovation from the audience, though many musicians give an encore regardless of the level of audience enthusiasm. Music chosen for an encore is most often a virtuosic **showpiece** or audience favorite.

end button. See **button**.

endpin. A spike or rod fixed to the bottom of a **cello** or **double bass** used to support the instrument on the floor. Most modern players use an adjustable endpin that retracts into the instrument and is secured by a thumb screw. Also called a spike or tailpin, the endpin is made of metal, wood, or **carbon fiber**, the end of which is sharpened to a point which can be anchored in the floor.

To prevent the endpin from slipping or damaging floors, cellists and double bassists use either an **endpin stop** or a rubber cap over the sharpened tip. Cellist **Paul Tortelier** innovated the curved Tortelier-style endpin, allowing the cello to be placed more horizontally while playing.

Double bass endpin modifications intended to redistribute the weight of the instrument include a bent metal endpin, an **egg pin**, and a **Laborie endpin**.

On the **violin** and **viola**, the **end button** is occasionally referred to as an endpin.

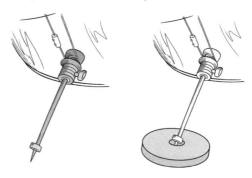

Figure 43. A typical **endpin** with a sharpened tip and one shown lodged in an **endpin stop**.

endpin rest, endpin stop. A device used to prevent the **endpin** of a **cello** or **double bass** from slipping on the floor. Endpin stop designs include a rubber or plastic disk that sticks to the floor, a strap anchored around a chair leg, and a wooden T braced behind both front legs of the chair. An endpin stop can also be called pinstop, donut, endpin anchor, spike holder, cello T, or rock stop.

endpin wheel. See **bass wheel.**

English violet. A bowed **string instrument** from the 18th century similar to the *viola d'amore* with six or seven melodic **strings** and as many as fourteen **sympathetic strings.**

enharmonic. Notes that are identical in pitch but spelled differently, such as D# and Eb. String players often think of notes in enharmonic equivalent to facilitate using **finger patterns** and to simplify string crossings.

ensemble.
1. A group of musicians who perform together.
2. The skill of playing well together, with unified timing and musical expression.

equal temperament. The modern system of **tempered tuning** in which the distance between each **half-step** within an octave is the same. Keyboards and **fretted string instruments** are fixed in equal temperament, allowing them to sound in tune in every key. Equal temperament was developed at the beginning of the 20th century, replacing earlier systems of **mean-tone temperament**, though **historically informed performance** musicians still use these historically relevant tunings, and groups without a fixed-pitch instrument, such as string **ensembles** and choirs, often use **just intonation** for its natural consonance.

ergonomic instrument. An instrument designed to fit the player in the most natural way possible. Ergonomic instruments are completely redesigned to facilitate ease of playing, a natural posture, and minimal physical strain. An ergonomic instrument may include an asymmetrical body shape to maximize the **resonance chamber** while keeping the string length short, and may use lightweight woods or other materials in its construction.

The **viola**, because of its large proportions, is the instrument most commonly redesigned for ergonomic reasons, with modern **luthiers** such as David Rivinus and John Newton creating striking ergonomic violas used by some of today's top professional players.

Ergonomic instruments help in preventing **tendonitis**, **carpal tunnel syndrome**, and other performance-related injuries. Some standard **string instruments** may have ergonomic modifications to facilitate a natural posture, such as **key pegs** on **cellos** and instruments with a **cutaway** treble shoulder.

ergonomics. The science of environment and equipment design intended to reduce fatigue and discomfort by creating an interface that is as natural as possible. Ergonomics are a significant factor in modern designs for string player's accessories, including **chin rests**, **shoulder rests**, and **cello chairs**. Some instruments are modified to facilitate a natural posture, such as **key pegs** on cellos, **cutaway instruments**, and **ergonomic instruments** that are completely redesigned to better fit the body. See **Alexander Technique** and **Feldenkrais** for information about teaching methods specifically focused on ergonomics.

erheben. (Ger.) To lift, as in a **lifted bowstroke.**

erhu. (Chin.) A Chinese bowed **string instrument** of the *huqin* family. A type of **spike fiddle**, the *erhu* has a long, round **neck** made of hardwood that passes through a small resonator. The resonator is a wooden tube, round or octagonal in shape, and is covered by a snake skin glued over one end. Two **strings** traditionally made of silk (though modern players often use **steel strings**) attach to the spike end of the neck where it protrudes below the resonator then pass over a low **bridge** sitting on the snake-skin membrane. The strings run under an adjustable **nut** of silk cord before attaching to **pegs** that pass dorsally through the top of the neck.

The *erhu* is played with a bamboo **bow** with the **horsehair** running between the two strings, which are not usually sounded together. The *erhu* player either pulls the bow hair outward to contact the higher (A4) string or inward to play the lower (D4) string. With no **fingerboard** to press against, the pitches are changed by stopping the strings lightly with the left hand. The *erhu* is held vertically, usually supported on the thigh.

Capable of great **virtuosity**, the *erhu* can be studied at the Chinese national **conservatory** and is a primary instrument in Chinese opera, **orchestras** playing Chinese national music, and many folk **ensembles.**

espressivo. (It.) Expressively, with emotion.

étude, **etude.** A study or exercise designed to help develop a particular skill. Some etudes are intended to transcend mere exercise, making for dazzling technical **showpieces**. For string players, this type of etude is often titled **caprice.**

EUB. See **electric upright bass**.

eurhythmics. See **Dalcroze eurhythmics**.

excerpts. Passages of music taken from the orchestral **repertoire** to be used in auditions. When orchestras hold auditions, they ask to hear a list of excerpts from orchestral **parts** that often isolate the most technically difficult and artistically demanding passages from the repertoire. While each orchestra compiles its own list of required excerpts, a set of commonly chosen standards has developed, allowing conservatories and schools of music to offer orchestral repertoire classes based on these excerpts.

expressive *glissando*. See *glissando*.

expressive intonation. A technique of **tuning** pitches based on the functionality of each note within a given key. Expressive intonation involves raising leading tones, lowering minor thirds, widening augmented seconds, and generally tuning each **pitch** relative to its role in the key being played. Using expressive intonation can be problematic when playing with piano or another fixed-pitch instrument.

extended position. A **finger pattern** on the **cello** in which each finger measures a consecutive **half-step** except the index finger, which stretches back to measure a whole-step. See also **closed position** and **finger pattern** for illustrations.

extended technique. Playing an instrument in an unconventional way. Extended techniques for string players include using the body of the instrument to create percussive effects, bowing with excessive pressure to produce **scratch tones**, playing on the **afterlength** behind the bridge, bowing on the **tailpiece**, stopping the **strings** with an object other than the fingers, and countless other innovations.

extension.
1. Stretching the fingers of the left hand beyond their normal frame to reach a note in another **position** without **shifting**. See also **position, shifting, finger pattern, hand frame,** and **octave hand frame**.
2. An added length of **fingerboard** on a **double bass**. See **C extension**.

eye. A decorative dot, usually abalone, inlaid into the wood of a **tailpiece, peg, button, frog,** or other **fitting**. An eye can also be called a pearl dot, and a dot

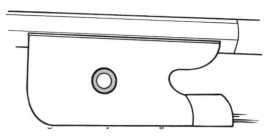

encircled by a metal ring is called a **Parisian eye**.

~ F ~

f-holes. A symmetrical pair of openings in the **top plate** of an instrument designed to enhance **resonance** by increasing the flexibility of the wood under the **bridge** and amplifying the lowest octave. The placement on either side of the bridge and the elegant shape of the f-holes are the result of exacting geometry based on the golden ratio. The physics of sound shows that it is air movement past the edges of a sound hole that enhances resonance, so the long, thin shape of the f-hole design reduces void and maximizes air movement along the plate edges. See also **resonance** and **soundhole**.

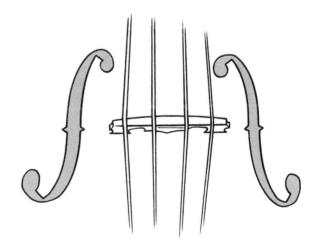

Figure 45. The usual design for **modern string family f-holes**.

Fagottgeige. (Ger.) See *viola di fagotto.*

fake book. A collection of **lead sheets** for popular songs showing only the basic melody, lyrics, and chord changes. Fake books are used primarily by **jazz** musicians, as they contain the fundamental information needed to play the melody, create harmonies, and improvise solos. Originally these lead sheets were printed illegally, with no royalties paid to the copyright holders, and were notoriously inaccurate. Hal Leonard, beginning with the sixth edition of *The Real Book*, offers legally published, updated fake books.

fall off. A **jazz** term for a quick downward slide at the end of a note. The fall off is accompanied by the gradual release of pressure as the finger slides away from the main pitch. The technique can be notated by a downward sloping line following the note-head. See also **drop, bend, doit, plop, scoop,** and *glissando.*

Figure 46. **Fall off** notation.

false harmonics. See **artificial harmonics.**

fantasia, fantasy. A type of free composition rooted in **improvisation.** For string players, a fantasy is often the vehicle for virtuosic showmanship. Also spelled **Fantasie** and **Phantasie.**

feather bowing. See **drum stroke.**

feedback. Electronic sound created when a loop exists between an audio input, such as a microphone or **pickup,** and an audio output, such as an **amplifier** or speaker. The sound from the speaker is picked up by the microphone and re-amplified through the speaker, then is picked up again by the microphone and re-amplified in a loop until a loud squeal is created at maximum amplification.

Many **electric instrument** designs are bodiless specifically to avoid feedback loops created between the **resonance chamber** of a hollow body and the pickup on the instrument.

feet. The supports at the base of the **bridge.** Feet must be hand carved to match the exact curve of the **top plate** on which they stand.

Feldenkrais Method. An educational system designed to enhance body awareness in order to reduce tension, alleviate pain, and free movement. The Feldenkrais

Method of Somatic Education, developed by Moshé Feldenkrais (1904-1984), focuses on the relationship between movement and thought, seeking to alter unconscious, stressful habits and cultivate a more relaxed, natural way of moving. Many musicians find study of the Feldenkrais Method invaluable in reducing physical strain and eliminating **tendonitis, carpal tunnel syndrome,** back pain, and other performance-related injuries. See also **Alexander Technique** and **ergonomics.**

ferrule. The U-shaped ring of metal around the **frog** of a **bow,** used to spread and secure the **horsehair** ribbon as it enters the frog. The ferrule is one of the **fittings** of a bow, usually made of nickel, silver, or gold.

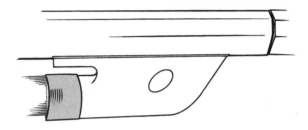

Figure 47. The **ferrule** on a **cello bow.**

fiberglass. A type of plastic made of glass fibers embedded in a resin. Fiberglass is used to make inexpensive **bows** and **cases** for **string instruments.**

fiddle.
1. A colloquial term for the **violin.**
2. A style of violin playing used in folk music. The many types of fiddle music include Appalachian, **bluegrass,** Cajun, Cape Breton, Celtic, English, French-Canadian, Irish, New England, Newfoundland, old-timey, Ontario, Scandinavian, Scottish, Shetland, Texas-style, and **swing.**
3. To play in a quick, carefree manner, or to **improvise.**

figuration. The **ornamentation** of a passage by embellishment and repeated patterns.

figured bass. Part of the **continuo** part common in the Baroque era notated with a fundamental bass line intended for a **cello,** *viola da gamba,* or similar instrument, and a numeric shorthand indicating **chords** to be played on keyboard, lute, or other chordal instrument. See also **continuo.**

filer un son. (Fr.) See *son filé.*

fill. A brief passage of notes used to add interest in the **break** between phrases of melody, used primarily in

jazz, pop, and folk music. Fills can be miniature improvised **solos** or may be a set motif for the song.

fine tuner. A device for making small adjustments to
tuning. Fine tuners are fitted into the string-holes of
the **tailpiece**, with a lever extending beyond the tailpiece onto which the end of the **string** is hooked. By
tightening or loosening a screw, this lever moves
closer or farther from the tailpiece, making minute adjustments in **pitch**. Also called adjusters or fine adjusters, fine tuners are most often made of metal or
carbon fiber.

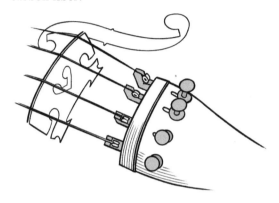

Figure 48. **Fine tuners**.

There is some contention about how many fine
tuners should be used. With the elasticity of synthetic
core strings, most modern string players only use
fine-tuners on steel strings, usually just the highest
string. Although using fine tuners makes tuning easier
than adjusting **friction pegs**, adding the devices
increases the possibility of buzzing, adds weight to
the instrument, and dampens the sound. The extended
lever alters the ratio of string length to the
afterlength, reducing the quality of **tone**, and since
fine tuners are often used for every string of a child's
instrument, many consider them a crutch for
beginners. To address these concerns, lightweight
tailpieces with integrated fine tuners have been
designed to maintain string length proportions and
minimize buzzing. Some players use **mechanical
pegs** in lieu of fine tuners.

finger angle. The way the finger of the left hand approaches the **fingerboard** when stopping the **string**.
   A soft or rounded finger angle means that the top
joint of the finger is at a gentle angle of about 45 degrees, placing the point of contact on the soft part of
the fingertip halfway between the nail and the pad. A
rounded finger angle allows flexibility of the top
joint, providing an **ergonomically** relaxed hand position in which the tip of the finger can roll easily in either direction to facilitate rich **vibrato** and minute

adjustments to **intonation**. Playing on the softer part
of the fingertip also creates a warmer **tone** with more
flesh between the bone and the string, and the gentle
angle allows for a greater reach.
   A square or tight finger angle means the top joint of
the finger is pulled into a sharp angle of 90 degrees or
more, placing the point of contact on the very tip of
the finger, near or on the fingernail. While playing on
the tip of the finger bone can create a more clear
sound, the extreme angle places stress on the joints
and limits the range that the finger can rock, lessening
vibrato and minute intonation adjustments. The
square angle reduces the reach of the hand, and wear
from fingernails can damage the fingerboard.
   A flat or straight finger angle means the finger approaches the string almost parallel to the fingerboard,
creating a contact point on the pad of the finger. Generally a flat finger angle does not allow for enough
clearance between strings, and limits the adjustment
of the finger; however, a flat finger angle is very useful in certain circumstances, such as playing in the extreme registers of the instrument, playing in high
thumb position on the cello and bass, making thick
portamento slides, and tuning **chords**, particularly
those containing the **doublestop** of a fifth.

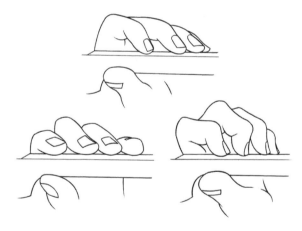

Figure 49. **Finger angles** shown on a **violin** or **viola**. A rounded
finger angle is shown above with a flat finger angle below left and
a square finger angle below right.

   A skilled player will have a default finger angle that
is rounded, using a flat finger angle for reach or color,
a square finger angle to grab tricky chords, or even a
combination of square and flat angles, as when a violinist reaches a tenth or a cellist uses extended **thumb
position**.

finger extension. See **extension**.

finger pattern. A system of organizing notes by grouping them into a particular spacing of the fingers. Finger patterns are one of the primary systems used to find pitches on fretless **string instruments**.

Fingers on string instruments are conventionally numbered 1 for the index finger, 2 for the middle finger, 3 for the ring finger, and 4 for the little finger. There are a variety of naming systems for identifying finger patterns, including names, numbers, and even colors. For the purposes of this article, a simple numbering system is used: no space between numbers indicates a **half-step**, a dash represents a **whole-step**, and a double dash measures an augmented second (a whole-step plus a half-step).

Violin and **viola** finger patterns are measurements of either half-steps, in which consecutive fingers are placed directly adjacent, or whole-steps, in which consecutive fingers are placed with a space the size of a finger width between them. The violin and viola use these four basic finger patterns:

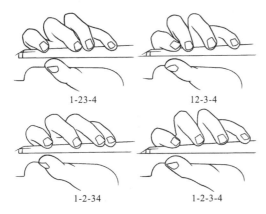

1-23-4   12-3-4

1-2-34   1-2-3-4

Figure 50a. The four basic **finger patterns** for **violin** and **viola**.

These four patterns can be used to play any major scale in any position. Most beginners on violin and viola start with the 1-23-4 pattern because it can produce simple G major, D major, and A major **scales** in first **position**.

For altered scales, augmented intervals, and chromatics, violin and viola use a variety of contracted and extended finger patterns, including:

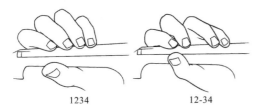

1234   12-34

Figure 50b. Contracted finger patterns for violin or viola: the **chromatic finger pattern** on the left and a common pattern on the right.

Other contracted and extended finger patterns for violin and viola include 12-34, 1-234, 123-4, 1234 (chromatic), 1--23-4, 12--34, 1-23--4.

Cello uses a wider set of finger patterns, proportional to the size of the instrument. Consecutive fingers typically play half-steps, with whole-steps skipping a finger. Cellists play with two basic finger patterns: closed position, with each finger on a half-step, and extended position, with the index finger stretching back to reach a whole-step.

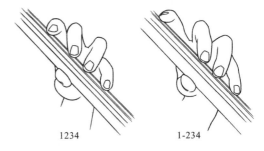

1234   1-234

Figure 50c. The two basic **finger patterns** for **cello**: closed on the left and extended on the right.

For work in high registers, cellists and double bassists also use **thumb position**, with a basic finger pattern of T-1-23.

T-1-23

Figure 50d. The **thumb position finger pattern** for **cello** or **bass**.

Double bass players use a basic **Simandl** pattern of 124.

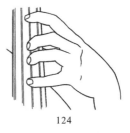

124

Figure 50e. The **Simandl finger pattern** for **double bass**.

See also **fingerboard mapping** and **hand frame**, **octave frame**, and **shifting**.

finger vibrato. A **vibrato technique** on **violin** and **viola** in which the pitch oscillation is created by finger movement using the base joint of the finger as the pivot point. Finger vibrato is used only in the rare instance that the hand is immobilized. See **vibrato**.

fingerboard. The long piece of wood beneath the **strings**, against which the player presses the strings to change the **pitch**. The fingerboard sits atop the **neck**, beginning at the **nut** and extending over the **belly** of the instrument.

The fingerboard of a standard **violin**, **viola**, **cello**, or **double bass** is fretless, smooth, and rounded to match the curve of the bridge, with a wedge shape that begins narrow near the nut and widens as it approaches the **bridge**. Fingerboards are carved with a very slight concave **scoop** along the length in order to avoid the strings buzzing against the wood. Additionally, many double basses and some cellos have a **Romberg bevel** beneath the lowest string to allow extra clearance. Fingerboards are typically made of **ebony**, a dark, smooth hardwood resistant to the grooves and troughs caused by the wear and tear of playing. Some fingerboards are made of **rosewood** or **maple**, often ebonized with a black stain to look like ebony. **Baroque instruments** may have fingerboards of light maple or laminated hardwoods, often decorated with ornate **inlay**.

As an instrument is played, troughs and grooves are gradually worn into the fingerboard, requiring periodic **planing** and eventually a complete replacement.

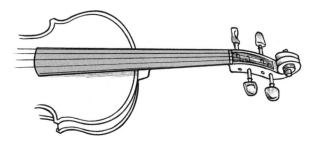

Figure 51. The **fingerboard** of a **violin**.

fingerboard mapping. Measuring of note spacing on a **string instrument** using the concept that the span of fingers can be set in a regular frame and that notes within this frame are organized by **finger patterns**. The fingerboard map is created by moving this structured hand frame through the **positions** of the instrument and across **strings**, creating an imaginary grid that guides a player to successfully navigate the entire fingerboard and play with good **intonation**. See also **finger pattern**, **hand frame**, **octave hand frame**, **position**, and **shifting**.

fingered extension. The simplest type of **C extension** on a **double bass**. A fingered extension has only a locking stop at the **nut**, allowing the bassist to engage the additional **string** length, and then reach back to finger pitches. The advantage of this system is that it allows the player to adjust **pitch** and play **vibrato**. The disadvantage is that the extended hand position makes it difficult to integrate the lowest pitches into passage work on the regular **fingerboard**. See also **C extension**, **chromatic extension**, and **machine extension**.

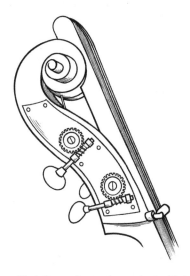

Figure 52. A **fingered extension** on the **double bass**.

fingered octaves. Playing **double-stop** octaves with an alternating **fingering** of first and third fingers followed by second and fourth fingers. Considered one of the most difficult techniques on the **violin** and **viola**, fingered octaves produce a more articulated passage than the standard consecutive first and fourth finger octave fingering.

fingered tremolo. See **slurred tremolo**.

fingering. The organization of the fingers of the left hand as they press the **strings** against the **fingerboard**, changing the string length and pitch.

Fingerings are indicated on printed music by Arabic numbers 1-4, with 1 being the index finger and 4 the little finger. The number 0 is used to indicate an **open string**. A skilled player will mark fingerings only when there is a change of position or unusual pattern, and may add symbols such as a slanted line before a number to indicate a shift or an *x* above the number to indicate an extension. Roman numerals are sometimes used to indicate **positions**, though since Roman numerals are also used to indicate a particular string, players tend to avoid this marking. A string player will assign fingerings to passages based on **fingerboard mapping**, taking into consideration artistic factors such as **tone color** and *portamento*, as well as technical factors such as **string crossings** and **shifting**. Fingering choices are complex and very personal, so while a student may receive fingerings from a teacher, and many editions of printed music include the fingerings and **bowings** of a famous player, eventually most musicians prefer to develop their own fingerings.

See also **extension, finger pattern, fingerboard mapping, hand frame, octave hand frame, position**, and **shifting**.

finial. A term for the **scroll** or **head** of the instrument. See **scroll**.

firm *staccato*. See **slurred** *staccato*.

first chair. The **principal** player of a **section** in an **ensemble** who is seated at the front of their section and closest to the conductor. See **conventions of orchestral playing**.

first position. The left-hand placement along the **fingerboard** in which the index finger sits on the first note of the string, usually a whole-step above the pitch of the **open string**. First position is considered the foundational starting hand placement in most string teaching methods, and is frequently chosen by players because it allows easy use of open strings. See also **shifting, fingerboard mapping, thumb position, half position**, and **extension**.

first violin.
1. The highest **violin part** in an orchestra or other **ensemble**. The first violin part traditionally carries the melody and is often more technically difficult than the second violin part.
2. A term for the **concertmaster**.

fittings. The pieces of an instrument that are not part of the fundamental structure of the body. Fittings include the **pegs, tailpiece, chin rest**, and **endpin**. Fittings can be changed according to the preference of the player without disturbing the construction of the instrument.

five-string bass. A **double bass** with an added fifth **string** used to expand the range of the instrument. For the modern classical player, a five-string bass is usually an orchestral bass with a fifth string tuned to low B as an alternative to the **C extension**. **Solo** basses and many **jazz** basses have the fifth string as an upper C string, added to extend the top range. The advantages of a five-string bass over an extension are

ease of fingering fast passages without having to reach back to the extension, and more accurate intonation than a chromatic or machine extension. The disadvantage is that the narrowed spacing between strings adds difficulty for both fingers and bow work. See also **C extension, chromatic extension, fingered extension**, and **machine extension**.

fixed-frog bow. An early **bow** design with no mechanism for adjusting the tension of the **horsehair**. The ribbon of hair can be wedged into a notch beneath the **frog**, but often the hair is simply tied around either end of the **stick**. Fixed-frog bows are still used for playing **rebec, vielle, mediaeval fiddle, bowed psalter**, and early **viols**. See also **clip-in-frog**, a type of fixed-frog bow.

Figure 53. Detail of the **frog** end of a **fixed-frog bow**.

flageolet. (Fr.) See **harmonic**.

flaming. The wavy figure in the **maple** of the **back plate** and **ribs** of an instrument, also called the curl. Because good flaming is an indication of high quality wood, some cheap instruments may have flaming painted or dyed artificially into the wood. Real flaming will undulate and show depth when held under a light and tilted.

flatback bass. A **double bass** construction with a back **plate** that has no arching. Flatback basses are made from thin sheets of solid wood glued to the **ribs** and reinforced on the inside with **bracing**. See also **break, double bass**, and **laminated bass**.

flautando, flautato. (It.) To play with a light, fast bowstroke, creating a translucent, flute-like tone. See **Table 1: Bowstrokes** for a list of strokes and their notation.

Flesch, Carl (1873-1944). Hungarian violinist and **pedagogue** whose logical approach to **technique** remains the basis of modern **violin** playing. Flesch studied at the Vienna **Conservatory** and the Paris Conservatoire, where he was awarded the *premier prix*, then quickly gained international acclaim for his performances as a soloist and **chamber musician**.

Known for his effortless technique and warm **tone**, Flesch was equally comfortable in the music of all eras, demonstrated by his historic five concerts given in 1905 in Berlin, where he played the standard violin **repertoire** in chronological order, presenting the works of over fifty composers from Corelli to Reger.

Alongside this successful career performing, Flesh maintained an active teaching studio as professor of violin, first at the Bucharest Conservatory, then at the Amsterdam Conservatory, the newly formed Curtis Institute, and the Berlin Hochschule für Musik. Flesh taught in a **master class** style, giving lessons in front of a small audience. His ability to diagnose and fix the technical and musical challenges of his students led to a legacy of successful performers, including Max Rostal, Szymon Goldberg, Henryk Szeryng, Ida Haendel, and Ginette Neveu. Flesch developed an analytical approach to playing the violin, placing focus on finding freedom of movement in both hands, a method documented in his treatise *The Art of Violin Playing, Books 1 & 2*. Flesch's *Scale System* remains one of the primary staples of violin training today.

flight case. A heavy-duty instrument **case** designed to offer extra protection for **double bass** players and **cellists** who need to check their instruments as luggage.

fluting. The concave channels carved into the wood on the back of the **scroll**.

flying *spiccato*. A thrown, bouncing **bowstroke** in which many notes are played **off the string** with the **bow** moving in the same direction. Flying *spiccato* is notated by the combination of a **slur** and **dots** over the notes and should not be confused with **flying staccato**, which is begun **from the string** and remains on or very close to the string. See **Table 1: Bowstrokes** for a list of strokes and their notation.

flying *staccato*. A **bowstroke** with a stopped **articulation** between notes bowed in the same direction with the **bow** springing away from the **string** slightly between notes. Flying *staccato* is initiated from the string, resulting in much less bounce than the thrown **flying** *spiccato* bowstroke. Flying *staccato*, also called *staccato volante* and *staccato à ricochet*, is indicated by the combination of a **slur** and **dots** over the notes. See **Table 1: Bowstrokes** for a list of strokes and their notation.

folding bass. See **collapsible upright bass**.

fouetté. (Fr.) A whipped **bowstroke** executed at the tip by lifting the **bow** and then slapping it back onto the **string** to create a biting **accent**. In *fouetté* the bow does not bounce, but remains in firm contact with the string. See **Table 1: Bowstrokes** for a list of strokes and their notation.

Franco-Belgian bow hold. The **violin bow hold** as taught by the **Franco-Belgian school of violin playing**, developed by **Charles-August de Bériot** and **Eugène Ysaÿe**. The Franco-Belgian hold is characterized by rounded, flexible fingers that drape over the stick and an index finger that contacts the bow at the first knuckle. The springy approach of this hold utilizes more flexing of the wrist and fingers than the stiffer **Russian bow hold**. The **Galamian bow hold** is a modified Franco-Belgian hold, with the index finger extending slightly away from the hand. Famous violinists with a primarily Franco-Belgian bow hold include Itzhak Perlman, Pinchas Zukerman, Maxim Vengerov, Gil Shaham, and Anne-Sophie Mutter.

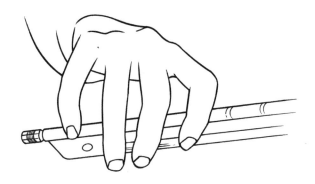

Figure 54. The **Franco-Belgian bow hold**.

Franco-Belgian school of violin playing. One of the two dominant systems for training violinists. The Franco-Belgian school grew from the French tradition and was developed at the Brussels Conservatory by **Charles de Bériot** and **Eugène Ysaÿe**. Through the work of **pedagogues Josef Gingold** and **William Primrose**, the school has become one of the most popular systems for training violinists. The legacy of great virtuosos with Franco-Belgian training includes Arthur Grumiaux, **Fritz Kreisler**, Jacques Thibaud, Joshua Bell, and Jaime Laredo.

The primary characteristic of violinists trained in the Franco-Belgian school is a virtuosic flair paired with refined elegance and flawless beauty of **tone** achieved by expressive **vibrato** combined with long, smooth bows pulled mainly from the forearm. See **Franco-Belgian bow hold** for more information. See also **Russian school of violin playing**.

frappez avec le bois de l'archet. (Fr.) Strike with the wood of the **bow**. See *col legno*.

free bowing. Play without preset **bowings**. The term is used most often in orchestral settings to indicate that the standard conventions of unified bowings do not apply. Instead, each performer is to choose bowings independently, often as they are felt in the moment. See also **conventions of orchestral playing** and **bowings**.

freelance. Work hired independently on a per-service basis rather than a salaried contract. See also **gig** and **pickup**.

French bow. A **double bass bow** that resembles a **cello** bow of the modern **Tourte** design and is held overhand. The French bow is also called a Bottesini bow, because it was made popular by virtuoso bassist **Giovanni Bottesini** in the 19th century. See also **French bow hold**, **German bow**, **German bow hold**, and **Tourte bow**.

Figure 55. A **French double bass bow**.

French bow hold. The technique of holding a French **double bass** bow. The **French bow**, also known as the Bottesini bow, resembles a **cello** bow and is held overhand with the palm facing the floor, fingers draped over the stick at the first knuckle, and the thumb touching the stick behind the second finger, against the edge of the **frog**.

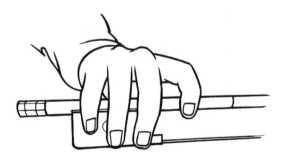

Figure 56. The **French bow hold** for **double bass**.

The French bow hold is the prevalent bass bow hold today, except in Germany and Austria, where the **German bow hold** remains popular. Because the French bow hold is thought to offer more finesse and the German bow hold to provide more power, many orchestral double bass players are proficient in both, choosing one or the other to suit the style of repertoire. See also **French bow**, **German bow**, and **German bow hold**.

French polish. See **shellac**.

French school of violin playing. The system for training violinists popular in 19th-century Paris. The French school was established by Viotti and developed through the founding of the Paris Conservatoire by Viotti's followers Baillot, Kreutzer, and Rode. The French school produced great performers, including **Sarasate**, **Wieniawski**, and **Vieuxtemps**, and continued through the teachings of **Flesch**. Eventually the French tradition was eclipsed by the more modern **Franco-Belgian school of violin playing** developed at the Brussels Conservatory by **Charles de Bériot** and **Eugène Ysaÿe**. Violinists trained in the French school played with a refined Classical elegance and beautiful **tone**. See also **Franco-Belgian school of violin playing**.

frequency. How quickly a **sound wave** moves, measured by cycles per second. The frequency of **waveforms** determines **pitch**, with the pitch rising as the frequency increases. A4 = 440 Hz. means the frequency of the sound wave is 440 cycles per second, producing the **standard tuning** A. See also **sound wave**.

fret.
1. A strip of metal, **gut**, or other material **inlaid** into the **fingerboard** or tied across the fingerboard at the **half-step**, used to guide the fingers to the correct **pitch**. Frets are unusual among the violin family of instruments, though they are found on some modern **electric instruments**, as well as on the *viola da gamba* and other **period instruments**.
2. To stop a note by pressing the string against the fingerboard, used mainly in **bluegrass** and folk genres regardless of whether the instrument has actual frets.

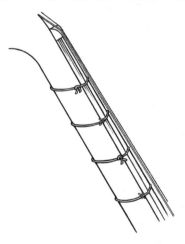

Figure 57. **Gut frets** tied across the **fingerboard**.

fretted. Having frets. See **fret**.

friction pegs. Tapered wooden dowels fitted through holes in the **pegbox** and used to tune the instrument. **Strings** are threaded through a hole in each **peg** and then wound around the dowel until the correct tension is reached. Strings are tuned by turning the pegs, which are held in place by pressure against the pegbox. Friction pegs are usually made of hardwood such as **ebony** or **rosewood**, chosen to match the other **fittings** of the instrument. The taper of each dowel needs to be custom carved to fit the holes in a specific instrument's pegbox. As the friction of tuning gradually wears down the wood, the pegs will sit closer and closer to the wall of the pegbox, eventually requiring replacement with a new set of pegs. Traditionally, most **string instruments** use wooden friction pegs with the exception of the **double bass**. See also **pegs**, **mechanical pegs**, **geared pegs**, and **key pegs**.

frog. The piece at the lower end of the **bow** that holds the **horsehair** away from the stick and houses the **screw** mechanism for adjusting the tension on the hair.

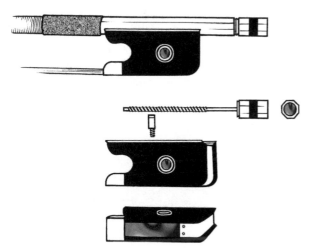

Figure 58. Details of the **frog** of a modern **Tourte bow**.

The frog is typically carved from **ebony**, though it can be made from a variety of hardwoods, tortoiseshell, or even ivory. Metal **mountings** on the frog include the **screw button**, the **ferrule**, the **slide**, the **back-plate**, and the **lining** between the frog and stick. The bow maker will often indicate an opinion of the quality of the stick by the choice of metal for the mountings, using nickel for the most ordinary bows, silver for finer bows, and gold mountings only for the stick of which the maker is most proud. The frog is often decorated with abalone in an **eye** on either side of the frog, a slide **inlay** on the bottom of the frog,

and a **pearl dot** on the end of the screw button. The corner of the frog of a **viola** or **cello** bow is usually rounded, distinguishing it from the square-cornered **violin** bow.

Most string players use a modern bow with an adjustable frog as designed by **François Tourte** in which a screw threads through an eyelet embedded in the frog. As the screw is turned, the frog is pulled back, causing the bow hair to tighten.

Double bass frogs follow one of two distinctly different designs: a **French bow** in the modern Tourte design, which looks like a large cello bow, or a **German bow**, descended from the **viol family**. The frog of a German bow is taller and more slender than its French counterpart.

Early bows prior to the Tourte design had a **fixed frog**, a **clip-in frog**, or a **crémaillère** adjustment system. See also **Bach bow** for details about the modern bow with a dynamic frog.

from the string. To begin a **bowstroke** with full contact between the **string** and the **horsehair**, usually at the start of an **off the string** passage. Starting from the string rather than dropping or throwing the bow from above the **string** provides greater control over the bowstroke and is one of the most valuable techniques orchestral players use to coordinate synchronized **section** playing. See **Table 1: Bowstrokes** for a list of strokes and their notation.

front of house.
1. The speaker system that faces the audience during an amplified performance. Front of house can also refer to the audio engineer who runs that speaker system.
2. The box office, ushering staff, concession stand, etc.

Frosch. (Ger.) The **frog** of the bow.

Fuchs, Lillian (1902-1995). American violist, pedagogue, and composer who was the first to perform and record **J. S. Bach's** six **cello suites** on the **viola**. Fuchs studied violin at Juilliard with Svecenski and Kneisel and debuted in New York on violin in 1926. As a member of the Perolé String Quartet, Fuchs switched to viola and began a career on the instrument, performing in **chamber music** concerts and touring as a solo violist.

As a **solo** violist, Fuchs concertized in the United States and across Europe, inspiring the composition of new works for the instrument, including Martinů's Madrigals for **violin** and **viola**, Duo no. 2 for violin and viola, and viola **sonata**.

Fuchs was an influential **pedagogue** of both viola and **chamber music**, and her books of etudes, *Twelve Caprices for Viola*, *Fifteen Characteristic Studies for Viola*, and *Sixteen Fantasy Etudes*, are a mainstay of viola technical training. She taught at the Aspen Music Festival, the Manhattan School of Music, and Juilliard.

fulcrum. The pivot point of a **lever**. In string playing, this usually refers to the idea that the **bow** itself is a lever, with the thumb functioning as the fulcrum. Using the thumb as a pivot point, the index finger applies weight to press the **hair** against the string. Without the thumb as a fulcrum, no amount of arm weight will create pressure on the bow. Even the **German bass bow hold** relies on the thumb as a fulcrum with the hand rotating up to send the other end of the bow down into the string. See **lever** for an illustration and more detail about the physics of the bow.

full orchestra. A large **ensemble** made up of **string instruments**, woodwinds, brass instruments, and percussion. A full orchestra is also called a symphony orchestra or philharmonic. See also **chamber orchestra** and **string orchestra**.

full-size instrument. An instrument considered the standard size for an adult player. See **size** for detailed information including the measurements for full-size **violin**, **viola**, **cello**, and **double bass**.

fully carved. Indicating that the top and back **plates** of an instrument have been shaped exclusively by hand carving. See also **laminated bass**.

~ G ~

G.P. General pause, meaning a measure in which no one plays. Also called *misura vuota*.

Gabrielli, Domenico (1659-1690). Italian composer and **cello virtuoso** who was among the first to write music featuring the cello. Gabrielli's *Seven Ricercare for Violoncello Solo* were the first pieces to be published for **solo** cello, and his two **sonatas** for cello and **continuo** demonstrate his highly developed technique. Many of Gabrielli's vocal compositions and pieces for trumpet feature a cello *obbligato*.

gadulka. A bowed **string instrument** from Bulgaria, traditionally used in dance. The gadulka has three or four main playing **strings**, with as many as ten **sympathetic strings**. The body is rounded in back, with both the **neck** and body carved from a single piece of wood. As the gadulka has no **fingerboard**, strings are stretched directly from the **tailpiece** to the **pegs**, with the playing strings crossing over the **bridge** and the sympathetic strings passing through it. One foot of the bridge is positioned atop the instrument while the other extends through the **sound-hole** to sit on the **soundpost**. The gadulka is played vertically, with a supporting strap connected to the tailpiece, and an underhand bow hold. The playing strings are most often tuned A4 – E4 – A4, and the resonating strings are tuned **chromatically**.

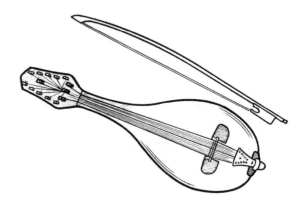

Figure 59. The **gadulka**.

Galamian bow hold. A modified Franco-Belgian **bow hold** in which the index finger is separated from the other fingers, as taught by pedagogue Ivan Galamian. See **Franco-Belgian bow hold** for details and an illustration.

galant. Elegant in style. The term is used as an expressive indication on music or in reference to an entire elegant style of art and literature popular in 18th-century Europe.

gamba bow. The **bow** used for playing a **viol**, commonly called a Baroque bow. The gamba bow was developed in the mid-15th century and was used primarily in the Renaissance and Baroque periods. The stick of a gamba bow is convex or sometimes flat, with a narrow **tip** and an open, **fixed frog**.

Figure 60a. A **gamba bow**.

The gamba bow is held underhand a few inches up from the **frog** with the stick between the thumb and index finger. This grip allows the player to use finger pressure directly on the hair to control tension while playing. The gamba bow is also called viol bow or *viola da gamba* bow.

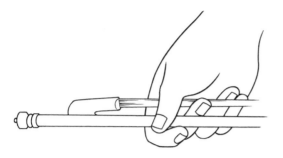

Figure 60b. The **gamba bow hold**.

gamba shape. A design for **double bass** in which the lower corners of the **C bouts** are curved into a C shape like those of a *viola da gamba*, rather than pointed like **violin** corners or rounded like **busetto** corners.

gamma. (It.) **Scale.**

gamme. (Fr.) **Scale.**

ganzer Bogen. (Ger.) The entire **bow.**

gardon. See *ütögardon.*

Gasparo da Salò (1540-1609). Italian **luthier** often credited with the invention of the **violin.** Gasparo was the son of a family of musicians who had a tradition of instrument making. Gasparo made a very successful career building **viols,** violins, **double basses,** at least one **cello,** and many tenor **violas.** Though these violas have mostly been cut down to a smaller size, they are highly regarded today for their quick response and a **tone** that is described as reedy. Gasparo's double basses have always been particularly prized, most famously the three-string bass played by Dragonetti. Gasparo's instruments are characterized by quality craftsmanship, elongated **sound-holes,** and occasionally a double ring of **purfling.**

gavotte. A French dance form popular in the Baroque era, in moderate common time with an upbeat. The gavotte is usually paired with a second gavotte of a contrasting character, and it is often included in the Baroque dance **suite.**

geared pegs. See **mechanical pegs.**

gebunden. (Ger.) **Legato** or **slurred.**

gedämpft. (Ger.) **Muted.**

gehalten. (Ger.) Sustained, held.

gehämmert. (It.) See *martelé.*

Geige. (Ger.) **Violin** or **fiddle.**

gekneipt. (Ger.) **Pizzicato.**

genre. A classification of music into categories defined by instrumentation, musical techniques, style, and context. Genres include classical, rock, **bluegrass,** and **jazz.** These genres are divided into sub-genres such as cool jazz, gypsy jazz, and jazz fusion.

Georgia bow, Georgia shuffle. A rhythmic **bowing** pattern of three notes **slurred** followed by a single note. See also **shuffle, double shuffle,** and **Nashville shuffle.**

gerissen. (Ger.) Torn, usually indicating a fast, aggressive **bowstroke.**

German bow. A **double bass** bow characterized by a tall, slender **frog.** Also known as the Simandl bow or the Butler bow, the German bow developed from the **viol family** and is still most prevalent in Germany and Austria. The German bow is grasped endwise, with the palm enclosing the frog and the fingers parallel to the stick. See also **French bow hold, French bow,** and **German bow hold.**

Figure 61. A **German double bass bow.**

German bow hold. The technique of holding a German **double bass** bow. Also known as a Butler or Simandl bow, the **German bow** has a taller **frog** than the French bow. The German bow is grasped endwise with the palm enclosing the frog and the fingers parallel to the stick. The index finger reaches along the stick to just touch the tip of the thumb. The two middle fingers curve around the frog and the little finger is positioned below the **slide,** touching the **ferrule.** The thumb sits atop the stick over the frog and touches the tip of the index finger. The German bow hold, derived from the bowing technique of the **viol family,** is most prevalent today in Austria and Germany. Because the German bow hold is thought to provide more power, and **French bow hold** is thought to offer more finesse, many orchestral double bass players are proficient in both, choosing one or the other to suit the style of repertoire. See also **French bow hold, French bow**, and **German bow**.

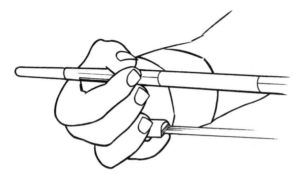

Figure 62. The **German bow hold** for **double bass**.

geschlagen. (Ger.) Beaten, meaning to beat the **string** with the **bow**, usually by swatting at the the string with an entirely vertical stroke. May be abbreviated *geschl*. See also ***battuto***.

gestossen. (Ger.) Accented.

gestrichen. (Ger.) Bowed.

geteilt. (Ger.) ***Divisi***, divided.

gettato. (It.) See **thrown bowstroke**.

gezogen. (Ger.) Sustained.

gig. A job or performance by a **freelance** musician. A gig is usually a single performance or studio session in which the musicians are hired as independent contractors rather than employees.

gig bag. A soft **case** for an instrument.

gigue, giga. (Fr., It.) An English dance form popular in the Baroque era, in lively compound meter with lilting rhythms, originating in the English **jig**. The gigue is one of the four foundational movements of a Baroque **suite**.

glissando. (It.) Generally used, a term for a **slide**. For modern string players, *glissando* refers to the **technique** of sliding rapidly through a scalar passage while using **vibrato** to distinguish each semitone. *Glissando* is most often written out with every **half-step** notated under a long slur. Alternately, it may notated by a wavy line between the starting and ending notes of the slide, or even by a straight line with the words "chromatic *glissando*" or "expressive *glissando*" to avoid confusion with ***portamento***, which is a

smooth slide notated by a straight line between notes.

Because some types of instrument do not have the capability of differentiating each note through a slide, *glissando* is commonly used as an all-purpose term for any type of slide between notes.

Figure 63a. ***Glissando*** from **Sarasate's** Zigeunerweisen, op. 20, no. 1, mm 42.

Figure 63b. ***Glissando*** from Richard Strauss' *Till Eulenspiegel's lustige Streiche*, op. 28, **solo violin**, mm 206.

glissez. (Fr.) See ***glissando***.

glue. See **hide glue**.

Goffriller, Matteo (1659-1742). Italian **luthier** who was the first important instrument maker of the Venetian school. Goffriller is best known for his **cellos**, which were made on a large **Amati** pattern and most of which were cut down to smaller dimensions in the mid-18th century. The great **virtuosos Pablo Casals** and Janos Starker performed on Goffriller cellos. Goffriller also made fine **violins** and a few prized **violas**.

grace note. A general term for any **ornament** notated in small print, indicating it is not included in the rhythmic distribution of the bar.

Figure 64. **Grace notes** from the third movement of Beethoven's **string quartet**, op. 18, no. 5, **viola** part, mm 18-19.

graphite fiber. See **carbon fiber**.

Grappelli, Stéphane (1908-1997). French jazz violinist best remembered for his collaboration with Django Reinhardt in the Quintette du Hot Club de France.

Grappelli was largely self-taught on both **violin** and piano, with four years of studies in theory at the Paris Conservatoire where he won a prize in **solfège**. To support himself through college, Grappelli played in silent movie theaters and dance bands.

In 1934 Grappelli and gypsy guitarist Django Reinhardt formed the Quintette du Hot Club de France, establishing the first distinctly European **jazz** idiom. Using **string instruments** only in an unusual instrumentation of violin, three guitars, and **double bass**, the band trail-blazed a new style known as **gypsy jazz**, music for dancing characterized by a vivacious **swing** rhythm and complex, **improvised solos**. The Quintette du Hot Club de France disbanded during World War II, and though Grappelli continued a fine career performing well into his 80s, it was his work with Reinhardt that made his most seminal contribution to violin in the jazz **genre**.

As a performer, Grappelli played with an elegant *suavité*, his half-closed eyes and enraptured smile conveying utter bliss. Often called the grandfather of jazz violinists, Grappelli pioneered the violin as a lead jazz instrument, inspiring and influencing generations of artists, particularly **Jean-Luc Ponty** and Didier Lockwood. Grappelli left a legacy of hundreds of recordings including sessions with Duke Ellington, Oscar Peterson, Stuff Smith, L. Subramaniam, Gary Burton, Paul Simon, André Previn, Mark O'Connor, Jean-Luc Ponty, and Vassar Clements. Grappelli made several albums with virtuoso **Yehudi Menuhin**, bringing jazz violin to the attention of the classical audience. Grappelli received a Grammy Lifetime Achievement Award and was inducted into the Jazz Hall of Fame.

Griffbrett. (Ger.) **Fingerboard**.

grip.
1. The piece of soft leather wrapping the stick of the **bow** between the **lapping** and the **frog**. The grip provides cushioning for the thumb when holding the bow and prevents wear on the stick. See **bow** for an illustration.
2. The way a player holds the **bow**. See **bow hold**.

ground bass. A variation form built over a repeated bass line melody. See also *ostinato*.

Guarneri family. A family of celebrated **luthiers** in Cremona during the 17th and 18th centuries. Andrea Guarneri (1626-1698), who apprenticed under Nicolò **Amati** alongside a young Antonio **Stradivari**, began the **violin**-making dynasty, followed by his sons

Pietro Giovanni Guarneri (1655-1720) and Giuseppe Giovanni Battista Guarneri (1666-1739). The most celebrated luthier of the Guarneri clan is Andrea's nephew Bartolomeo Giuseppe (1698-1744), who is known as "del Gesù;" because of the initials "I.H.S." inscribed on his **labels**. The instruments of Guarneri del Gesù are among the most valued, particularly the 1724 "*Il Cannone*" violin owned by **Paganini** and the 1742 "**Wieniawski**" violin named for its famous owner.

gudok. A folk **string instrument** from Russia, traditionally used in dance. Also spelled "hudok," the gudok has three **strings** played with various tunings, often with two strings tuned in unison, and the third tuned up a fifth. The flat **bridge** allows all three strings to be played simultaneously. Occasionally a gudok has several **sympathetic strings** below the sounding board. The instrument has no **fingerboard** or **frets**, is played with a **bow**, and is held vertically, balanced on the player's knee. The gudok is also called a sigudök.

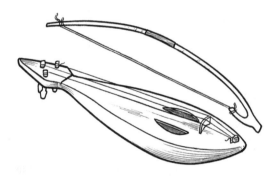

Figure 65. A **gudok** and **bow**.

guitar shape instrument. See **cornerless instrument**.

guitarre d'amour. (Fr.) See **arpeggione**.

guseto. See **cornerless instrument**.

gusle. A bowed **string instrument** from the Balkans. The gusle has one or two **horsehair strings** that pass over an animal skin-covered wooden body carved in the shape of a spoon. The strings attach to **pegs** that protrude through the top of the **neck** just below the **head**, which is carved into the shape of an animal, most often a horse or eagle. The gusle is held vertically between the knees like a **cello** and is played with a sort, convex **bow**.

gut strings. Strings made from a cord of stretched animal intestines, also called **cat gut**. Cat gut is processed from cattle, sheep, or goats, with the name probably deriving from a shortening of "cattle gut."

Gut strings are made of a gut core that is most often wound with aluminum or silver. While most modern string players use synthetic or steel strings, gut strings are still popular, particularly on **baroque instruments** and in **historically informed performance**. See also **steel strings**, **strings**, and **synthetic strings**.

gypsy fiddle, gypsy violin. A highly virtuosic, improvisatory style of fiddling derived from gypsy musicians of Hungary, Romania, and Eastern Europe. Gypsy fiddle has been a source of inspiration for **violin showpieces** including *Zigeunerweisen* by **Sarasate** and *Tzigane* by Ravel.

gypsy trill. See **vibrato trill**.

~ H ~

H. See **Hoboken**.

haegŭm. (Kor.) A Korean **spike fiddle** similar to the *erhu*.

hair. The strip of **horsehair** on a **bow**. See **horsehair**.

hair tension. How tightly the **horsehair** on a **bow** is pulled. Hair tension is an important element in the physics of the bow, affecting every **bowstroke**, particularly those requiring bounce. A bow with too high hair tension will not have the suppleness to pull a rich **tone** or the flexibility to bounce in a lively **spiccato**. In addition, too much tension can warp the stick of the bow, causing permanent damage. Hair that is too loose will have no power and may even allow the stick to scrape against the string.

As horsehair is affected by even small changes in temperature and humidity, it is important to monitor and adjust the hair tension. The modern **Tourte bow** used by most string players features a **frog** with a **screw** mechanism for making fine adjustments to the hair tension. Early designs such as the **fixed-frog** and **clip-in frog** bows had no mechanism for adjustment —by no means a limitation, as players pulled the hair with their fingers while playing to modify the tension. Releasing the hair tension when a bow is not in use prevents warping of the stick.

half position. The lowest possible placement of the left hand along the **fingerboard** in which the hand is aligned so that the index finger sits on the first possible note of the string, a **half-step** above the pitch of the **open string**, leaving the second finger placed on the note that usually marks **first position**, and the entire **hand frame** one half-step lower than **first position**. Half position is mostly used in passages heavy with accidentals, particularly those altering the **open strings**, and may result from a player making a passage easier by thinking of the pitches **enharmonically**. See also **position**, **shifting**, **finger pattern**, **fingerboard mapping**, and **extension**.

half shift. An archaic term indicating a **shift** the distance of a second.

half-size. A small instrument, intended for a child. In spite of its name, a half-size is proportionally only slightly smaller than a full-size. See **sizes** for specific measurements on sizing of **string instruments**.

half-step.
1. The distance of a minor second between two notes.
2. The smallest spacing between consecutive fingers. For the **violin**, **viola**, and **cello**, the half-step is an important element of **finger patterns** and **fingerboard mapping**. The half-step measurement can be linear, as between two notes of a **scale** a semitone apart, or cross-string with the distance of a minor sixth or diminished fifth being created by the same close spacing of consecutive fingers. **Double bass** is the exception, not only because it is usually tuned in fourths, but also because the **fingerboard** spacing is so large that half-steps are often played with nonconsecutive fingers, particularly in the standard 124 finger pattern. See **finger pattern** for illustrations.

hammer-on. An ascending, slurred **grace note ornament** used primarily in **bluegrass**.

hand frame. The measuring of note spacing on a **string instrument** using the concept that the span of fingers can be set in a consistent frame, and that by moving this structured hand frame through the **positions** of the instrument, a player can successfully navigate the **fingerboard** and play with good **intonation**. See also **finger pattern**, **fingerboard mapping**, **octave hand frame**, and **shifting**.

hand vibrato. A **vibrato** technique on **violin** and **viola** in which the pitch oscillation is created by hand movement using the wrist as the pivot point. Hand vibrato is also called wrist vibrato. See also **arm vibrato**, **finger vibrato**, and **vibrato**.

Handbassel, Handbassl. (Ger.) A small **cello**.

hārangī. See *sārangī*.

Hardanger fiddle. A traditional bowed **string instrument** from Norway, closely related to the **violin**.

Figure 66a. A **Hardanger fiddle**.

The Hardanger fiddle, or *Hardingfele*, has four playing **strings** like a violin, and four or five **sympathetic** under-strings. Highly decorated, a Hardanger fiddle usually has a carved lion or woman's head **scroll**, elaborate abalone **inlay** along the **fingerboard** and **tailpiece**, and black ink decorations called rosing on the body of the instrument. Sometimes pieces of bone are used to decorate the **pegs** and edges of the instrument.

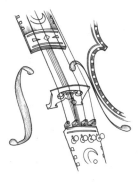

Figure 66b. Detail of the **sympathetic strings** and **bridge** of a **Hardanger fiddle**.

Hardingfele. See **Hardanger fiddle**.

harmonic. An overtone created when a **string** is touched lightly at a **node**, causing segments of the string on both sides of the finger to vibrate simultaneously. Harmonics played on open strings are called **natural harmonics** and are notated simply with a "o" fingering above the note-head. Harmonics played on a stopped string are called stopped, false, or **artificial harmonics** and are notated with a solid note-head for the stopped pitch and a **diamond note-head** for the lightly touched harmonic. In general, a solid note-head with a "o" shows the final sounding pitch of the harmonic, which may be played at a location on the fingerboard other than the pitch notated, while a diamond note-head shows where on the fingerboard the node will be found, most often producing a higher pitch than the note-head placement would normally indicate. On rare occasions, the harmonic is notated with three note-heads: the solid note-head for the stopped note, the diamond note-head for the harmonic node, and a cue-sized note-head, often in parentheses, indicating the sounding pitch. See also **diamond note-head** and **node**.

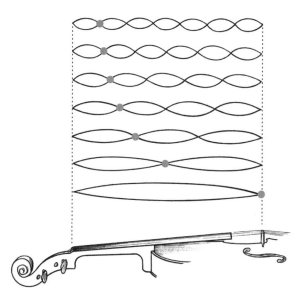

Figure 67. The location of **natural harmonic nodes** along a **string** and the vibration patterns they produce.

harmonic tuning. See **just intonation**.

hat pegs. A type of **machine tuner** used on **double bass** with an **ebony** shaft attached to a metal **worm gear**, capped by an ebony knob. Hat pegs are also called hat tuners, peg tuners, and top hat pegs.

hazelficte. See **bearclaw**.

head.
1. The wooden part at the end of the **neck** of a **string instrument**, including the **pegbox** and **scroll**, made of **maple** to match the body. In some cases, the head can be carved in the shape of an actual head.

Figure 68. The **head** of an instrument carved into a figure in place of the typical **scroll**.

2. The piece of wood at the **tip** of the **bow**, into which the **horsehair** is anchored. The head of the bow is carved from the same block of wood as the stick and holds the hair away from the stick to allow tension to be put on the hair. See **bow** for an illustration.
3. The main theme of a song, usually the A phrase in a standard AABA verse-chorus form. In **jazz**, "playing the head" usually means starting at the top of the **chart**.

headstock. See **head**.

heavy gauge string. A **string** with a high tension. Heavy gauge strings provide more volume but may be more difficult to play than a medium or light gauge string. See **strings** and **string gauge**.

heel.
1. The **frog** end of the **bow**. Playing at the heel means playing *au talon*, or very near the frog.
2. The curved base of the **neck** where it joins the body of the instrument between the top **bouts**. The heel fits

over the edge of the top **plate** with a groove and is met by the **button** on the back plate.

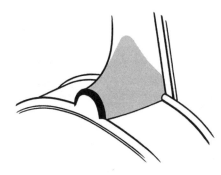

Figure 69. The **heel** of the **neck** of an instrument.

Heifetz, Jascha (1901-1987). Russian-American violinist, considered by many to have been the greatest violinist of the 20th century.

Heifetz began **violin** under his father, who was a professional violinist, then at age ten began studies with **Auer** in St. Petersburg. By age eleven, Heifetz was already so accomplished that he was invited to play Tchaikovsky's violin **concerto** with the Berlin Philharmonic and two years later he performed Glazunov's concerto under the direction of the composer. Soon after the Heifetz family emigrated to the United States in 1917, Heifetz made his Carnegie Hall debut, a stunning success that launched him into instant stardom.

Heifetz was admired for his flawless **technique**, which he executed in his signature, statuesque stance with the violin held high, exerting great power with his **Russian bow hold**. He performed with such consistent perfection that critics were left with little to fault, though some found his interpretations cold. With concert tours that took him around the world, including tours of Australia, Asia, and Palestine, Heifetz often used his fame to the benefit of others. In 1919 at the Metropolitan Opera House he gave a recital with Rachmaninoff at the piano, raising an incredible $7.8 million to defray the United States' costs of World War I. During World War II, Heifetz gave benefit concerts for the Red Cross and British War Relief, and he performed for thousands of service men and women, often in war zones.

Heifetz commissioned and premiered new violin concertos including those by Walton, Rózsa, and Korngold. He championed Sibelius' concerto and Prokofiev's second concerto, performing them often and making the first recordings of the works. By the end of his career, Heifetz had made hundreds of recordings, almost all of which remain in print. He was one of the first musicians to be well known to an audience through recordings before they had the opportunity to hear him in person.

Heifetz created a collection of **transcriptions** and **arrangements**, many of which have become part of the standard violin **repertoire**, including Dinicu's *Hora Staccato*, Ponce's *Estrellita*, Prokofiev's *March from the Love of Three Oranges*, and Gershwin's *Porgy and Bess*.

Dedicated to the task of preserving the art of the violin, Heifetz served on the faculty of the University of Southern California from 1962 to 1983.

Helmholtz's scale. See **just intonation**.

hemiola. A musical figure in which two groups of three beats are replaced by three groups of two beats, creating a momentary sense of a changed meter.

Herabstrich, Herstrich. (Ger.) **Down-bow** (archaic).

Heraufstrich. (Ger.) **Up-bow** (archaic).

hertz. The unit of **frequency** of **sound waves**, measuring the number of cycles per second and abbreviated Hz. **Standard tuning** is A4 = 440 Hz. See also **sound wave**.

Herunterstrich. (Ger.) **Down-bow** (archaic).

hidden shift. Changing **positions** by **shifting** to a note that is not audible. A hidden shift allows the player to find a position and set the **hand frame** using a strong finger or familiar reference point. For example, in the notoriously difficult opening phrase of Mendelssohn's **violin concerto**, the two leaps of sixths are to be executed by first-finger hidden shifts, followed by stopping the string on the high pitch with the fourth finger.

Allegro, molto appassionato

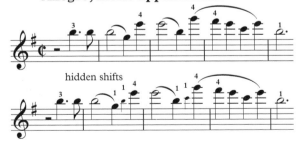

Figure 70. **Hidden shifts** in the opening of Mendelssohn's **violin concerto**, op. 64, mm 2-6, shown in the small notes below.

Because the arrival note of the shifting finger is never heard, the shift is considered hidden. See also **shifting**, **finger pattern**, and **fingerboard mapping**.

hide glue. The glue traditionally used by **luthiers** in the construction and repair of **string instruments**. Made from boiled animal hide, the glue is valued for its elasticity, which allows the parts of the instrument to expand and contract, and for the ease with which it can be dissolved to open the instrument for repairs.

Hinaufstrich, Hinstrich. (Ger.) **Up-bow** (archaic).

HIP, HIP movement. See **historically informed performance**.

historical edition. See **critical edition** and *Urtext*.

historically informed performance. The practice of performing a piece of music using the instruments and techniques contemporary to the time period in which it was composed.

Historically informed performance, or HIP, emerged as a movement in the 1970's that looked to treatises and other documents to find information on the styles, techniques, and instruments used by musicians in particular eras and localities. Considerations for HIP performances may include tuning to a lower reference pitch, using various **tuning** systems, interpreting the composer's marks according to the conventions of the time, reading alternative **clefs** and notation systems, playing on baroque or classical instruments that have not been modernized, and using **gut strings**, **fixed-frog bows**, and other equipment appropriate to the era of the composition.

While no amount of musicological research will ever truly reveal how music sounded in times prior to the development of recording technology, HIP performances offer an insightful, often vivid approach to music, and have led to the revival of musical instruments such as the lute, **arpeggione**, *viola da gamba*, and fortepiano.

Historically informed performance is also called period performance or authentic performance. See also **baroque pitch**, **baroque instrument**, **baroque bow**, **viol family**, and **just temperament**.

Hoboken, Hob. The cataloging system of Franz Joseph Haydn's works, often used in lieu of **opus numbers**, abbreviated Hob. or H. See also **thematic index**.

Holz. (Ger.) Wood. For string players, *Holz* usually refers to the **stick** of the **bow**.

homophony. Music composed of a melody over a **chordal accompaniment**, as opposed to **polyphony**, which is constructed of two or more simultaneous melodic lines.

hooked bow. A **bowstroke** in which two notes are played on the same **bow** with a stop between them. Hooked bows are used to manage **bow distribution**, especially in rhythms with uneven note values and when executed well should sound like separate bows. Hooked bows are notated by a **slur** and **dots** above the notes. See **Table 1: Bowstrokes** for a list of strokes and their notation.

horn violin. See **stroh viol**.

horsehair. The coarse material on a **bow** used to grip and pull the **strings**, cut from the tails of horses. The preferred horses for bow hair are stallions from cold climates such as Siberia, Mongolia, and Argentina, as their tail hair grows strong to cope with frigid winters and is usually cleaner than the tail of a mare. Most string players use white horsehair, with some **double bass** and **cello** players preferring black hair for its coarseness or the blending of black and white hairs together into a combination called **salt and pepper**. Horsehair wears smooth with playing, so a bow typically needs a **rehair** at least once a year.

Synthetic fibers are occasionally used on cheap bows in place of real horsehair.

hudok. See **gudok**.

humidifier. A device designed to add moisture to the air. Because **string instruments** may crack or split a seam in dry conditions, it is wise to use a humidifier anytime the humidity falls below 30% as measured by a **hygrometer**. Types of humidifiers specifically designed for musicians include a small sponge inside the **case** or a **dampit** that fits through the **f-holes** to release moisture directly to the air inside the instrument.

huqin. A family of bowed **string instruments** originating in China, the best known of which is the **erhu**. *Huqin* (pronounced "hoo-chin") are made in a wide array of sizes and forms, all characterized by a small **soundbox** attached to a long, round **neck**. *Huqin* are played by bowing between two **strings** while lightly pressing the strings to change the pitch. The *huqin* family of instruments is used in Chinese opera and the Chinese National Orchestra. The many varieties of *huqin* include the *jinghu, xiqin, tiqin, zhonghu,* and *bangzi*. See **erhu** for more detailed information.

hurdy-gurdy. A mechanical **string instrument** that uses a **rosined** wheel turned by a crank in place of a **bow**. The hurdy-gurdy is made in a variety of shapes, sizes, and designs, all of which use mechanical keys that press against the **strings** to change the pitch and have **drone strings** that sit on extra, buzzing **bridges**. Also called a *vielle à roue,* the hurdy-gurdy is related to the **nyckelharpa** and sounds like a bagpipe.

Figure 71. Playing a **hurdy-gurdy**.

huur. (Mong.) A type of Mongolian **spike fiddle** of the *huqin* family of instruments. The *huur,* also called the *khuur,* is built in three designs: box-bodied, ladel-bodied, or tube-bodied, most of which have two **strings** stretched over a skin membrane. The **head** of the instrument is often carved into the shape of a horse, swan, or serpent. The *huur* is held vertically between the knees like a **cello** and played with a convex **bow** held underhand.

hygrometer. A device used to measure the amount of humidity in the air. Many instrument **cases** are fitted with a hygrometer to indicate when to use a **humidifier**, which for **string instruments** is anytime the moisture level falls below 30%. See also **dampit**.

~ I ~

improvisation. The playing of extemporaneously created music. Improvisation is usually achieved by embellishing upon and varying an existing melody, or by creating new material that fits over a preset chord progression. Improvisation is the defining element of jazz, with many jazz tunes being merely a set of chords over which the musicians take turns improvising solos. Other musical **genres** that use improvisation include **bluegrass** and rock, particularly progressive rock and jam bands. In **art music**, improvisation was a highly valued skill from the Medieval through the Romantic eras, when string players were expected to embellish and **ornament** their parts and to showcase their improvisation skills in the **cadenzas** of **concertos**. Since the first half of the 20th century, coinciding with the advent of recording technology, art music rarely includes improvisation.

inlay. Decorative materials set into the wooden surface of the instrument. Most **string instruments** have functional inlay in the form of the band of wood **purfling** outlining and reinforcing the edges of the top and bottom **plates**. Additional inlay for ornamentation is often abalone, including **eye dots** on **end button**, **tailpiece**, **pegs**, or **frog**. More elaborate inlaid designs may include shell, bone, or metals.

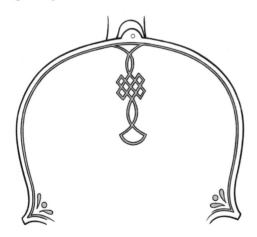

Figure 72. Decorative **inlay** on the back of an instrument.

inside player. The musician sharing a **music stand** in **orchestra** who is sitting further from the edge of the stage than his **stand-partner**. See also **conventions of orchestral playing**, **outside player**, and **stand-partners**.

insurance. A guarantee of compensation in the case of damage or loss to a valuable item. Because of the fragility and high value of most **string instruments**, musicians buy special insurance policies for their instruments, which are often not covered under homeowner's or renter's insurance. **Orchestras**, the musician's union, and some music societies offer group rates for instrument insurance.

international standard pitch. See **standard pitch**.

intonation. The degree of accuracy in **pitch**. On fretless **string instruments**, good intonation is achieved by playing on well-tuned **strings**, stopping the notes in the precisely correct places on the **fingerboard**, and adjusting the pitch in relationship to the particular tonal center being played. Playing with consistently good intonation is one of the greatest challenges for any string player. See also **finger pattern** and **fingerboard mapping**.

inverted mordent. Lower mordent. The term has occasionally been used to indicate an upper mordent, leading to some confusion. See **mordent**.

inverted turn. See **turn**.

Irish fiddle. A style of **violin** playing in the traditional music of Ireland, characterized by frequent use of **ornamentation**, rhythmic **slurring**, and sparse use of **vibrato**. Irish fiddle is also called Celtic fiddle. See also **bow treble**, **cut**, **double cut**, **roll**, and **tap**.

Italian notation. **Double bass** music notated at actual pitch rather than the standard **transposing clef**, which sounds an octave lower than written.

~ J ~

jam. Improvise. A jam session is a group of musicians improvising together on a familiar tune, and a jam band improvises in performance.

jazz. Music of African-American origin characterized by **improvisation**, syncopation, and complex harmonies. Jazz developed in the southern United States at the beginning of the 20th century as a mix of African and European musical traditions and has grown into an international music encompassing a vast array styles. Aside from the **double bass**, which plays a key role in the jazz **rhythm section**, bowed **string in-**

struments are not part of a typical jazz **ensemble**, with the notable exception of **gypsy jazz**, which often includes a violinist playing lead.

jeté. (Fr.) An **off the string bowstroke** in which the **bow** is thrown onto the **string**, bounces several times in the same direction, then is lifted off again. *Jeté* is slower and more controlled than *ricochet* or **flying spiccato**. See **Table 1: Bowstrokes** for a list of strokes and their notation.

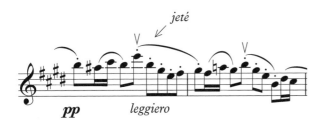

Figure 73a. *Jeté* from the third movement of Mendelssohn's **violin concerto**, op. 64, mm 8-10.

Figure 73b. Extended *jeté* later in the same movement, mm 127-129.

jig. An **Irish fiddle** dance form in a lively 6/8. See also *gigue*.

Joachim, Joseph (1782-1840). Hungarian violinist known for his **pedagogical** legacy, his numerous **concerto cadenzas**, and his close collaboration with Johannes Brahms. Joachim studied in Leipzig under the guidance of **Ferdinand David** and Felix Mendelssohn, followed by a performance career that included serving as **concertmaster** in Weimar under Franz Liszt and extensive touring of Europe. Joachim formed the celebrated Joachim Quartet, one of the first **string quartets** to give public concerts, often performing new works by contemporaries. Joachim advised numerous composers on string writing and inspired the dedication of many great works in the violin **repertoire**, including pieces by Brahms, Schumann, **Sarasate**, Bruch, and Dvořák. Joachim's personal motto *"Frei aber einsam"* [Free but lonely] provided his friends Robert Schumann, Albert Dietrich, and Johannes Brahms the musical kernel of their F-A-E Sonata, including the Brahms *Sonatensatz* Scherzo. In Berlin Joachim created a dis-

tinctly new school of violin playing. His students include **Leopold Auer**, Willy Burmeister, Sam Franko, Bronisław Huberman, Maud Powell, and Andreas Moser.

jouhikko. (Fin.) A traditional bowed lyre from Finland used in folk music. The *jouhikko* usually has two or three **strings** made of **horsehair** which are pressed with the back of the fingers to change the pitch.

just intonation. A tuning system based on the natural overtone series. Just intonation is naturally used in string **ensembles** and choral groups working without a fixed-pitch instrument such as a piano or guitar. Because the pitches of just tuning are particular to a key, instruments with fixed pitch will only sound in tune in one key, a limitation that caused just intonation to gradually be replaced by a variety of **tempered tunings**, including **mean-tone temperament** in the 16th century and eventually the modern system of **equal temperament**. Just intonation is also referred to as harmonic tuning or Helmholtz's scale.

~ K ~

K, KV, K-V. Abbreviations for *Köchel-Verzeichnis*, the cataloging system of **W. A. Mozart's** works in lieu of **opus numbers**. See also **thematic index**.

Kadenz. (Ger.) **Cadenza**.

Kammermusik. (Ger.) **Chamber music**.

Kämpfer, Joseph (1735-1796?). Hungarian **double bass** player who was the first to have a career touring with the double bass as a **solo** instrument. Kämpfer's fluid **technique** and beautiful **tone** made an important contribution to the popularization of the double bass.

Karr, Gary (b. 1941). American **double bass** player and **pedagogue** who founded the International Institute for the String Bass which has since become the International Society of Bassists. Born into a family of double bassists, Karr studied with Herman Reinshagen, Warren Benfield, and Stuart Sankey. Karr's international **solo** career began in 1962 when he appeared as a featured soloist in Leonard Bernstein's nationally televised New York Philharmonic Young People's Concerts. Karr has furthered double bass playing immeasurably through his method books, his pioneering of new techniques, and his extensive commissioning, performing, and recording of new **repertoire** for the instrument.

keman. (Turk.) **Violin**.

key pegs. A design of **cello** tuning pegs in which the removal of the heads from the C and G pegs allows the player to hold the cello in a more **ergonomic** position. The key peg is turned by fitting a removable square key tool into the slot in the peg shaft. Key pegs are also called posture pegs or krovoza pegs.

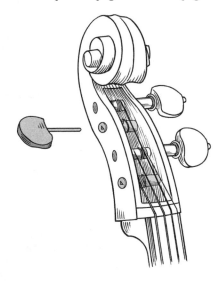

Figure 74. A **key peg** for the **cello**.

khuur. See *huur*.

kickoff. A short, rhythmic **lick** leading into a **fiddle** tune used to establish the tempo and key.

kinesthetics. The ability to sense the position, location, and movements of the limbs and body. String players rely heavily on their kinesthetic sense in the navigating of the **fingerboard** and in **bow** work. See also **Alexander Technique**, **Dalcroze Eurhythmics**, and **Feldenkrais System**.

kit. See *pochette*.

klein discant Geig. (Ger.) See *violino piccolo*.

klezmer. The traditional folk music of the Ashkenazi Jews from Eastern Europe rooted in dance music for Jewish weddings. The typical klezmer band consists of some combination of **violin**, clarinet, flute, accordion, and cimbalom, with the possible addition of brass instruments, cello, and percussion. While klezmer is known for its highly **ornamented**, virtuosic instrumental style, many klezmer bands also fea-

ture a singer. Klezmer music has experienced a revival in the 20th century and has been incorporated into **jazz** and other popular **genres**.

Kniegeige. (Ger.) **Viola da gamba**.

Köchel, Köchel-Verzeichnis. (Ger.) The cataloging system of **W. A. Mozart's** works in place of **opus numbers**, abbreviated K., KV, or K-V. See also **thematic index**.

kontra. (Ger.) Sounding an octave lower. See also **transposing instrument**.

Kontrabass. (Ger.) **Double bass**.

Konzert. (Ger.) Concert or **concerto**.

Konzertmeister. (Ger.) **Concertmaster**.

Koussevitzky, Serge (1874-1951). Russian-born conductor, composer, and **double bass** player best known for his championing of living composers and the founding of Tanglewood. As a double bass soloist, Koussevitzky toured performing primarily his own **arrangements** and compositions, including his 1905 double bass **concerto**. Koussevitsky began conducting with an **orchestra** he founded in 1921 and followed with a quarter-century as music director of the Boston Symphony Orchestra, becoming one of the greatest advocates for contemporary American music.

Kreisler, Fritz (1875-1962). Austrian-American violinist and composer beloved for his elegant style and charming salon pieces.

Kreisler was a child prodigy who gained admission to the Vienna **Conservatory** at the age of seven and studied **violin** with Massart at the Paris Conservatoire where he won the *premier prix* at age twelve. Kreisler toured America from 1888 to 1889, and then returned to Vienna where he left his musical career to study medicine and art. In 1896, Kreisler resumed performing and enjoyed an international career as one of the most popular violinists of the 20th century.

Highly regarded among his peers, Kreisler was awarded the London Philharmonic Society's gold medal in 1904. Elgar wrote his violin **concerto** for Kreisler, who gave the **premiere** in 1910 with Elgar conducting. In 1923, **Eugène Ysaÿe** dedicated his fourth **solo sonata** to Kreisler.

Kreisler possessed an unmistakable **tone**, a silky sweet **resonance** created by graceful **bow** work and a continuous **vibrato**, which he used even in faster passages. He played with an effortless perfection, never making a show of his **virtuoso technique**. As one of the first great violinists to record and broadcast extensively, Kreisler had a tremendous influence on later generations.

In the tradition of the virtuoso performer-composer, Kreisler wrote many charming **salon pieces** to showcase his own personal style of playing, including *Caprice Viennois, Liebesfreud, Liebesleid,* and *Schön Rosmarin.* In addition, he composed dozens of pieces in the "olden style," which he attributed to 18th-century composers such as Pugnani and Francoeur. All of these works remain in the standard **repertoire** alongside his **cadenzas** for the Beethoven and Brahms concertos, his many **transcriptions** of works by Dvořák, **Paganini**, and **Tartini**, and the virtuosic **showpiece** *Recitativo and Scherzo Caprice,* op. 6, dedicated to Ysaÿe.

Kreutzer, Rudolphe (1766-1831). French violinist, composer, and **pedagogue** important for his role in founding the **French school of violin playing** together with **Baillot** and **Rode** at the Paris Conservatoire.

As a violinist, Kreutzer was recognized as a child prodigy and gained work in the chapel **orchestra** of Louis XVI and Louis XVIII. In 1802, after the revolution, Kreutzer played in Napoleon's chapel orchestra and private orchestra.

It was on a concert tour to Vienna in 1798 that Kreutzer met Beethoven, who heard the violinist perform. It should be noted that Beethoven's famous op. 47 violin **sonata**, nicknamed the "Kreutzer," was originally written for English violinist George Bridgetower, who **premiered** the work with Beethoven at the piano in 1803, and that Beethoven revised the dedication to Kreutzer only after having a quarrel with Bridgetower. There is no evidence that Kreutzer knew of the dedication or ever performed the sonata.

Kreutzer's greatest contribution to his field was his pedagogical work helping establish the Paris Conservatoire and his co-authorship of the school's violin curriculum. Kreutzer taught at the Institut National de Musique starting in 1793, then became professor of violin at the Paris Conservatoire from its founding in 1795 until his retirement in 1826. His work in helping found the French violin school of playing was a legacy inherited by **Wieniawski, Vieuxtemps, Sarasate,** and **Ysaÿe,** virtuoso performers who revolutionized the role of the violin into a superstar solo instrument, challenged today only by the piano.

As a composer, Kreutzer wrote violin **concertos, chamber music,** and operas, though only his forty-two **etudes** gained a place in the standard **repertoire** (it is thought that only forty are original to Kreutzer). As foundational exercises for mastering **technique,** valued for their methodical approach and focus on left hand **extensions,** the etudes remain core training for both **violin** and **viola.**

Kreuz. (Ger.) Sharp.

krovoza pegs. See **key pegs**.

kurz. (Ger.) Short.

KV. Abbreviation for *Köchel-Verzeichnis,* the cataloging system of **W. A. Mozart's** works in lieu of **opus numbers**. See also **thematic index**.

~ L ~

L. H. Left hand, often used to indicate **left-hand pizzicato.**

L'arte del arco. (It.) *The Art of Bowing,* a set of fifty variations on a theme by **Arcangelo Corelli** forming a book of **etudes,** each developing a different technique of **baroque violin** playing.

label. A slip of paper glued to the inside of the back **plate** of an instrument identifying the **luthier** and year the instrument was made. The label, visible through the **f-hole,** is not reliable proof of the authenticity of an instrument as it can easily be removed, replaced, or forged. On the **bow,** the maker is identified by the **stamp** on the **frog.**

Laborie endpin. A removable end pin for **double bass** designed by Christian Laborie that is inserted into a conical hole drilled into the lower **block** near the **back plate** of the instrument. The Laborie endpin is

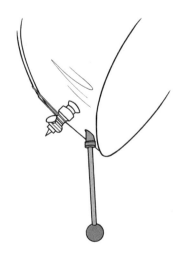

Figure 75. A **Laborie endpin** on the **double bass**.

made of a graphite rod tipped with a rubber ball. By changing the angle to the double bass and redistributing the weight, the Laborie design is intended to facilitate ease of left hand work and produce a larger **tone**. The Laborie endpin is also called the Rabbath endpin or the Laborie-Rabbath endpin. See also **endpin, tilt-block**, and **egg pin**.

Laforge, Théophile (1863-1918). French violist and **pedagogue** who created the first dedicated **viola** studio at the Paris Conservatoire. Laforge began his career as a violinist, having studied with Eugène Sauzay at the Paris Conservatoire where he was awarded the 1886 *premier prix* in **violin**. He joined the Paris Opéra orchestra as a violinist, and then took a position as **principal** viola of the Orchestre de Paris.

In 1894, ninety-nine years after the violin and **cello** programs were begun, and in the face of great opposition from those who believed that viola **technique** was indistinguishable from violin technique and the instrument was suited only to inferior violin players, Laforge became the first professor of the viola as an instrument distinctly independent from the violin. During his tenure, Laforge commissioned and inspired many new works for the viola, making great strides for the development of his instrument.

Lage. (Ger.) **Position**.

laminated bass. A **double bass** made from plywood that is pressed into the shape of the instrument **plates** and finished with a thin veneer of hardwood. Because laminated basses are machine-made from cheaper materials than hand-carved basses, they are relatively inexpensive, and tend to be more durable. Some **luthiers** make a hybrid double bass with a carved **top plate** for warmth of sound combined with laminated back and ribs.

lancé. (Fr.) See *détaché lancé*.

langueur. (Fr.) A two-fingered **vibrato** technique used on the **viol** and other fretted instruments in which one finger holds down the string while the next finger flutters in a trill-like movement. Also called two-finger vibrato, vibrato trill, and close shake.

lapping. The material wrapped around the **stick** of the **bow** above the **grip**. Also called **winding**, lapping protects the stick beneath the index finger of the **bow**

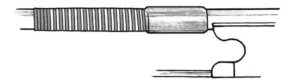

Figure 76. **Lapping** protecting the **stick** of the **bow**.

hold from wear and tear. Traditionally made of whale bone, lapping on modern bows can be a variety of materials including rubber, plastic, leather, or metal thread.

låtfiol. (Swed.) A type of Swedish **violin** with two to eight **sympathetic strings** running beneath the **fingerboard**. The *låtfiol* is also called a *låtfela* or a Swedish **drone**-fiddle. See also **hardanger fiddle** and *nyckelharpa*.

lay out. A **jazz** term instructing a player to stop playing for a section or song. See also **tacet**.

lead, playing the. Playing the principal melody, particularly in the genres of **bluegrass** and **jazz**. See also **backup** and **lead sheet**.

lead sheet. Sheet music showing only the basic melody, lyrics, and chord changes. A lead sheet is used primarily by **jazz** musicians to play the tune, create an accompaniment, and **improvise solos**. Lead sheets, sometimes called fake sheets, are printed in collections known as **fake books**.

leader. **Concertmaster**, mainly used in England.

ledger lines. Small horizontal lines extending above or below the staff to accommodate notes beyond the range of the staff.

left hand *pizzicato*. Plucking with the hand that is stopping the **strings**. Left hand *pizzicato* is accomplished by pressing the first, second, or third finger hard onto the note, then pulling the string to the side and releasing with a higher finger of the same hand, creating a percussive pop.

The technique is a favorite **virtuoso** pyrotechnic found in many string **showpieces**, often combined with *battuto* notes swatted with the bow. Left hand *pizzicato* works particularly well on open strings and can be useful when making a quick transition between *pizzicato* and **arco**. Left hand *pizzicato* is notated by a + symbol over the note-head.

Variation 9

Figure 77. **Left hand *pizzicato*** from the ninth variation of **Paganini's** 24th **Caprice**, op. 1. Notes with the + symbol are plucked with the left fingers while notes with **bowing** indications are played *battuto.*

legato. (It.) Smooth and connected.

legatura. (It.) **Slur.**

léger. (Fr.) Lightly.

leggiero. (It.) Lightly.

legno. (It.) Wood, as in the **stick** of the **bow**. See *col legno.*

Leier. (Ger.) **Hurdy-gurdy.**

lever. A simple machine in which a beam pivots over a **fulcrum** in order to move an object at a second point by a force applied at a third. In string playing, this usually refers to the idea that the **bow** itself is a third-class lever used to apply pressure to the **string** using hand rotation at one end of the stick. With the thumb as the pivot point or fulcrum, the index finger applies enough weight for the far end of the bow to grab and move the string. Without this leverage, no amount of arm weight will create pressure on the bow. The **German bass bow hold** also operates as a lever, with the thumb as a fulcrum on top of the stick and the hand rotating up to send the other end of the bow down into the string.

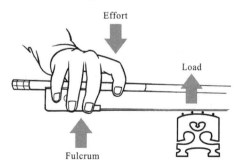

Figure 78. The bow functioning as a lever with the index finger applying weight (effort) and the thumb serving as a pivot point (fulcrum) in order to move the string (load).

liberamente. (It.) Freely in regard to rhythm and tempo.

libre. (Fr.) Free.

lick.
1. In **jazz**, rock, and other popular music **genres**, a lick is a short musical idea. Licks are usually single-note melodic lines played by a **solo** musician either as the building block of an **improvised solo** or as a **fill** between melodic phrases.
2. In **art music**, a lick is a short, fast, virtuosic passage (informal).

Liebesgeige. (Ger.) **Viola d'amore.**

lifted bowstroke. The technique of removing the **bow** from the **string** between notes. The lifted bowstroke is a controlled movement in which the player raises the bow upward from the string, as opposed to a thrown bow stroke such as *spiccato* in which the player throws the bow onto the string, causing it to bounce. Particularly common in music written prior to the development of the modern **Tourte bow**, the lifted stroke is used between notes of a dotted rhythm or along a moving line to achieve a lively, detached **articulation**. See **Table 1: Bowstrokes** for a list of strokes and their notation.

light gauge string. A string with a light tension. Light gauge strings provide more clarity but may create a small sound. See **string gauge** and **strings**.

linings. The thin strips of wood glued inside the **ribs** where they join the back and **table** of the instrument. Made of flexible softwood, the linings connect to the **blocks** to reinforce the shape of the instrument and support the ribs.

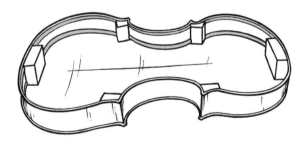

Figure 79. **Linings** reinforcing the seams inside an instrument.

linseed oil. Oil extracted from flax seeds used as one of the principal ingredients in **string instrument varnish.**

lira.
1. A small bowed **string instrument** from the Medieval era, related to the **rebec**.
2. A short name referring to the *lira da braccio* or *lira da gamba*.
3. A Ukrainian type of **hurdy-gurdy**, also called the lera or the relia.

lira da braccio. An early bowed **string instrument** with five playing **strings** running over the **fingerboard** and two **drone** strings to the side of the fingerboard. A relative of the *vielle*, the *lira da braccio* has a violin shape, a wide fingerboard, a nearly flat **bridge**, and a leaf-shaped **head** with frontal **pegs**. The *lira da braccio* is held horizontally on the shoulder and tuned like a **violin** with the fifth string at G4 and the drone strings tuned to D3 and D4.

Figure 80. A *lira da braccio.*

lira da gamba. The bass version of the *lira da braccio.* The *lira da gamba* is a large bowed **string instrument** with 12, 14, or 16 playing **strings** running over a **fretted fingerboard** and two **drone** strings to the

side of the fingerboard. The *lira da gamba* is held between the knees like a **cello** and tuned in successive fifths with two drone strings in octaves. With a nearly flat **bridge**, the *lira da gamba* can easily play **chords**. The *lira da gamba* is also called a *lirone*.

lira organizzata. (It.) A Ukrainian type of **hurdy-gurdy** that is combined with a small set of pipes. The crank that plays the strings on the *lira organizzata* also operates a bellows for the pipes.

lirone. See *lira da gamba.*

loco. (It.) Play in the proper location, usually found following an **8va** or **sul** G marking.

long bow. A **bowstroke** in which the entire length of the **hair** is used, usually in *legato*.

long roll. See **roll**.

loop end. A **string** that is finished with a loop to be attached to the hook of a **fine tuner**. See also **ball end**.

louré. (Fr.) A **bowstroke** in which each note under a **slur** is gently pulsed. While the amount of **articulation** can be varied, *louré* is always essentially *legato* with the pulses created by adding and releasing weight. Also called *portato*, *louré* is notated by the combination of slur and lines over each note. See **Table 1: Bowstrokes** for a list of strokes and their notation.

lower mordent. See **mordent**.

lower saddle. See **saddle**.

Luftpause. (Ger.) A momentary breath in music indicated by a comma or V between notes. For string players, a *Luftpause* is often achieved with a **retake**. Also called *Atempause, caesura, Cäsur,* or *Zäsur.*

lunga. (It.) Long.

Lupot, Nicholas (1784-1824). French **luthier** considered the finest of the French school and often called the French **Stradivari**. Born into a family of instrument makers, Lupot studied **lutherie** with his father, then apprenticed with François-Louis Pique before opening his own shop in Paris. Lupot's work steadily improved throughout his career, and his best work began around 1810. Starting with Stradivari's design as his model, Lupot created finely crafted instruments finished with a transparent reddish **varnish**. With a production almost entirely of **violins**, Lupot set the standard by which all future French luthiers would be measured.

lutherie. (Fr.) The art of making **string instruments**. See also **luthier**.

luthier. (Fr.) Someone who makes and repairs **string instruments**. See also **lutherie**.

lyra viol.
1. The smallest of three sizes of bass **viol**.
2. A style of playing the bass **viol** in the 17th century using extensive *scordatura* to facilitate **polyphonic** playing in particular keys and reading music written as **tablature**.

lyre gamba. See *viola bastarda*.

~ M ~

m. d. (Fr.) *Main droite*, or right hand.

m. g. (Fr.) *Main gauche*, or left hand.

M. or M. M.
1. **Metronome** marking, usually followed by the number on a metronome that corresponds to pulses at the desired tempo.
2. Measure number (m) or measure numbers (mm), followed by the numbers of the corresponding measures.

machine extension. A mechanized **C extension** for the **double bass** using a set of **levers** mounted next to the regular **fingerboard** which function similar to the keys on a bassoon. By pressing the keys, a player engages a lever to **stop** the **string** at any pitch on the fingerboard extension. The advantage of a machine extension is that the placement of the keys adjacent to the regular hand **position** on the fingerboard allows a player to integrate the lowest pitches into passage work on the regular fingerboard. The disadvantage is that the machine does not permit the player to spontaneously adjust **pitch** or play **vibrato**. Additionally, the machine may make unwanted clicking sounds. The machine extension is also called a mechanical ex-

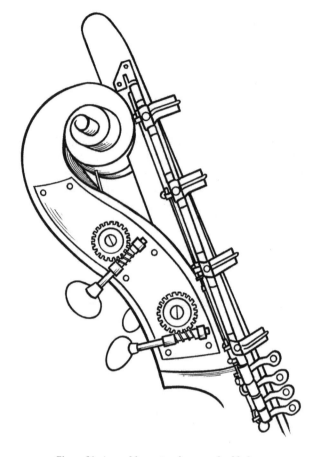

Figure 81. A **machine extension** on a **double bass**.

tension. See also **C extension**, **chromatic extension**, and **fingered extension**.

machine head. A metal mechanical tuning **peg** that uses a **worm gear**. See **mechanical pegs**.

machine tuner. See **mechanical pegs**.

machines. A short name for the mechanical lever system on a **double bass** extension. See **machine extension**.

Maggini, Giovanni Paolo (1580-1632). Italian **luthier** whose developments influenced the art of **violin** making. At the age of seven, Maggini was apprenticed under **Gasparo da Salò** in Brescia. Once he began working independently, Maggini developed an individual style of instrument making, frequently experimenting with design to improve the **tone**, and the instruments he made at the end of his career are most valued. Maggini's work is characterized by high-quality woods, fine craftsmanship, large **sound-holes**, and a warm, mellow tone. Many of his instruments have a double ring of **purfling** and ornamental motifs inlaid into the back. Maggini is known to have made at least sixty violins, nine **violas**, two **cellos**, and one **double bass**.

maggiore. (It.) Major key.

magnetic pickup. A transducer using a magnet mounted on the instrument to convert **string** vibrations into an electric signal. This signal is used to amplify, modify, or record the sound of the instrument. Magnetic pickups read the vibrations of each string, requiring steel-core or steel-**wound strings**. While magnetic pickups are popular on electric bass, most string players use a **piezo pickup**. See **pickup** for an illustration.

main. (Fr.) Hand. Used in phrases such as *main droite*, meaning right hand, and *main gauche*, meaning left hand.

majeur. (Fr.) Major key.

manche. (Fr.) **Neck** of the instrument.

mando-bass. A very large **mandolin** with the same tuning as a **double bass** (E1 – A1 – D2 – G2). The mando-bass is held upright like a double bass and is supported on an **endpin**. See also **mandolin**.

mandocello. A large **mandolin** tuned like a **cello** (C2 – G2 – D3 – A3). See also **mandolin**.

mandola. An alto **mandolin**, tuned like a **viola** (C3 – G3 – D4 – A4). See also **mandolin** and **mandocello**.

mandolin. A plucked **string instrument** of the **lute** family with a rounded body and a **fretted fingerboard**. The mandolin has eight **strings**, most commonly tuned in adjacent unison pairs, each a fifth apart. The finger spacing and string tuning of the

Figure 82. A **mandolin**.

mandolin are the same as a **violin**. Originally popular in 18th-century Italy, the modern mandolin is a mainstay in **bluegrass** and country western music today. See also **mandola**, **mando-bass**, and **mandocello**.

manica. (It.) **Shift** of **position**.

manico. (It.) **Neck** of the instrument.

maple. A **tonewood** of the Acer genus, most often chosen for making the back, sides, and **neck** of instruments in the **modern string family** because of its ability to transmit sound vibrations. Maple is also used to make instrument **bridges**.

marcato. (It.) With a strongly marked **articulation**.

mariachi. The traditional folk music of Mexico, also called *son* style. The typical mariachi band consists of as many as eight violinists, several trumpet players, and at least one guitarist.

markiert. (Ger.) *Marcato*.

martelé. (Fr.) A vigorous, detached **bowstroke** created by a heavy, biting start released into a fast, floated bow which reaches a complete stop before beginning the next stroke. *Martelé* is notated by wedges or **accents** above the notes.
    Also called *martellando, martellato, martello, gehämmert*, and hammered. See **Table 1: Bowstrokes** for a list of strokes and their notation.

martellando, martellato, martello. (It.) See *martelé*.

master class. A seminar given by a highly accomplished musician who teaches a series of individual lessons before an audience. A master class usually features polished pieces played by advanced students with the idea that all students and other teachers in the audience can benefit from the master teacher's comments.

mean-tone temperament. A type of **tempered tuning** used in the Renaissance in which the fifths measured out from a central or mean tone are tuned slightly narrower than perfect fifth of **just intonation**. Mean-tone temperament, which allows a keyboard to play in tune in five to six closely related keys, was gradually replaced by the modern system of **equal temperament**. Mean-tone temperament is still used today in some **historically informed performances**.

measured vibrato. A technique used in the 17th and 18th centuries of creating a pulse in the **tone** by regular, controlled changes in bow **pressure** similar to *portato*.

mechanical extension. See **machine extension**.

mechanical peg. A **tuning peg** that uses gears to improve ease and accuracy of **tuning**. Traditionally most **string instruments** use wooden **friction pegs**, which are held in place by pressure against the **pegbox**. Mechanical pegs are intended to address challenges of friction pegs, which are adversely affected by weather, as changes in humidity shrink or expand the wood, causing pegs to stick or suddenly slip. Friction pegs eventually wear down, requiring **rebushing** of the pegbox and new pegs.

Some **violins**, mainly **fiddles**, use mechanical pegs with a **worm gear**, similar to those on a guitar or **mandolin**, but these are not popular due to the weight of the mechanism. With a few exceptions, classical string players still primarily use friction pegs, taking pride in mastering the skills needed to operate them successfully. This is slowly changing, due to newly developed **geared pegs**, which look like friction pegs but have a hidden mechanism inside, allowing for minute adjustments without the difficulty of friction pegs.

Double basses are the exception, with most instruments using worm gear tuners, and instruments designed to be electric also commonly use some type of mechanical pegs.

Mechanical pegs are also called mechanical tuners, machine tuners, geared pegs, gear heads, and machine heads. See also **worm gear**, **geared pegs**, and **fine tuners**.

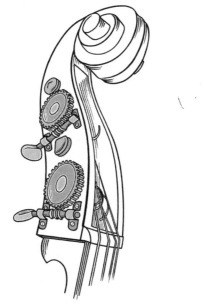

Figure 83. **Worm-gear mechanical pegs**.

medieval fiddle. A predecessor to the **violin**, found depicted in medieval artwork. The medieval fiddle is characterized by a guitar-shaped body, a low **bridge**, and frontal **pegs** holding four or five **strings** which use a variety of tunings. The medieval fiddle has experienced a revival as part of the **historically informed performance** movement.

medium gauge string. A string with a medium tension. Medium gauge strings are the choice of most players as they provide a balance of clarity, volume, and playability. See **string gauge** and **strings**.

memorization, conventions of. In the performance of **art music**, there are established conventions of when a piece should be memorized and when reading from sheet music is permitted. In general, any piece that is a **solo** showcase is expected to be performed from memory. This includes **concertos**, **showpieces** with piano accompaniment, and solo works such as those by **J. S. Bach**. In the performance of **orchestra** music, **chamber music**, and any music that is fundamentally collaborative, the use of sheet music is expected. This includes **sonatas** with piano in which the pianist is considered an equal partner rather than an accompanist, as well as **duos** between any two string players.

mensur. The vibrating length of **string** stretched between the **nut** and the **bridge**.

Menuhin, Yehudi (1916-1999). American violinist and conductor who used his fame to promote music as philanthropy. Menuhin was a child prodigy who at the age of eleven stunned audiences at his Carnegie Hall debut by performing a mature Beethoven **violin concerto**, and at age thirteen performed the concertos by Bach, Beethoven, and Brahms in a single concert with the Berlin Philharmonic.

Menuhin commissioned and premiered significant new works from more than forty composers, including Bartók, Bloch, Foss, and Walton. Menuhin's studio work leaves him one of the most prolifically recorded artists of the 20th century, including a **jazz** album in collaboration with **Stéphane Grappelli**.

A dedicated violin **pedagogue**, Menuhin published several books on technique and violin repertoire, advocating a relaxed, **ergonomic** approach to playing. He founded the Menuhin School to provide full-time education for young musicians.

As a humanitarian activist, Menuhin gave over five hundred performances during World War II for U.S. and Allied troops, many of them in theaters of war, served as president of the International Music Council, founded Live Music Now!, which sponsors performances of young professionals in hospitals, prisons, and special schools, and inaugurated the Assembly of the Cultures of Europe.

messa di voce. (It.) A gradually swelling crescendo followed by a slow diminuendo used to shape a single long note.

metronome. A device that produces a regular, adjustable pulse. The metronome is a valuable tool used by musicians for rhythmic training, measuring and communicating tempos, and maintaining good **ensemble**.

The numbers on metronomes measure the number of pulses per minute, which are usually adjustable within a range of 40 to around 200. A metronome marking indicating the desired tempo is notated in music as **MM**, followed by the number of beats per minute (MM = 120), or as the kind of note receiving the beat followed by the number of beats per minute ($\quarternote$ = 120).

The original metronome design was an inverted double weighted pendulum which generated a click every time it swung past center and could be adjusted to swing slower or faster by sliding the weight up and down the rod. These mechanical metronomes are still available, although they are rarely used by modern string players who prefer electronic or digital designs.

Electronic metronomes use a quartz crystal to maintain the accuracy of the pulse and are made in a wide variety of designs, from credit-card-sized devices that produce only an adjustable click to elaborate, programmable metronomes that provide uneven beat meters, cross-rhythm subdivisions, and tap-pad tempo recognition. Most electronic metronomes include some visual pulse along with the click and many have a silent setting. Even simple electronic metronomes usually play a tuning note of A4 = 440 Hz, with some models generating the entire chromatic spectrum with adjustable **pitch**.

Digital metronome programs are able to make the most complex features of an electronic metronome available online or as a smart phone application. Music software and **synthesizer** keyboards usually include a programmable digital metronome feature.

See also **click track**.

mettez la sourdine, mettez sourd. (Fr.) Use the **mute**.

microtone. An interval smaller than a **half-step**. There is no standard notation in Western music to indicate microtones. See also **quarter tone**.

MIDI instrument. An instrument designed to be used as a controller for a synthesizer. **String instruments** using MIDI have a multi-pin output attached to a **pickup** and are typically bodiless electric designs that make no **acoustic** tone so as to allow complete control of the sound through the synthesizer. MIDI instruments are polyphonic, creating a separate digitized signal for each string. While an external MIDI converter can be used with any **electric instrument**, it will produce only a monophonic output.

Mingus, Charles (1922-1979). American **jazz double bass** player, composer, and bandleader whose virtuosic **technique** and dynamic approach to the instrument elevated the double bass into the spotlight of the jazz band. Mingus' focus on complex texture, layered rhythm, and conversational **improvisation** characterized his orchestral treatment of jazz composition. Charles Mingus started double bass in high school in Los Angeles, then studied with Red Callender and Herman Rheinschagen. Mingus toured in the big bands of Louis Armstrong and Lionel Hampton, and he performed with Billy Taylor, Duke Ellington, Stan Getz, Art Tatum, Bud Powell, Charlie Parker, and Dizzy Gillespie. In 1955 he founded a new jazz workshop in which he dictated a part to each player.

minuet. A stately dance form in 3/4 time, originating in 17th-century France. The minuet is often a movement in a **suite**, **sonata**, **quartet**, or **symphony**. Also spelled *menuet* (Fr.), *menuetto* (It.), *Menuett* (Ger.), and *minuete* or *minué* (Sp.).

Mitschlag. (Ger.) The simultaneous **plucking** and **bowing** of a note.

mittel. (Ger.) Middle. Used to designate a **middle gauge string**.

mixed bowing. The combination of different bowing patterns or bowstrokes in a single passage. Mixed bowings can be particularly challenging, as in the rapid alternation between *sautillé*, *spiccato*, and **slurs** in the final movement of Mozart's 39th symphony (see figure 84). See also **Table 1: Bowstrokes** for a list of strokes and their notation.

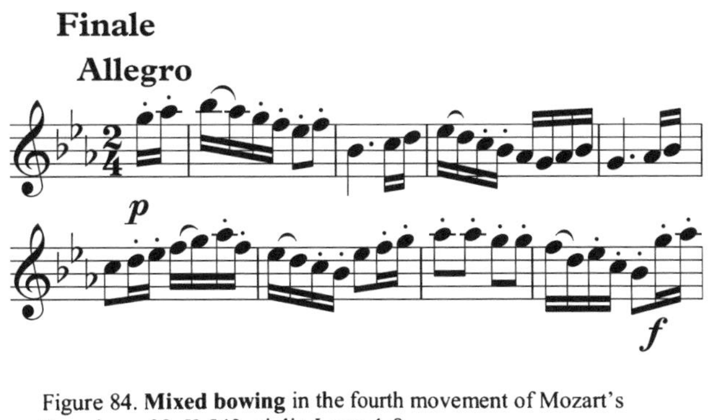

Figure 84. **Mixed bowing** in the fourth movement of Mozart's Symphony 39, K 543, violin I, mm 1-8.

MM.
1. Metronome marking indicated in beats per minute. See also **metronome**.
2. Measure numbers.

mode. A set of seven **scales** each built from a different note of the diatonic scale. Each mode has a distinctive interval pattern, which may be conveniently understood by beginning on the final and following the white keys of the piano until the next final is reached. Inspired by the ancient Greeks, the modes are: Ionian (C final), Dorian (D final), Phrygian (E final), Lydian (F final), Mixolydian (G final), Aeolian (A final), and Locrian (B final). Western **art music** most commonly uses the Ionian mode, which creates a major scale, and the Aeolian mode, which creates a natural minor scale. Folk music, **jazz**, **fiddle**, and other popular music **genres** often use Mixolydian and Dorian modes.

modern string family. The group of **string instruments** belonging to the **symphony orchestra**, also called the modern violin family. The modern string family includes the **violin**, **viola**, **cello**, and **double bass** in their modern forms. This term is used in this text to distinguish these from instruments of the general **string family**, which also includes plucked instruments such as the harp, guitar, and **banjo**. The term modern string family is also used to differentiate from the term **violin family**, which expands beyond modern instruments to encompass **baroque instruments** and violin variants such as the **Hardanger fiddle**, *basse de violon*, and *violino piccolo*.
　　See also **viol family** and **violin family**.

monitor. A speaker system that faces in towards the musicians on stage, used to help them hear themselves during an amplified performance. Additionally, a musician may use a personal monitor in the form of a headphone or earphone. The sound in monitors may be mixed to emphasize the lead instrument or vocals rather than having all instruments blended together like the **front of house** sound.

mordent, mordant. An **ornament** created by a single, quick alternation between the indicated note and either the note above or the note below. The upper mordent, also called a *Pralltriller*, is notated by a squiggle above the note (see figure 85a), while the lower mordent, also called an inverted mordent, is notated by a slashed squiggle above the note (see figure 85b).

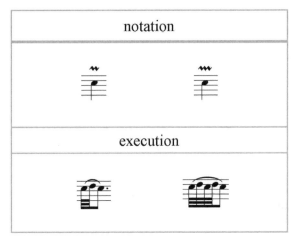

Figure 85a. A **mordent** and a double mordent with their executions.

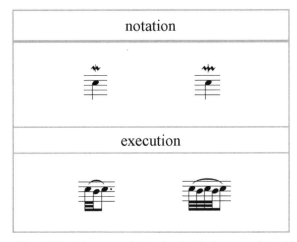

Figure 85b. A lower mordent and a double lower mordent with their executions.

morendo. (It.) Gradually dying away.

mortice, mortise. A cavity or slot in a piece of wood, prepared to receive a matching projection. On **string instruments**, the mortise most often refers to the slot cut into the upper **ribs**, **block**, and top **plate** of the instrument to receive the **heel** of the **neck**, which is glued rather than bolted together.
　　The term mortice can also refer to the cavity in the **frog** and **tip** of the **bow**, where the **horsehair** is held in place with a **wedge**. On the bow, the wedge is not

glued into the mortice but rather is held in place with the pressure of the hair tension against the wedge of wood lodged in the mortice opening.

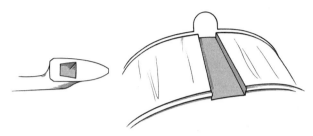

Figure 86. A **mortice** in the **tip** of a **bow** for securing the **hair** on the left, and a mortice in the **top block** for attaching the **neck** on the right.

mountings. The metal elements on the **frog** of the **bow**, including the **screw button, ferrule, slide, backplate**, and the **lining** between the frog and stick.

Mountings serve to reinforce and strengthen the frog, and they are sometimes engraved with ornamental designs. The choice of metal for the mountings may indicate the maker's opinion of the quality of the stick: nickel for the most ordinary bows, silver for finer bows, and gold mountings reserved for a stick of which the maker is most proud.

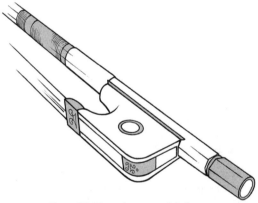

Figure 87. **Mountings** on a **viola bow**.

Mozart, Leopold (1719-1787). Austrian composer, violinist, and **pedagogue**. Although writings about Leopold Mozart's work, like his life itself, are eclipsed by his role in his prodigy son's career, the senior Mozart was a highly regarded composer and teacher, and he was the author of the foundational treatise of **violin technique**, *Versuch einer gründlichen Violinschule*.

As a violinist, Mozart played in the **orchestra** of the Archbishop of Salzburg from 1743 and was appointed court composer and vice-*Kapellmeister* there in 1762. Mozart continued this work after young Wolfgang's talents began to manifest themselves, but he eventual-

ly became so dedicated to the training and promotion of his son that his own position in the court suffered.

Mozart's famous treatise *Versuch einer gründlichen Violinschule* [A Treatise on the Fundamental Principles of Violin Playing] was first published in 1756, the same year as Wolfgang's birth. The work was well received and republished with revisions by the author for a second edition in 1770 and a third edition in 1787. Mozart was so well regarded as the leading pedagogue of violin in Europe that his *Versuch* was translated and published in Dutch in 1766 and French in 1770. Still in publication today, the book expounds on the Italian method inherited from **Tartini**, including chapters on the execution of **ornamentation**, the timing of particular rhythmic figures, and the treatment and embellishment of **trills**, as well as a glossary of technical terms, all illustrated with musical examples. Mozart's treatise serves as the fundamental source for information about 18th-century performance practice and is an invaluable resource for musicians involved in **historically informed performance**.

multiple stop. Two or more notes played simultaneously. See **chord, double stop, polyphony**, and **voice leading**.

music stand. A device for holding sheet music in a position where the musician can read it while playing. Music stands are made in a wide variety of sizes and designs. Most allow for adjustment of the height and tilt of the desk, and many can be folded up to facilitate transportation or storage. Accessories for music stands include **stand extensions** to accommodate large scores, shelves for holding pencils or a **metronome**, and clip-on **stand lights**. Modern **digital music stands** hold a touch screen displaying the music and have features such as automated page turns and adjustable lighting. See also **stand partners**.

music theory. The study of the fundamental elements of music, including notation, melody, harmony, rhythm, structure, texture, and compositional techniques. Music theory is one of the core subjects studied by students at a **conservatory** or school of music.

musical saw. See **saw, musical**.

mute. A device that dampens the vibrations of the **bridge**, creating a quieter, softer **tone**. Mutes are made from a variety of materials and designs, each affecting the sound in a different way. Orchestral players use a rubber **Tourte mute** that attaches to the **strings** for ease of sliding on and off the bridge. **Practice mutes** are heavy pieces of rubber or metal that encase the entire bridge, dampening the sound of the instrument to almost silent. Sometimes called hotel mutes, these are intended to facilitate quiet practicing and are not generally used in performance. *Con sordino*, *sord.*, *mit Dämpfer*, and *sourdine* are common indications in music to use a mute. *Senza, senza sordino*, *Dämpfer ab*, and *sans sourdine* are the corresponding indications to remove the mute again. The shorthand symbol for using a mute is ⋔ and ⋓ for removing the mute again.

Figure 88. Three types of **mute**: a heavy **practice mute** top left, a rubber **Tourte** mute to right, and a wooden mute below.

mute instrument. See **silent instrument**.

~ N ~

Nachschlag. (Ger.) A two-note **ornament** placed at the end of a **trill**.

nagybőgő. (Hungarian) **Double bass**.

nail *pizzicato*. The **extended technique** of plucking the **string** with the fingernail rather than the fingertip, creating a biting, metallic **tone**.

Nashville shuffle. A rhythmic **bowing** pattern of two **slurred** notes followed by two single notes. See also **shuffle**, **double shuffle**, and **Georgia shuffle**.

natural harmonics. See **harmonics** and **node**.

neck. The piece of wood supporting the **fingerboard**, connecting the body of the instrument to the **scroll** and **pegbox**. The neck is usually made of unvarnished **maple** carved as one piece into the **scroll**. The **heel** of the neck is glued to the **top block** and **button** using a **mortise** joint.

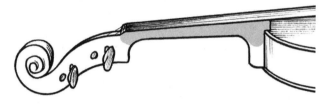

Figure 89. The **neck** of a **violin** or **viola**.

neck graft. The operation replacing the **neck** of an instrument, including the **heel**, which joins the neck to the body, in which the original **scroll** and **pegbox** are removed and reset onto the new neck in order to preserve the integrity of the instrument.

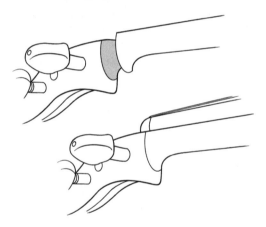

Figure 90. A **neck graft**.

A neck graft can be used to repair a broken neck, an injury common for **cello** and **double bass**, or it may be part of refitting a bass to be a **five-string**. Most often a neck graft is an indication of the modernization of an instrument that was built before the mid-19th century. With the need for performers to produce louder, more brilliant sound to fill concert halls, and the increasingly demanding technical requirements of virtuosic music, instruments of the **violin family** were modified with a higher **bridge** and a longer, angled **neck**. Most instruments made before 1840 have been converted to this modern design, including those made by the celebrated **luthiers Stradivari** and **Guarneri**. Initially, replacing the neck meant losing the scroll, an important signature of the maker, until Parisian luthier **Jean Baptiste Vuillaume** developed a technique for grafting a new neck onto an instrument using a dovetail joint to reattach the original scroll.

Evidence of a neck graft can be found in the seams left on the neck just where the pegbox begins. While a neck graft can indicate an antique instrument, many newer instruments are made to look as though they have grafted necks, either as a detail in replicating a fine old instrument or as an unfortunate effort to trick a buyer into believing a new instrument is an antique. With the growing interest in **historically informed performance**, some modernized instruments are being restored to their original neck design.

new violin family. A consort of eight **violins** of graduated sizes, one at each half octave, designed by American **luthier** Carleen Hutchins in the 1960s. The new violin family instruments range in size from a seven-foot contrabass violin to a miniature piccolo violin tuned an octave above the standard violin, all sharing the **acoustic** characteristics of a violin.

newgrass. A sub-**genre** of **bluegrass** music that incorporates instruments, songs, and styles from other genres including **jazz**, art music, and rock. Newgrass bands often play **electric instruments** and may incorporate drums, piano, **cello**, or other instruments not usually associated with bluegrass.

nickelharpa. See **nyckelharpa**.

nicks. The tiny notches cut into the center of **f-holes** on the **top plate** of an instrument. The inner nicks indicate the placement of the **bridge** and are used to measure the **string length**.

Niederstrich. (Ger.) **Down-bow** (archaic).

nocturne. A **character piece** with a dreamy, reflective mood.

node. The point of rest between two vibrating portions of a **string**. In string playing, a node is the exact location on a **string** where a **harmonic** can be played. See also **harmonic** and **sound wave**.

Nonnengeige. (Ger.) Nun's fiddle. See **trumpet marine**.

notching. The practice technique of using a **metronome** to increase the speed of a passage by playing slowly at first, then at each successive notch on the metronome until reaching the desired tempo.

note bending. See **bent note**.

note buone. (It.) Notes receiving natural rhythmic stress, such as those on the first beat of each bar. *Note buone*, or "good notes," are emphasized with strong **down-bows**, as part of the **rule of down-bow** in use from the late 15th century.

note-for-note solo. An exact reproduction of a previously **improvised** solo, learned from a recording. See also **transcription**.

notes inégales. The practice of taking notes that are written with even time values and playing them in groups of uneven values, usually alternating long and short. Most popular in France during the 17th and 18th centuries, *notes inégales*, or "unequal notes," is also standard practice in **jazz**, where it is called **swing**, or swung notes.

nun's fiddle, nun's violin. See **trumpet marine**.

nut.
1. The raised block of **ebony** at the narrow end of the **fingerboard**, supporting the **strings** as they pass into the **pegbox**. In coordination with the **bridge**, the nut raises the strings above the fingerboard and defines the vibrating length of the open strings. The nut is grooved to guide the strings in correct spacing and to create friction as the strings pass, relieving some tension on the **pegs**. Reshaping or replacing the nut is part of an instrument **adjustment**. The nut is also sometimes called the upper saddle.
2. The **frog** of the **bow**.

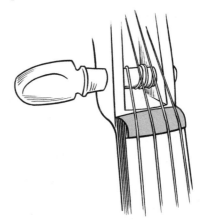

Figure 91. The **nut** at the end of the **fingerboard**.

nyckelharpa. A traditional bowed **string instrument** from Sweden, also called a keyed **fiddle**. The nyckelharpa has four playing **strings** crossing over the **bridge** and twelve **sympathetic strings** passing through the bridge. A mechanism of about thirty-seven simple gravity-operated keys is positioned beneath the strings in place of a **fingerboard**, each with a wooden pin, or tangent, situated at **half-step** intervals along the strings. When the player presses on a key, the tangent is pushed against the string, changing the pitch. The nyckelharpa is held horizontally, either balanced on the lap or supported by a shoulder strap, and played with a short **bow**.

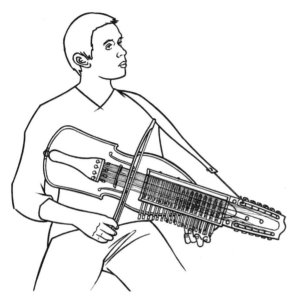

Figure 92. Playing the **nyckelharpa**.

~ O ~

obbligato.
1. (It.) Obligatory, referring to an instrumental part which must not be omitted. This meaning is most commonly applied to music from the Baroque era, particularly keyboard parts which are fully realized and not **continuo**.
2. Optional, referring to an accompanying part, often a countermelody or decorative line which may be omitted as necessary.

   It is up to the performer to decide which of these contradictory interpretations applies in a specific case. In general, music from the Baroque era will follow the first definition while more recent music will follow the second.

octave 8va. Play an octave higher than written.

octave 8vb. Play an octave lower than written.

octave frame. The measuring of note spacing on a **violin** or **viola** using the concept that the span of fingers can be set in a frame of one octave, and that by moving this structured hand frame through the **positions** of the instrument, a player can successfully navigate the **fingerboard** and play with good **intonation**. The octave frame is shaped by placing the first finger on the lower note and the fourth finger on the higher note of an octave, then using **finger patterns** to measure the remaining notes within the octave. An exercise for

Octave frame

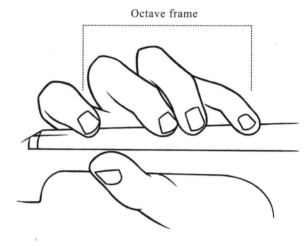

Figure 93. Measuring an **octave frame**.

training the use of the octave hand frame is Otakar Ševčík's *Preparatory Studies in Double-Stopping*, numbers 1 and 2, to be mastered in every key. See also **shifting, finger pattern, fingerboard mapping**, and **extension**.

octet. A **chamber music** ensemble comprised of eight players, each playing an independent part, or the music written for that **ensemble**. See **chamber music**.

octobass. A gigantic **double bass** with a sounding range of an octave below the standard double bass. Designed in 1850 by French luthier **Jean-Baptiste Vuillaume**, the octobass stands twelve feet tall and has three **strings** which are stopped by lever-operated bars that press against **frets** on the **fingerboard**.

off the string. Any **bowstroke** in which the **bow** bounces so that the **hair** loses contact with the **string**. Off the string strokes may be **thrown** or dropped from above the string, or initiated **from the string**. These strokes include *jeté, ricochet, spiccato*, and (arguably) *sautillé*. Off the string is also called *saltando* in Italian and *springender Bogen* in German. See also **bowstroke, on the string**, and see **Table 1: Bowstrokes** for a list of strokes and their notation.

ohne. (Ger.) Without. *Ohne* is often found in the phrase *ohne Dämpfer*, meaning "without mute."

on the string. Any **bowstroke** that is executed with the bow hair remaining in contact with the string. On-the-string strokes include *collé, détaché, louré, martelé,* and *staccato.* On the string is also called *à la corda* in French and *alla corda* in Italian.

See also **off the string,** and see **Table 1: Bowstrokes** for a list of strokes and their notation.

ondeggiando, ondeggiante, ondeggiamento. (It.) The slurred alternation between notes on two **strings,** creating a wavy movement of the bow arm. Also called by the French term *ondulé.* See also **bariolage** and **tremolo.**

Figure 94. A passage of *ondeggiando* from the first movement of Brahms' **Sonata** no. 3 for Violin and Piano, op. 108, mm 121-122.

ondulé. (Fr.) Undulating. See *ondeggiando.*

open string. A **string** played at full length without any fingers **stopping** a note, indicated by the finger number 0.

orchestra. A large **ensemble** made up of **string instruments,** woodwinds, brass instruments, and percussion. An orchestra is also called a symphony, a symphony orchestra, or a philharmonic. See also **chamber orchestra, string orchestra,** and **conventions of orchestral playing.**

orchestral playing conventions. See **conventions of orchestral playing.**

orchestral tuning. Standard tuning for **double bass,** as opposed to **solo tuning.** Orchestral tuning is E1 – A1 – D2 – G2.

orchestration. The adaptation of a composition for the instrumentation of an **orchestra** or other large **ensemble.**

ornament. A decorative embellishment to the musical line. Historically, music carried the expectation that the performer would add ornaments, leaving many ornaments merely implied by the style of music.

When notated, ornaments are often represented by a symbol, which may have a variety of interpretations. Not only do types of ornaments vary widely based on the culture and **genre** of music, but various ornaments and the means of executing them have gone in and out of style through history, leaving musicians with a bewildering array of traditions that can be vague and even contradictory. In particular, the music of the Baroque era is highly ornamented, involving an elaborate collection of ornaments and rules for their use. With growing interest in **historically informed performance,** many scholarly studies are available, offering practical guidelines to the art of baroque ornamentation (see the bibliography). See also **appoggiatura, grace note, mordent, Nachschlag, trill,** and **turn.**

ornamentation. The art of embellishing the musical line. Ornamentation is found in all **genres** and eras of music, perhaps most strikingly as a **virtuosic technique** in the **art music** of the Baroque era. Ornamentation is most often a form of **improvisation,** executed freely at the discretion of the performer. Even when ornamentation is notated in written music, either as an **ornament** symbol or fully written-out, tremendous freedom is given to the performer in determining the exact timing and execution of the ornament.

ossia. (It.) An alternative passage that may be played instead of the original, usually notated in small print above the original passage in the music.

ostinato. (It.) A melodic pattern that is constantly repeated throughout a passage or complete piece. See also **riff.**

ôtez les sourdines. (Fr.) Remove the **mute.**

outro. The coda or ending of a song, used by **jazz** musicians as the final equivalent to the intro.

outside player. The musician sharing a **music stand** in an **orchestra** who is sitting closer to the edge of the stage than his **stand-partner.** See also **inside player, stand-partners,** and **conventions of orchestral playing.**

overhand bow. See **French bow.**

overstand. The distance between the top of the instrument and the bottom of the **fingerboard,** measured at the edge of the **top plate** next to the **heel** of the **neck.**

overtone. A tone that is a part of the **harmonic** series which resonates above a note being played. Overtones are an integral element of string **intonation** and beauty of sound. Players achieve good intonation by listening for the complex, resonant **tone** that indicates that a finger is placed in exactly the correct spot to activate the overtones. Intervals are tuned by listening for when the overtones of the two pitches align. The overtones produced by one note will create **sympathetic vibrations** in other **open strings**, activating their overtone series as well, creating a sound that is rich and resonant.

~ P ~

pad. A sustained chordal background played to support a singer or lead instrumentalist. See also **shoulder pad**.

Paganini, Nicolò (1782-1840). Italian violinist and composer of legendary stature. Initially taught by his amateur musician father, Paganini was only twelve when he played for the famous violinist Alessandro Rolla, who was so impressed that he declared he could teach the boy nothing further. The first nine years of Paganini's career were spent playing in the court **orchestra** at Lucca, a position he left in 1810 to pursue a **solo** career, beginning with tours of Italy, then broadening to all of Europe.

As his fame as a touring **virtuoso** grew, Paganini played more and more of his own **concertos** and **showpieces**, treating audiences to brilliantly creative and shamelessly flashy displays of his pyrotechnic skills. These pieces contained effects and techniques never before heard: **double-stop harmonics**, *ricochet* **bowstrokes**, and a rapid alternation between *battuto* and **left-hand** *pizzicato*.

Paganini's extraordinary career as a superstar virtuoso was shrouded in a mystique carefully cultivated to attract audiences. At the time his gaunt appearance, wild persona, and seemingly impossible abilities drew accusations that Paganini had made a pact with the devil. Modern musicologists believe that Paganini may have suffered from Marfan syndrome, giving him long, exceptionally flexible fingers that allowed him to reach three octaves across four strings, a feat unattainable for most violinists even by today's standards.

Of Paganini's numerous virtuosic pieces, many remain in the standard repertoire. His first violin concerto, originally written in Eb with the solo violin

tuned *scordatura*, is usually performed in a transposed D major today. His 24 Caprices for Solo Violin, op. 1, represent the pinnacle of virtuosic violin **technique**. Dedicated "To the artists" and initially judged unplayable, the caprices have become standard fare for professional violinists and are used to set the bar as a required part of the admission audition to many conservatories. The caprices have been transcribed for **viola** and are even played by virtuoso **cello** and **double bass** players.

pardessus de viole. (Fr.) The smallest member of the **viol family**, tuned an octave above the tenor viol.

Parisian eye. A decorative dot encircled by a metal ring inlaid into the wood of a **tailpiece**, **pegs**, **button**, **frog**, or other **fitting**.

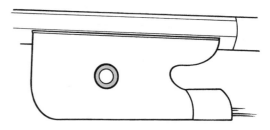

Figure 95. A **Parisian eye inlaid** on the **frog** of a **cello bow**.

parlando. (It.) A declamatory style in which the music imitates speech.

part. The sheet music of one instrument extracted from a score and printed for a single player or **section**.

partita. A **suite** or set of contrasting dance movements, such as **J. S. Bach's** three partitas for solo violin.

passacaglia. (It.) A musical form of continuous variations over an *ostinato* bass line.

pearl dot. See **eye**.

Peccatte, Dominique (1810-1847). French bowmaker whose work is considered second only to **Tourte**. Peccatte apprenticed with Persoit, then went to work for **Vuillaume** in Paris where he made **violin** and **viola bows** mostly in Vuillaume's self-rehairing design. In 1838 Peccatte took over the shop of **Lupot**, where he made bows of excellent playing qualities with round sticks and hatchet **heads** in the style of Tourte. Peccatte's brother François and nephew Charles continued the business, but it is the bows by Dominique Piccatte that remain in high demand by players today.

pedagogue. A specialist in the art of teaching. Music, as a living art form in which the skills of playing can only be learned from another person, relies heavily on pedagogues who fill the crucial need of training a new generation of players. The lineage of all great **virtuoso** string players can be traced to a handful of master teachers through a musical family tree.

pedagogy. The art of teaching. A **pedagogue** is someone who is an expert in pedagogy.

peg bushing. See **bushing**.

peg dope. A waxy paste applied to the contact surfaces of **friction pegs** to lubricate sticking pegs and add friction for pegs that slip. Peg dope is made in a small stick similar to lipstick and can be found at any **luthier** or violin shop.

pegbox. The part of the **head** of a **string instrument** which houses the tuning **pegs**. The pegbox sits at the end of the **neck** just beyond the **nut** and is usually finished with a decorative **scroll**. Traditional **friction pegs** are fitted through tapered holes in the side walls of the pegbox. **Mechanical pegs** are attached to the outside walls of the pegbox.

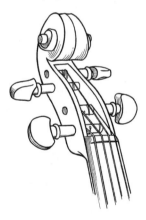

Figure 96. The **pegbox** and **scroll**.

pegs. Tapered wooden dowels fitted through holes in the **pegbox** at the **head** of the instrument. **Strings** are threaded through a hole in each peg, and then wound around the dowel until the correct tension is reached. Strings are tuned by turning the pegs.

Traditionally, most **string instruments** use wooden **friction pegs**, held in place by pressure against the pegbox. While **mechanical pegs** are available, most string players use friction pegs, taking pride in mastering the difficulties of wedging the pegs into their

holes at just the right tension. **Double bass** players are the exception, using primarily **worm gear** tuners, mechanical pegs similar to those used on guitar.

Friction pegs are usually made of a hardwood such as **ebony** or **rosewood**, chosen to match the other **fittings** of the instrument. Pegs can be carved in a variety of shapes and sometimes have ornamental **inlay**. The taper of each dowel needs to be custom carved to fit the holes in a specific instrument's pegbox. As the friction of tuning gradually wears down the wood, the pegs will sit closer and closer to the wall of the pegbox, eventually requiring replacement with a new set of pegs and a **rebushing** of the pegbox. See also **mechanical pegs**, **geared pegs**, **hat pegs**, and **key pegs**.

Figure 97. Standard **ebony friction pegs**.

perfect pitch. The inherent ability to identify a note without the benefit of an external reference. People who possess this ability can identify pitches in a manner similar to the way most people can identify colors. Perfect pitch, also called absolute pitch, is found in about one out of every ten thousand people, and is more common in speakers of tonal languages such as Chinese or Vietnamese. See also **relative pitch**.

performance practice. See **historically informed performance**.

period.
1. The amount of time elapsed between iterations of a wave form. See **sound wave**.
2. A musical structure usually built of a pair of phrases, the first ending with a weak cadence and the second culminating with a strong cadence.
3. An era of history.

period instrument. An instrument built with the structure and materials contemporary to a particular era, such as a **baroque instrument** or **transitional bow**. Period instruments are often played as part of a **historically informed performance**. See also **baroque instrument** and **viol family**.

period performance. See **historically informed performance**.

perlé. (Fr.) A series of articulated notes in a single **bow**, notated by the combination of a slur and dots over the notes. *Perlé* is generally more delicate than the closely related **slurred** *staccato* stroke. See **Table 1: Bowstrokes** for a list of strokes and their notation.

Figure 98. *Perlé* from Haydn's **Concerto** for **Cello Hob.** VIIb: 5, III, mm 120-123.

perlon. A synthetic fiber similar to nylon. Perlon is used to make **synthetic strings**. See **strings**.

pernambuco. A reddish wood of the Caesalpinia genus, also called brazilwood, used to make **bows** for **string instruments**. Pernambuco, currently a protected species, is so scarce that bowmakers have formed the International Pernambuco Conservation Initiative (IPCI) to rescue the tree.

pesante. (It.) Heavy in character.

Pettiford, Oscar (1922-1960). American **jazz** double bassist, cellist, and band leader known for his contributions to the role of the **double bass** in **bebop**. Born into a large musical family, Pettiford learned many instruments while playing with his family's travelling band. As a double bass player, Pettiford worked with many of the jazz greats including Thelonious Monk, Dizzy Gillespie, Miles Davis, and Duke Ellington. Pettiford was the first jazz double bass player to expand the work of **Jimmy Blanton** into the **genre** of bebop, establishing the double bass as an equal to the wind instruments, and Pettiford's work playing **solos** on amplified **cello** trail-blazed the instrument as a member of the jazz **ensemble**.

phono fiddle. See **stroh viol**.

phrasing. Grouping notes into a musical sentence to express meaning. String players shape phrasing through the use of dynamic inflection, flexible timing, and change of **articulation**, as well as variation in **bow distribution** and **contact point**. The notation for the duration of a musical phrase is often a long slur spanning several measures, not to be confused with **slurs** indicating **bowings**. See also **tempo rubato**.

physiology. The scientific study of the body's vital functions, including all physical and biochemical processes. Understanding the body and how it functions is very helpful in mastering the physical challenges of string playing. See also **Alexander Technique, Feldenkrais Method,** and **kinesthetics**.

piacere. (It.) See *a piacere*.

piano quartet. A **chamber music ensemble** usually comprised of **violin, viola, cello,** and **piano**. See also **chamber music**.

piano quintet. A **chamber music ensemble** usually comprised of a **string quartet** and **piano**, with a few notable exceptions such as Schubert's "Trout" Quintet for **violin, viola, cello, double bass,** and piano. See also **chamber music**.

piano reduction. The adaptation of a composition for **orchestra** or other large **ensemble** onto two staves for piano. For string players, a piano reduction is often the orchestral accompaniment of a **concerto** that has been condensed into material that can be played on a piano, allowing the soloist to rehearse and even perform the piece without assembling a **full orchestra**.

piano trio. A **chamber music ensemble** comprised of **violin, cello,** and **piano**. See also **chamber music**.

Piatti, Alfredo (1822-1901). Italian cellist and composer whose *Cello Method* is a mainstay in technical studies. The son of an **orchestra** director, Piatti started musical studies with his father on **violin**, then learned **cello** with Gaetano Zanetti. Piatti entered the Milan **Conservatory** at age ten to study with Merighi, and made his debut in 1837 playing his own **concerto**. In 1844 attention from Liszt helped Piatti launch his career as a soloist, **quartet** member, and cellist in London's Italian Opera orchestra.

As a performer, Piatti was one of the last to play without an **endpin**, and he was known for his clear, unsentimental style. As a private teacher and professor at the Royal Academy of Music, Piatti's many students included Robert Hausmann, William Whitehouse, Leo Stern, William Henry Squire, and Hugo Becker. Piatti's contribution to cello literature includes editions of previously neglected pieces which have since joined the standard **repertoire**.

picchettato. (It.) A thrown **off the string bowstroke** with several notes bounced in the same direction, notated by the combination of a **slur** and dots over the notes. See also *jeté, perlé,* and *ricochet,* as well as **Table 1: Bowstrokes** for a list of strokes and their notation.

piccolo violin. See *violino piccolo.*

pickup.
1. A device that captures the vibrations of an instrument and converts them into an electronic signal, which can then be amplified, modified, and recorded. String players usually use either a **magnetic pickup** or a **piezo pickup**.

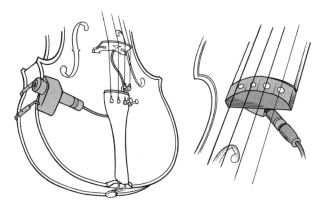

Figure 99. Two types of **pickup** used on string instruments: a **piezo pickup** on the left and a **magnetic pickup** on the right.

2. A pickup band or group is an **ensemble** of **freelance** musicians assembled for a particular engagement.
3. A note or short sequence of notes preceeding the downbeat. A pickup is also called an anacrusis or upbeat.

picqué. (Fr.) Obsolete spelling of *piqué.*

piezo pickup. A transducer using a piezoelectric contact microphone mounted on the instrument to convert vibrations to an electric signal, which is then used to amplify, modify, or record the instrument. Since the piezo pickup must contact the instrument directly, it is usually mounted on or near the **bridge**. Most piezo pickups use a single ceramic disc or plastic film, placed below the foot of the bridge or imbedded directly into the bridge. Some piezo pickups use a strap across the belly of the instrument or are attached directly to the surface of the instrument with putty. Others have individual pickups for each **string**, placed just beneath the strings as they cross the bridge. Peizo is pronounced "pee-ay-zo."

Piezo pickups are the most common choice of **violin**, **viola**, **cello**, and **double bass** players because they are generally less expensive and easier to add to

an **acoustic** instrument than a **magnetic pickup**. See **pickup** for an illustration.

pikieren. (Ger.) See *piqué.*

piqué. (Fr.) A small, biting **bowstroke** with a quick release that may leave the string. *Piqué* is the basic stroke used in **shoe-shine bowing**. See **Table 1: Bowstrokes** for a list of strokes and their notation.

pitched noise. See **scratch tone.**

pizzicato. (It.) Play by plucking the **strings**. *Pizzicato* is usually done with the right hand instead of **bowing**, though plucking with the left hand is a virtuosic skill displayed in some **showpieces**. The notation for *pizzicato* is usually the abbreviation *pizz.* above the staff, which applies to all following notes until the music is marked **arco**. See also **Bartók** *pizzicato*, **left hand** *pizzicato*, **snap** *pizzicato*, and **strumming**.

plate tuning. See **tap tuning**.

plates. The thin pieces of carved wood that are the top and back of the instrument. The top plate, alternately called the table, the face, or the belly, is typically carved from a slab of spruce. The top plate is arched to bear the pressure from the **bridge**, with **f-holes** carved into it to release the sound, and a **bass-bar** glued to the underside to help transmit vibrations. The back plate is carved from **maple** and includes the **button** which attaches to the **heel** of the **neck**. The plates are carefully hand carved, as their precise shape and thickness determines the sound of an instrument.

See **tap tuning** for information about how the **resonance** of the plates can be used to determine the ideal graduation of plate thickness. See also **top plate** and **back plate**.

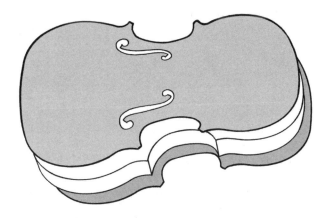

Figure 100. The top and back **plates** of an instrument.

playing angle.

1. The tilt of the instrument in relation to the player. The **violin** and **viola** usually have a playing angle with the **top plate** of the instrument tilted on a horizontal axis towards the treble side, allowing the **f-holes** to face the audience. This angle offers ease of reaching every **string** with the bow and helps to project the sound towards the audience. In some instances, a player may temporarily flatten the playing angle to increase brilliance on the highest string and facilitate reaching particularly high passages, or may increase the playing angle to gain power on the lowest string. Achieving the best, most comfortable playing angle on violin and viola depends in large part on a player's choice of **shoulder rest** and **chin rest**.

   The **cello** is most commonly held with a playing angle parallel to the chest, with some players occasionally rotating the instrument on a vertical axis towards the bow arm for work in the high register and away from the bow arm for the low register.

   The playing angle of the **double bass** varies largely depending on whether the bassist is standing or sitting as well as the **genre** of music being played.

2. The set of the **neck** and **fingerboard** of an instrument in relation to the **top plate** of the instrument. The playing angle of a **violin** or **viola** is usually rotated about a millimeter towards the treble side, with the bridge cut to match. This setup is intended to facilitate a slightly lower bow arm when playing on the bottom strings. A rotated playing angle is less common on **cello** and **double bass**.

3. Playing angle can also refer to **bow angle**, meaning the relationship between the bow and the bridge, or **finger angle**, meaning the way the left hand fingers approach the fingerboard.

plop. A **jazz** term for sliding into a note from above. The technique can be notated by a downward sloping line preceding the note-head. See also **fall off**, **bend**, **drop**, **scoop**, and *glissando*.

Figure 101. **Plop** notation.

pluck. See *pizzicato*.

pochette. (Fr.) A miniature **violin** used by dance masters from the 17th to the 19th century. The *pochette* is designed with a regular **fingerboard** and **neck** attached to a tiny body in order to fit into the coat pocket (*pochette* is French for "little pocket") of the dance master in order to free his hands while showing

his students the steps. Some *pochettes* are shaped like tiny violins, while others are carved from a simple boat-shaped stick of wood. Too small to hold on the shoulder, *pochettes* are held along the arm or resting on the chest, and are played with a short **bow**. A *pochette* is also called a pocket fiddle, kit, or kit fiddle.

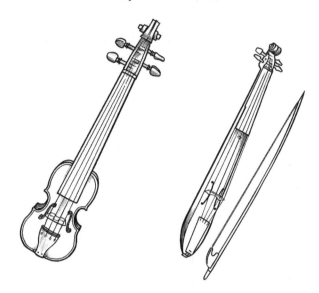

Figure 102. Two designs of *pochette*.

pocket. The center of the beat. Playing "in the pocket" means placing each beat exactly in time. One can also play "ahead of the pocket," "at the front of the pocket," "in back of the pocket," and "behind the pocket."

pocket fiddle. See *pochette*.

point. Tip of the **bow**.

pointe. (Fr.) **Tip** of the **bow**.

pointiller. (Fr.) *Sautillé*.

polyphonic bow. See **Bach bow**.

polyphony. Music constructed from two or more simultaneous melodic lines, as opposed to **homophony** which is constructed from a melody over chordal accompaniment. **String instruments** have the capability to create polyphony through the use of **double-stops** and **voice-leading** by placing one melody on each string. Demanding an extensive knowledge of the **fingerboard** by the composer and tremendous technical skill on the part of the performer, polyphony on a solo string instrument can produce stunning results, as exemplified by the four-voice fugues for **solo** violin written by **J. S. Bach**, who was himself a very accomplished violinist (see figure 103).

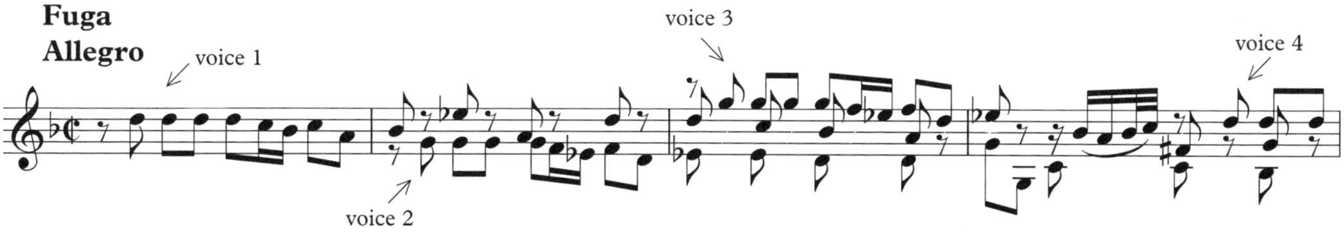

Fuga
Allegro

Figure 103. Complex **polyphonic** writing for **violin** from **J. S. Bach's** Sonata no. 1 for Solo Violin BWV 1001, Fuga, mm 1-4. The entrance of each voice of the fugue is labeled.

ponticello. (Fr.) **Bridge**. Most often found in the phrase *sul ponticello*, meaning to **bow** very near or on top of the bridge to create a harsh, metallic **tone**.

Ponty, Jean-Luc (b. 1942). French violinist known for trailblazing a featured role for the **violin** in the **genres** of **jazz** fusion and rock. Ponty received the finest classical training, graduating from the Paris Conservatoire with the *premier prix* at the age of seventeen. After three years as a professional **orchestra** musician, Ponty left the classical stage to launch a unique career in jazz and rock. A pioneer in electrifying the violin, Ponty found that merely amplifying his **acoustic** instrument was limiting.

Starting in 1969, he focused on developing the violin as an **electric instrument**, performing with a five-string electric violin, a **violectra**, and a violin synthesizer, experimenting with **MIDI instruments**, distortion boxes, phase shifters, and wah-wah pedals. Ponty has toured internationally, leading jazz-rock bands and collaborating with legends such as Frank Zappa, Elton John, and Chick Corea. Ponty has recorded many albums, twelve of which consecutively reached the top five on the Billboard jazz charts.

Pop's rosin. A particularly soft, sticky brand of **rosin** preferred by many **double bass** players.

Popper, David (1843-1913). Austrian cellist and composer whose *High School of Cello Technique*, op. 73, remains one of the foremost studies for mastering **cello** technique. Popper auditioned into the Prague **Conservatory** at age twelve on violin, but in order to fill a need in the school he switched to cello, studying with Julius Goltermann. At eighteen Popper won a position with the Löwenberg Court **Orchestra** where he quickly became **principal**, and at age twenty-five he became principal in the Vienna Philharmonic. Popper was a member of the Hellmesberger **Quartet** and Hubay Quartet and he performed with his pianist wife on tour. In 1886 he was appointed by Liszt to the faculty of the Hungarian Royal Academy of Music, where he established the cello and **chamber music** programs. Popper was a champion of new music for

cello, and he composed more than seventy-five works, mostly for his own performance.

portamento. (It.) The smooth slide between two **pitches**, used for expressive effect. *Portamento* can be implied by the style of the music or can be explicitly notated by a straight line connecting the two notes. See also *glissando*.

f molto sostenuto

Figure 104. A smooth line indicating *portamento* in Debussy's **Cello Sonata**, I/ Prologue, m. 29.

portando. (It.) See *portamento*.

portato. (It.) A slightly detached, pulsing **bowstroke**, notated by the combination of **slurs** and dashes. *Portato* is also called by the French term *louré*. See **Table 1: Bowstrokes** for a list of strokes and their notation.

position.
1. The placement of the left hand along the **fingerboard**. Positions are numbered starting from the farthest end of the fingerboard where the **string** meets the **nut**. First position is when the hand is aligned so that the index finger sits on the first note of the string, usually a whole-step above the pitch of the **open string**. To reach second position, the entire hand is reset so that the index finger sits on the second note of the string, and so on along the diatonic scale. Traveling from one position to another, or **shifting**, is accomplished by moving the entire **hand frame** to be centered around the new position.

Positions are sometimes notated by Roman numerals, particularly in music that is intended for students, although Roman numerals are most often used to indicate a desired string rather than position.

See also **shifting, finger pattern, fingerboard mapping, thumb position, half position**, and **extension**.

2. The way in which the instrument is held in relation to the body while playing. For example, a classically trained violinist may have a high position, with the instrument placed on the collarbone and held under the corner of the jaw, while a bluegrass fiddler may have a low position with the instrument placed against the chest and supported by the left hand. See also **rest position** and **playing angle**.

posture. The way in which the body is held while playing. Because the design of **string instruments** demands substantial physical energy to play, often while the body is set into a fundamentally unnatural position, finding and maintaining a healthy posture is always challenging for string players. Although ideal posture is unique to the physique of a particular player and instrument, a good set-up should provide the most effective **position**, maximize sound production, and facilitate **shifting, intonation**, and **vibrato**, all while minimizing tension, fatigue, and the risk of injuries.

With the development of **ergonomics** in the 20th century, the quest for healthy posture has inspired innovations for musicians such as redesigned **ergonomic instruments**, flexible **shoulder rests**, adjustable **chin rests, cello chairs**, and **key pegs**. The physical interaction with the instrument is being constantly reworked and there are many conceptual training methods known to help musicians develop healthy posture, including **body mapping, Alexander Technique**, and **Feldenkrais Method**.

posture pegs. See **key pegs**.

poussé. (Fr.) **Up-bow**.

power chord. A **chord** with only the root, fifth, and octave, commonly used in rock music.

practice instrument. See **silent instrument**.

practice mark, practice spot. The blemish on the skin where an instrument is held. Violinists and violists commonly develop a practice mark on the left side of the neck just below the jaw where the pressure from holding the instrument creates a callus. While many players wear the mark proudly as a badge of being a serious musician, others try to minimize the mark by placing a cloth between the **chin rest** and the neck, gluing a pad directly onto the chin rest, or using a chin rest made from a hypoallergenic material. Musicians should be sure to keep their chin rest and the skin it touches clean to prevent the blemish from be-

coming infected. A practice spot is commonly called fiddle neck or a violin hickey.

practice mute. A heavy rubber or metal **mute** encasing the entire **bridge**, dampening the sound of the instrument to almost silent. Sometimes called hotel mutes, these are intended to facilitate quiet practicing and are not generally used in performance. See also **mute**.

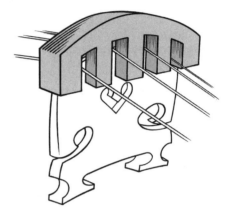

Figure 105. A heavy **practice mute** encasing the **bridge**.

Pralltriller. (Ger.) Upper mordent. See **mordent**.

premiere, *première*. (Fr.) The first performance of a piece of music.

pressure.
1. The force exerted upon the bow from above, created by muscle effort, as opposed to **weight** which is force exerted from below, created by gravity. Whether a musician should use pressure, weight, or a combination of the two is one of the fundamental components in different schools of **bow hold**. See also **German bow hold, French bow hold, Franco-Belgian bow hold, Russian bow hold**, and **lever**.
2. The force exerted upon the **string** by the fingers of the left hand, necessary to **stop** a note.

Primrose, William (1904-1982). Scottish viola player whose high-profile career furthered the perception of the **viola** as a **solo** instrument. Encouraged by his **violin** teacher **Ysaÿe** to switch to the viola, Primrose blended violinistic technique with the warm **tone** of the viola, earning a place on the international concert stage alongside **Heifetz** and Piatigorsky. Known for his effortless performances of **Paganini's** violin **caprices** on viola, Primrose wrote **transcriptions** and **arrangements** for viola, many of which are technically dazzling. Primrose commissioned and premiered Bartók's viola **concerto**, and inspired composers such as Britten, Milhaud, and Rochberg to compose for the viola. As a **pedagogue**, Primrose taught internationally and wrote several viola **technique** books, including *The Art and Practice of Scale Playing on the Viola* and *Technique Is Memory*. The first international competition for viola, called the Primrose International Viola Competition, was created in 1979 in his honor, and Primrose has a star on the Hollywood Walk of Fame.

principal. The leader of a **section** of players in an **orchestra**. The typical orchestra has five string principals: the **concertmaster**, who is **principal** of the **first violin** section, the principal **second violin**, the principal **viola**, the principal **cello**, and the principal **double bass**.

The principal string players form a **string quartet** circled around the conductor, except the principal bassist who usually stands behind the cello section. Principals follow the lead of the concertmaster, making all musical and technical decisions for their respective sections, unifying their timing, bow work, phrasing, and musicality with each other, just as a string quartet would.

Bowings are determined by the principals and should match those chosen by the concertmaster. Often, principals meet as a quartet prior to the first rehearsal to coordinate bowings and musical ideas.

Principals lead their section in making entrances, playing the right dynamics, and interpreting the gestures of the conductor by cueing with large physical gestures that enable their section players to anticipate and synchronize.

The **stand partner** of each principal is the assistant principal, who helps in communication with the section and is prepared to sit principal should the need arise. Some orchestras have expanded principal opportunities which may include co-concertmasters, co-principals, and associate principals. In a professional orchestra, the concertmaster and other principal players receive a higher salary than section players as a reflection of their additional responsibilities.

See also **conventions of orchestral playing**.

pronation. The rotational movement of the forearm from the elbow that turns the back of the hand inward. For **string instrument** players, the term pronation is usually used to describe rotating the forearm of the bow arm towards the player. Pronation is a way to operate the **lever** of the **bow** by increasing weight on the index finger and leverage of the thumb without raising the shoulder or upper arm. Whether and how much to pronate the bow hand is a primary factor in schools of bow technique.

On **cello**, pronation can also refer to the approach of the left hand to the **fingerboard**, tilting the hand back

towards the index finger by rotation of the forearm, rather than using a square hand **position**.

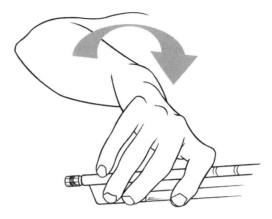

Figure 106. **Pronation** of the **bow** arm to facilitate using the bow as a **lever**.

psaltery. See **bowed psaltery**.

pull-off. A descending slurred **grace note ornament** used in **bluegrass**.

Pulte. (Ger.) **Music stand** shared by two players in an **orchestra**. See also **stand-partners**.

Pultweise. (Ger.) By stand, usually found in instructions for distributing *divisi* lines.

punta. (It.) **Tip** of the **bow**.

pupitre. (Fr., Sp.) **Music stand** shared by two players in an **orchestra**. See also **stand-partners**.

purfling. The strip of **inlay** glued into a narrow channel cut into the outer edges of the **plates** of an instrument, reinforcing the wood against cracks. Traditionally, purfling is a sandwich of three thin strips of wood: a light band of poplar between two bands of pearwood, dyed a dark black, though **ebony** or whale bone can occasionally be used. Inexpensive instruments may

Figure 107. **Purfling** inlaid along the edge of an instrument's back **plate**.

only have lines painted onto the surface of the wood to imitate purfling. Because of the high level of skill required to inlay purfling, particularly at the corners where the strips meet in the **bee sting**, purfling is one of the signature marks used to authenticate an instrument's maker. Some **luthiers** show off their skill with a double ring of inlay, or decorative weavings of inlay on the back.

Pythagorean intonation. A system of **just intonation** tuning attributed to Pythagoras in which the relationships of all intervals are based on the perfect fifth.

~ Q ~

quadruple stop. Four notes sounding simultaneously.

quarter tone. An interval of half a semitone. Although there is no standard notation in Western music to indicate quarter tones, one common system is shown here:

| 1/4 | 3/4 | | 1/4 | 3/4 |
| sharp | sharp | | flat | flat |

Figure 108. A notation system for indicating **quarter tones**. The tones are arranged in ascending, then descending, pitch order and are shown in context between **half-steps**.

quartet.
1. An **ensemble** of four players.
2. The music composed for an ensemble of four players.
See **chamber music, piano quartet,** and **string quartet.**

Quartgeige. (Ger.) A *violino piccolo* tuned a fourth higher than a standard **violin.**

quinte. (Fr.) A term for the **viola** or viola player.

quintet.
1. An **ensemble** of five players.
2. The music composed for an ensemble of five players.
See **chamber music, piano quintet,** and **string quintet.**

~ R ~

R. H. Right hand.

Rabbath endpin. See **Laborie endpin.**

rabeca, rabeca chuleira. (Port.) A type of folk **violin** found in northern Portugal and Brazil. Descended from the medieval **rebec**, the *rabeca* is tuned in fourths or fifths in the same range as the violin. The shorter *rabeca chuleira* is usually tuned an octave above the standard violin. The *rabeca* is also called the *rabeca rabela, chula de Amarante, chula de Penafiel,* or *ramaldeira,* depending on the region.

ravanhatta. An ancient bowed **string instrument** from India and Sri Lanka, similar to the **erhu.** The *ravanhatta* is made of a coconut shell resonator covered by skin and attached to a bamboo neck. It has two primary **strings,** a melodic string made of horsehair, and a **drone** string made of steel, and can also have any number of **sympathetic strings.** The curved **bow** passes between the two primary strings and has bells attached to provide rhythm. The instrument is held in the left hand, supported against the lower torso, and facing the player. Also called *ravanatta, ravanahatha, rawanhattha, ravanastron,* or *ravana hasta veena.*

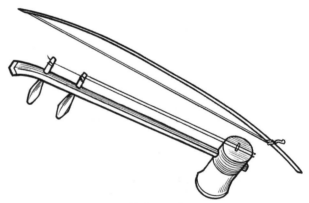

Figure 109. A *ravanhatta.*

real book. A legal, updated **fake book.**

rebab. A traditional bowed **string instrument** from the Middle East, used as the lead instrument of a Javanese gamelan **ensemble.** The rebab is a type of **spike fiddle** with a long wooden spike piercing the length of a heart-shaped wooden body covered by parchment. The spike supports the **strings** and serves as an **endpin** below the instrument. Two brass strings stretch from the leg of the spike below the body across a wooden **bridge** on the parchment membrane to long tuning **pegs** in the upper portion of the spike. With no **fingerboard**, the pitch is changed with just a touch on the string. The **bow** is strung loosely with horsehair, which the player pulls to varying degrees of tension to control sound and volume. The rebab is held vertically with the foot of the spike resting on the floor.

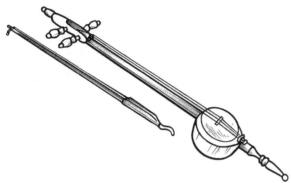

Figure 110. A **rebab** and **bow**.

rebec. A bowed **string instrument** popular in the European Middle Ages and Renaissance music. Derived from the Arabic **rebab** and considered an ancestor of the **violin**, the rebec has a pear-shaped wooden body and **neck** carved from a single piece of wood. The rebec has a carved wooden **bridge**, an attached, sometimes **fretted fingerboard**, and a matching **tailpiece**. Standardly violin-sized with three **strings** tuned in fifths, rebecs are made in a variety of sizes and tunings. A **consort** of rebecs might range from the small soprano rebec, which is held horizontally against the chest or under the chin, to the large bass rebec which is held vertically on the lap. The rebec is also called rebeca, rebecq, rebet, ribeca, rebecum, rabel, rebequin rebecha, or rebeckha.

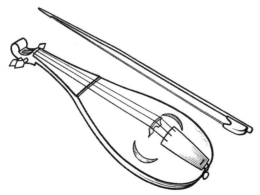

Figure 111. A **rebec** and early **bow**.

rebound. See **retake**.

rebushing. See **bushing**.

recital. An intimate concert, usually in a small venue, featuring an individual musician performing **solo** or a small group playing **chamber music**. Since the 1880s when the practice was begun by Franz Liszt, instrumental recitals have become one of the most important formats of performance in **art music**. The typical solo recital program is around two hours of music built around a **sonata** or two from the Classical or Romantic repertoire, often combined with a solo work of **J. S. Bach** and finished off with several **showpieces** or character pieces. Many musicians give specialized or themed recitals, such as programs featuring the works of a single composer or music from a particular nationality. Historically great string players including **Jascha Heifetz** and **Pablo Casals** performed **concertos** with a **piano reduction** on their recitals, though this has fallen out of fashion and is considered inappropriate by some.

recitative, *recitativo*. (It.) A style of singing in opera and oratorio that resembles speech, often free of strict rhythm.

reduction. The adaptation of a composition for **orchestra** or other large ensemble into one playable by a smaller ensemble or piano. See also **piano reduction**.

reel. An **Irish fiddle** dance form in a fast 4/4 tempo characterized by frequent use of **bow rocking**.

register. Part of the range of an instrument. The notes in upper range form the high register, while the deepest notes are called the low register.

rehair. Replacing the ribbon of **horsehair** on the **bow**. A rehair is needed any time the hair becomes worn smooth, is stained with oil from the hand, or loses enough strands that the ribbon is no longer spread evenly. An active string player may get a rehair as often as every four to six months.

relative pitch. The trained ability to identify the intervals between notes, regardless of their relation to **concert pitch**. Relative pitch is one of the skills honed in aural skills or ear training classes, as it is particularly valuable to string players, singers, and other musicians who depend on their ear to find the notes on their instrument. Relative pitch has not been shown to develop into **perfect pitch**. See also **perfect pitch**.

relia. See **lira**.

repertoire.

1. The collection of pieces that a player has prepared and ready to perform at any time.
2. The entire body of works regularly performed. For example, the **cello suites** of **J. S. Bach** are a mainstay of the cello repertoire.

repertory. See **repertoire**.

replacement fingering, replacement shift. Playing two consecutive notes of the same pitch with different fingers by **shifting** between the notes. A replacement fingering can be used to move the **hand frame** to a new **position** while sustaining a note, or may be chosen to place an expressive *portamento* between two melodic notes of the same pitch.

resin. See **rosin**.

resonance. The rich, full quality of sound enhanced in **string instruments** by the wood of the **resonance chamber** and the **sympathetic vibrations** and **overtones** of the **strings**.

resonance chamber. The hollow soundbox of an instrument. On the **modern string family**, the resonance chamber is the entire hollow body of the instrument. Vibrations from the **strings** are transmitted through the **bridge** to the **top plate** of the instrument, are then spread along the top plate by the **bass bar** and to the **back plate** by the sound post. These vibrations of the wood of the resonance chamber cause the air within the chamber to vibrate, creating **sound waves** that escape through the **f-holes** to travel to the listener's ear.

resonating strings. See **sympathetic strings**.

rest position. How the instrument is held while not being played. Violinists and violists often have a rest position with the instrument tucked under the right arm when they are standing, or set upon the right knee when they are seated.

restez. (Fr.) Remain in one **position**, play without **shifting**.

resultant tone. See **Tartini tone**.

retake. To bring the **bow** back to the **frog** between notes by lifting the bow and placing it back on the string near the frog, creating a circular motion with the hand. A retake is needed for consecutive **down-**bows, particularly between **phrases** or on **chords**. A retake can also be used to create a strong **articulation** on a dotted rhythm by playing a fast down-bow on the long note, then retaking to place the short note near the frog for an *au talon* up-bow. Using a retake is most often at the discretion of the performer and can be notated by a comma between notes.

Sostenuto, ma non troppo

Figure 112. **Retake** markings usually added to Beethoven's *Egmont* Overture, **viola**, mm 1-3. Although Beethoven did not include **bowing** indications in this piece, using consecutive down-bows with retakes is a common way to execute the *marcato* direction below the half notes. An additional retake is taken during the rest, providing an energized end to the second half note and preparing the **bow** for the relatively short eighth-note pick-up.

reverb, reverberation. An echoing **resonance** that may occur naturally when sound is reflected off the walls of a room, or may be electronically produced through an **amplifier** or **synthesizer**.

ribbon. See **horsehair**.

ribs. The six pieces of curved hardwood that are the sides of the instrument. The ribs are typically made of flamed **maple** that is bent using heat to match the shape of the top and back **plates**. The ribs are glued to the **blocks** at the top, bottom, and corners of the instrument, and reinforced by the **linings** along the joint between the ribs and the plates. See **laminated bass** for more information about **double basses** with laminated ribs.

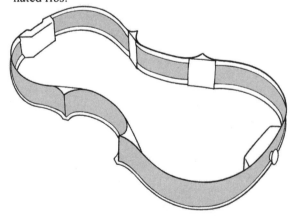

Figure 113. The curved **ribs** of a **violin** or **viola**.

Richardson-Tertis viola. See **Tertis viola**.

ricochet. (Fr.) A **thrown bowstroke** executed in the upper half of the **bow**, causing the **stick** to rebound several times in the same direction. The speed of these rebounds is controlled by the placement of the initial throw: the closer to the **tip**, the faster the stick bounces. *Ricochet* is notated by a combination of dots and **slurs** over the notes. See **Table 1: Bowstrokes** for a list of strokes and their notation.

Figure 114. The most famous example of *ricochet* from Rossini's *William Tell Overture*, **violin** 1, mm 243-246.

riff. A short melodic, rhythmic, or harmonic figure that is repeated to form the accompaniment for solos. See also **ostinato**.

rinforzando. (It.) Stressed, accented. *Rinforzando* is notated with *rf* or *rfz* over the affected note.

ripieno. (It.) The **tutti** section in a *concerto grosso*, as opposed to the *concertino*, or **solo** player(s).

Rivinus instruments. **Violins** and **violas** designed by **luthier** David Rivinus with **ergonomics** as the primary motivation. Rivinus instruments are built to reduce tension, avoid **tendonitis**, and maximize **resonance** through a complete rethinking of shape, materials, and player interface. The asymmetrical bodies, reshaped **bridges**, and additional **sound holes** make Rivinus designs bold and controversial. See also **ergonomic instrument.**

rock stop. A type of **endpin stop** that has a small metal cup inside a ring of rubber which sticks to the floor to prevent the **endpin** from sliding.

rockabilly bass.
1. A **double bass** specially set up to play **slap bass**. A rockabilly bass may have a higher action, a reinforced structure, covered **f-holes** or no f-holes, and a painted body.
2. The technique of playing double bass in the rockabilly style, characterized by aggressive, percussive string slapping and bass stunts such as standing on the **C bouts** or sitting astride the instrument. See also **slap bass.**

rocking bow. See **bow rocking**.

Rode, Pierre (1774-1830). French violinist, **pedagogue**, and composer important for his role at the Paris Conservatoire, where, together with **Baillot** and **Kreutzer**, he co-authored the **conservatory's violin** method. Of Rode's many violin **concertos**, **string quartets**, and **duets**, only his twenty-four **caprices** remain part of the standard **repertoire**, considered one of the most important foundational **technique** studies used in training violinists today. As a student of **Viotti**, Rode served as a vital link in the pedagogical legacy of great violinists through his student Joseph Böhm, who in turn taught the great master **Joseph Joachim**.

roll. An **ornament** common in **Irish fiddle** music, particularly **jigs**. The roll is a slurred five-note **turn** that starts on the melody note, plays a third above, the melody note again, a second below, and then returns to the melody note. A long roll ornaments a dotted quarter note, and a short roll ornaments a quarter note.

rolled chord. See **arpeggiation**.

Roman numeral indications.
1. Direction for which **string** is to be played for a marked passage or note. The strings are assigned numerals, with IV being the lowest string and I being the highest. This is the most common usage of Roman numerals in string music.
2. Instruction for which **position** should be used for a passage. The positions are assigned numerals, with I being first position, II being second position, and so on. This system is used primarily in student music to assist a player who is learning to play in positions.

romance. A piece expressing a sentimental, tender mood.

Romberg, Bernhard Heinrich (1767-1841). German cellist and composer who made many important advances in the **technique** and construction of the **cello**. Romberg was **Jean-Louis Duport's stand partner** in the Berlin court orchestra, and as a soloist he toured Europe performing on the highest level, including the first Vienna performances of Beethoven's op. 5 cello **sonatas** with the composer at the keyboard. Romberg completed his *Méthode de violoncelle* in 1839, which was immediately adopted as the teaching manual for the Paris Conservatoire. His legacy of students includes Pierre Norblin, Count Mathieu Wielhorsky, Adolf Press, Friedrich Kummer, and August Prell. Romberg, who played a 1711 **Stradivari** cello, made several significant innovations to the instrument and its technique. He had the **fingerboard** lengthened and its curve flattened beneath the C **string**, allowing greater clearance for the string's vibrations, a design that is still called the **Romberg bevel**. Among other developments, Romberg is credited with thinning the cello **neck**, introducing the **frog**-held **Tourte bow** to Germany, and simplifying cello notation to only three clefs.

Romberg bevel. A flattened area of the **fingerboard** beneath the lowest **string**, intended to give the thick string more clearance to vibrate without buzzing against the fingerboard. Designed by cellist **Bernhard Romberg**, the bevel is found most often on **double bass**, sometimes on **cello**, and very rarely on **viola**. A Romberg bevel is also called an E bevel.

rosewood. A strong, fragrant wood of the Dalbergia genus used to make **fittings** for **string instruments**. Rosewood is currently a protected species.

rosin. A form of hardened pine resin that is rubbed on the **horsehair** of a **bow** to increase friction and help grab the **string**. Rosin for string playing is distilled from oil of turpentine and mixed with wax, metal, and other ingredients in a large variety of recipes, with color varying from light amber to dark brown. Rosin powders into a white dust during playing, settling onto the stick of the bow and top of the instrument. It is important to wipe off this **rosin dust** regularly before it hardens into a sticky residue. Some players are allergic to pine-based rosin dust, suffering from watery eyes and sneezing while playing. A synthetic, hypoallergenic rosin has been developed for these musicians. The best type of rosin is a matter of individual taste, though it is generally understood that thicker strings benefit from softer, stickier rosin. Many **double bass** players prefer the particularly soft **Pop's rosin**.

rosin dust. The white powder residue that settles on the stick of the **bow** and top of the instrument. Rosin dust should be regularly wiped off with a soft cloth before it can harden and potentially damage the finish of the instrument. Musicians who experience watery eyes and sneezing while playing a **string instrument** may be allergic to rosin dust and should switch to a special synthetic, hypoallergenic rosin. See also **rosin**.

Rostropovich, Mstislav (1927-2007). Russian cellist, pianist, and conductor known for his immense contribution to expanding the **cello** literature by inspiring and commissioning more new works than any other cellist.

Rostropovich began his musical studies with his pianist mother and cellist father. After studies with Kozolupov at the Moscow **Conservatory**, Rostropovich won competitions in Moscow, Prague, and Budapest and was awarded the Stalin Prize.

Rostropovich built an international career first with concert tours as a cellist, then as a conductor, eventually becoming music director of the National Symphony. He served on the faculty of the Moscow and Leningrad conservatories.

A champion of new music, Rostropovich **premiered** more than one hundred pieces, many of which were the product of lifelong partnerships with composers including Benjamin Britten (Cello **Sonata** op. 65, **Symphony** for Cello and **Orchestra** op. 68, and three **suites** for unaccompanied cello), Dmitri Shostakovich (two cello **concertos**), Sergei Prokofiev (second cello concerto), Leonard Bernstein (*Three Meditations*), and Alfred Schnittke (second cello concerto).

Rostropovich was internationally recognized for his human rights advocacy, and his numerous awards include the Presidential Medal of Freedom (USA), the National Order of the Legion of Honour (France), and the Award of the International League of Human Rights.

roulé, roulet. (Fr.) Rolling the **stick** of the **bow** between the fingers and thumb while playing. *Roulé* is a **tone**-building exercise designed by influential violin **pedagogue Lucien Capet**.

roundback. A **back plate** that is carved into an arch to mirror the **top plate**. The term roundback applies particularly to **double bass**, to distinguish it from the common **flatback** construction.

rubato. (It.) Play with a flexible tempo to heighten expressive **phrasing**. See also *tempo rubato* and **agogic accent**.

Ruggieri, Francesco (1620-1695). Italian **luthier** of the Cremona school who apprenticed under **Amati**. Ruggieri is best known for his work developing a smaller, more playable **cello** than had been previously made.

rule of down-bow. An important concept in **baroque bowing** technique dictating that the strong beats of a measure are always played with a **down-bow** while the weak beats are played with an **up-bow**.

run. A rapid scalar passage. See also **lick**.

Russian bow hold. The **violin bow hold** as taught by the **Russian school of violin playing**, developed by **Henryk Wieniawski** and **Leopold Auer**. The Russian hold is characterized by long fingers that lean into the stick, a marked **pronation** of the bow arm, and a strong index finger that contacts the bow at the second knuckle. This hold treats the bow as a **lever**

tipped across the **fulcrum** of the thumb, finding flexibility in allowing the stick to rotate atop the thumb rather than through the springy finger and wrist movements of the **Franco-Belgian hold**. Famous violinists with a primarily Russian bow hold include **Jascha Heifetz**, Nathan Milstein, Mischa Elman, and **Yehudi Menuhin**.

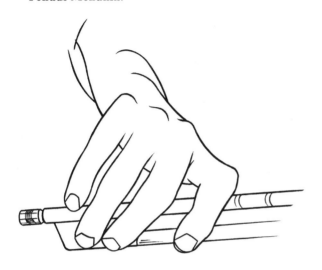

Figure 115. The **Russian bow hold**.

Russian school of violin playing. One of the two dominant systems for training violinists. The Russian school was developed at the St. Petersburg **Conservatory** as part of a campaign to attract Europe's finest musicians to Russia. **Henri Vieuxtemps** was the first teacher at the St. Petersburg Conservatory, a post taken over by **Henryk Wieniawski** and then **Leopold Auer**, who was the central **pedagogue** of the Russian school for forty-nine years. The reach of the Russian school broadened when Auer immigrated to the United States in 1917, and it has become one of the most popular schools of violin playing taught around the globe. The legacy of great virtuosos with Russian training includes Mischa Elman, **Jascha Heifetz**, Nathan Milstein, Efrem Zimbalist, **David Oistrakh**, Gidon Kremer, Vadim Repin, Maxim Vengerov, Daniel Hope, Aaron Rosand, and **Isaac Stern**.

The primary characteristics of violinists trained in the Russian school are a brilliant, clean left-hand technique combined with a strong, powerful approach to **tone** production that is achieved by a heavy, weight-based approach to bow work. See **Russian bow hold** for more information. See also **Franco-Belgian school of violin playing**.

RV. Abbreviation for *Verzeichnis der Werke Antonio Vivaldis*, Peter Ryom's system for cataloging the mu-

sic of **Antonio Vivaldi** in lieu of opus numbers. See also **thematic index**.

Ryom number. See **RV**.

~ S ~

saccadé. (Fr.) A jerked **bowstroke** that accents the second, third, or fourth note under a slur. *Saccadé*, also called the Viotti bowing, is notated with a sf under the accented note (see figure 116). See also **Table 1: Bowstrokes** for a list of strokes and their notation.

Figure 116. *Saccadé* bowing in **Kreutzer's Etude** no. 2

saddle. The small piece of **ebony** at the base of the **top plate** of an instrument over which the **tail gut** passes as it connects the **end button** to the **tailpiece**. The saddle is set into the edge of the top plate, flush with the **end block**, and serves to prevent the pressure of the tail gut from cutting into the wood of the instrument. It is sometimes called the lower saddle, to differentiate it from the nut, which can be referred to as the upper saddle.

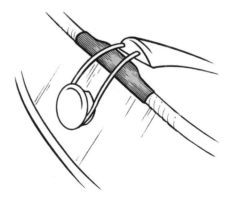

Figure 117. An **ebony saddle** supporting the **tail gut**.

Saite. (Ger.) **String**.

salon music. Short, lighthearted compositions of a charming nature intended for performance as entertainment in a private home rather than as **art music** in the concert hall. **Fritz Kreisler**'s *Liebesleid, Liebes-*

freud, and Edward Elgar's *Salut d'Amour* are characteristic examples of salon music.

salt and pepper bow hair. A mixture of black and white **horsehair** on the **bow**, used as a compromise between the smoothness of white hair and the relative coarseness of black hair.

saltando, saltato. (It.) A general term for a bouncing **bowstroke**. *Saltando* may be executed as *jeté*, *ricochet*, *sautillé*, *spiccato*, or even **flying** *spiccato*, depending on the notation and style of the music. See **Table 1: Bowstrokes** for a list of strokes and their notation.

saltellando. (It.) A rarely used term for **slurred** *staccato*, executed either on or off the string.

sample, sampled sound. A short recording of an instrument's sound that is replayed electronically. **String instrument** sounds are recorded one note at a time with various **tone colors** and **articulations** to be used by **synthesizers** and music notation software.

sanjo ajaeng. (Kor.) See *ajaeng*.

sarabande. (Fr.) One of the movements of the Baroque instrumental dance **suite**, characterized by a stately mood in slow triple time. *Sarabande* is also spelled *saraband*, *sarabanda*, and *zarabanda*.

sārangī. A bowed **string instrument** from South Asia, characterized by a short **neck**, a skin-covered wooden **resonance chamber**, and a large number of **sympathetic strings**. The *sārangī* has three **gut playing strings** that cross over an ornate bone **bridge** and as many as forty metal sympathetic strings that run through the center of the bridge. The three playing strings pass over a second raised bridge at the upper end of the neck, and the sympathetic strings pass over two additional small bridges below. The *sārangī* is held vertically with the player seated cross-legged while leaning the pegbox of the instrument against the left shoulder. With no **fingerboard**, the *sārangī* is played by touching the fingernails or cuticles of the left hand to the sides of the strings. The *sārangī* is used in folk **ensembles** and is one of the most important instruments in North Indian classical music. Also called *sārang*, *sarān*, *sarāng*, *sarāngā*, and *hārangī*.

Sarasate, Pablo de (1844-1908). Spanish violinist and composer best known for his contributions to **violin** literature, both in the works he inspired and those he composed.

Sarasate entered the Paris Conservatoire to study violin with Delphin Alard in 1856 and won the *premier prix* the following year at age fourteen. His career as a concert violinist was launched in 1859 with tours across Europe, bringing instant success and fame. Sarasate broadened his touring to include both North and South America and enjoyed a career as one of the most famous musicians on the international stage.

A vibrant virtuoso, Sarasate played with a distinctly Spanish **bravura** style, an image enhanced by performances of his own folk-song inspired Spanish compositions. Admired by the composers of his day, Sarasate inspired the dedication of many important new works including Bruch's second violin **concerto** and *Scottish Fantasy*, Lalo's *Symphonie espagnole*, **Wieniawski's** second violin concerto, and Saint-Saëns's *Introduction et rondo capriccioso*, first and third violin concertos. Sarasate championed these works, incorporating all of them into his **repertoire**.

As a composer, Sarasate primarily wrote Spanish-flavored **showpieces** for his own performance, many of which remain in the standard repertoire, including *Zigeunerweisen* [Gypsy Airs], op. 20; *Fantasy on Bizet's Carmen*, op. 25; *Introduction et tarantelle*, op. 43; and many of the pieces from his four albums of Spanish dances.

sautillé. (Fr.) A rapid, bouncing **bowstroke** played just above the **balance point**. Although *sautillé* is generally considered an uncontrolled **off the string** stroke, the secret to a great *sautillé* is that the stick bounces but the hair does not actually leave the string. *Sautillé* can be indicated by dots over the note-heads, or by the word *saltando*, or it may simply be understood as appropriate to the style of the piece. See **Table 1: Bowstrokes** for a list of strokes and their notation.

saw, musical. A flexible handsaw played by holding the handle between the knees and bending the blade while **bowing** along the flat edge. The musical saw is found in the folk music of Russia and rural America, and is a popular vaudeville instrument. Shostakovich wrote a part for musical saw in his opera *The Nose*, and Khachaturian included a musical saw in the score for his first piano **concerto**, a part now usually played by a **violin**.

saw stroke. A **bluegrass** term for playing a separate **bow** on every note. See *detaché*.

scala. (It.) **Scale**.

scale. A sequence of notes arranged in stepwise order of pitch, either ascending or descending. Because scales are one of the fundamental building blocks of music, the understanding and drilling scales are foundational training exercises for all string players. See also **arpeggio, chord, chromatic scale,** and **mode.**

scherzando. (It.) Playful, joking.

Schuppanzigh, Ignaz (1776-1830). Austrian violinist who was the first to make a career primarily performing in a **string quartet.** Schuppanzigh founded the Razumovsky Quartet in 1808, an **ensemble** that **musicologists** consider the first professional string quartet, who made a living performing in public concerts in Vienna. Schuppanzigh is remembered mostly as a champion of Beethoven. With the Razumovsky Quartet, Schuppanzigh gave the **premieres** of the string quartets op. 16, 20, 59, 95, 97, 127, 130, 132, and 135. Schuppanzigh was instrumental in helping to organize and lead the the premiere of Beethoven's Ninth Symphony.

scoop.
1. A **jazz** term for a quick upward slide into the beginning of a note. The scoop is accompanied by the gradual increase of pressure as the finger slides into the main pitch. The technique can be notated by a upward sloping line preceding the note-head. See also **fall off, plop, bend, drop, doit,** and *glissando.*

Figure 118. **Scoop** notation.

2. The concave curve carved into the length of the **fingerboard,** providing enough clearance for the **strings** not to **buzz** against the fingerboard.

scordatura. (It.) Play using a nonstandard tuning. *Scordatura* allows for new **tone** colors, fast passages with large leaps, changed location of string crossings, and the possibility of **drone** notes in any key.

Famous examples of **violin** *scordatura* in Western **art music** include Biber's "Mystery" and "Rosary" Sonatas, Saint-Saëns's *Danse macabre,* and Mahler's fourth symphony. Mozart uses a *scordatura* for the solo **viola** in *Sinfonia concertante* with all four **strings** tuned up one **half-step** to give the instrument a more brilliant tone to balance its violin counterpart and provide easier fingerings for the key of E-flat. It is rare for modern viola players to retune, preferring instead to play a transposed part.

Cello pieces using *scordatura* include the Fifth Solo Suite BWV 1011 by **J. S. Bach** and Kodaly's Sonata, op. 8.

Double bass, with its unique evolution encompassing various tunings, number of strings, and extension options, is the **modern string family** instrument most

often found to use *scordatura.* Using **orchestral tuning** as a standard (E1 – A1 – D2 – G2), the most common double bass *scordaturas* are **solo tuning** (F#1 – B1 – E2 – A2) and a fifths tuning one octave below the cello (C1 – G1 – D2 – A2).

In the **fiddle** and **bluegrass genres,** *scordatura* is commonly used to turn the string adjacent to the melody string into a drone for the key of the tune, such as the classic fiddle tune "Bonyparte's Retreat" that uses a D3 – D4 – A4 – D5 tuning for a high drone and a low drone in D major.

Scordatura tuning notes are indicated at the beginning of the piece, and the music is usually notated so that the player reads and fingers it as if the instrument were in standard tuning.

See also *accordatura.*

Figure 119. *Scordatura* in the tradtional **fiddle** tune "Bonyparte's Retreat." The **tuning** is indicated in the staff at the upper right, and the melody has been notated in actual sounding pitches.

scratch tone. The **extended technique** of playing with an extremely heavy, slow **bow,** producing an unpitched noise.

scratch track. A rough recording, usually of the rhythm section only, used as a reference for musicians working in a recording **session.**

screw. The mechanism for adjusting the **horsehair** tension of a modern **bow.** The screw threads through an eyelet embedded in the **frog.** As the screw is turned, the frog is pulled back, causing the bow hair to tighten. The screw is hidden within the stick above the frog, extending beyond the butt of stick with a knob, known as the **screw button.**

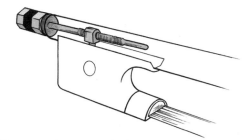

Figure 120. The **screw** mechanism embedded in **frog** end of a modern **Tourte bow.**

screw adjuster. The mechanism in the **frog** of a modern bow used to adjust the tension of the **horsehair**. See **screw**.

screw button. The knob end of the **screw** mechanism used to adjust the **horsehair** tension of a modern **bow**. The screw button has two metal rings around a wooden core, usually matched to the wood of the **frog**. The metal, part of the **mountings** of the bow, can be nickel, silver, or gold. The button is shaped to match the octagonal facets of the end of the stick.

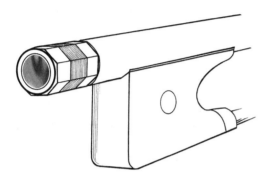

Figure 121. The **screw button**.

screw eye. A decorative dot on the end of the **screw button** on the **frog** of a **bow**.

scroll. The decorative carving at the end of the **neck**, usually shaped into a curl and sculpted from the same block of **maple** as the neck and the **pegbox**. The elegant shape of the volute, or curl, flares into protruding **ears** as the turns tighten and ends in the **eye** at the very center. The scroll is an artistic signature of the instrument's maker, showing off woodworking skill and artistry. Occasionally the scroll is carved into a figure such as the head of a person or an animal.

Figure 122. The graceful **volute** of a **scroll**.

Seaton saddle. See **tilt-block**.

sec, secco. (Fr., It.) Dry.

second violin. The lower **violin part** in an **orchestra** or other **ensemble**. The second violin part traditionally harmonizes, accompanies, or doubles the melody and is usually less technically difficult than the **first violin** part.

section.
1. A general grouping of instruments by family in an **orchestra** or other large **ensemble**: for example, the brass section or the percussion section.
2. A group of string musicians within an orchestra all playing the same part in unison. See **conventions of orchestral playing** for details about the role of section players and **principals** within the orchestra.

section leader. See **principal**.

sectional. A rehearsal of the players of a **section** of an **orchestra**. A sectional rehearsal usually includes only the players of a single section, though it can include all five string sections or a division of upper or lower strings. Sectionals may be led by the conductor, the **concertmaster**, the section **principal**, or an outside expert hired to give a coaching, and are a valuable tool for solving challenges particular to that group of musicians and the **part** they are playing. See also **conventions of orchestral playing**.

segue. Continue without pause.

Sentiment. (Ger.) See **arpeggione**.

senza. (It.) Without.

senza sordino. (It.) Without the **mute**.

septet.
1. An **ensemble** of seven players, each with an individual part.
2. The music composed for an ensemble of seven players.
   See also **chamber music**.

session.
1. Time spent working in a recording studio. Musicians who work primarily for recording studios are known as session musicians.
2. Informal gatherings of musicians playing together and improvising, often in Irish pubs or **jazz** clubs. See also **jam**.

set-up. The parts of an instrument that can be adjusted or changed to improve **tone** or playability, including the **bridge, soundpost, fingerboard, nut, saddle, tailpiece,** and **end button.** Reshaping, resetting, or replacing the elements of the set-up is part of an instrument **adjustment.**

sextet.
1. An **ensemble** of six players, each with an individual part.
2. The music composed for an ensemble of six players. See also **chamber music.**

sforzando. (It.) Suddenly accented. *Sforzando* is notated by *sfz* under the affected note.

shake. Early term for a **trill.** See also **close shake.**

shellac. A resin secreted by the female lac bug found on trees in India and Thailand, that when mixed with alcohol is used to seal and finish woods. Shellac is applied to **modern string instruments** instead of **varnish** on the **neck** between the **heel** and **pegbox** in order to provide a smooth **shifting** surface for the hand. Shellac on a string instrument is also called French polish.

shift, shifting. The movement of the forearm to reset the entire **hand frame** in a new **position** along the **fingerboard.** Shifting is usually executed by sliding a fingertip along the **string** without changing the shape of the hand.
    A shift is commonly notated in fingering as a dash before a finger number, slanting up or down to indicate the direction of the shift.
    See also **hand frame, finger pattern, fingerboard mapping, hidden shift, replacement shift,** and **crawling fingering.**

shoe. The thin piece of metal lining the channel where the **frog** joins to the stick of the **bow,** designed to guide the movement of an adjustable frog, strengthen the edges of the frog, and protect the **stick** from wear as the hair tension is tightened and released.

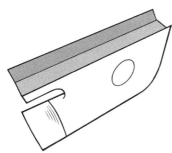

Figure 123. The metal **shoe** lining the top of the **frog.**

shoe-shine bowing. A **bowstroke** used for dotted rhythms, with the long note played **up-bow** and the short note played **down-bow,** all near the **frog.** The feel of the stroke is similar to that of shining a shoe. See **Table 1: Bowstrokes** for a list of strokes and their notation.

Figure 124. **Shoe-shine bowing** as commonly used in the "March to the Scaffold" from Berlioz's *Symphonie Fantastique,* *viola* mm 140-142.

short roll. See **roll.**

shoulder pad. A piece of material, often a sponge or soft cloth, placed between the back of a **violin** or **viola** and the player's shoulder used to aid in holding the instrument. A shoulder pad prevents the instrument from slipping and helps reduce strain on the muscles of the neck, back, and shoulder. While shoulder pads come in a variety of materials and shapes, the most popular type is a small cosmetic sponge attached directly to the back of the instrument with rubber glue. Use of a shoulder pad or **shoulder rest** is very common, although many violinists and violists prefer to hold the instrument without any aid.

    See **shoulder rest** for information about the more rigid type of support devices which are held away from the back of the instrument.

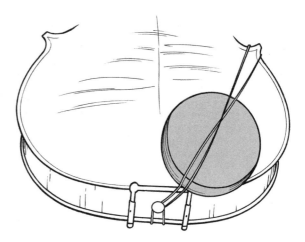

Figure 125. One common type of **shoulder pad**: a sponge held in place by a rubber band.

shoulder rest. A device attached to the back of a **violin** or **viola** designed to help hold and support the instrument. A shoulder rest is a fairly rigid length of plastic, wood, **carbon fiber**, or similar material held away from the back of the instrument by feet which clamp to the bottom edges of the **bouts**. Violinists and violists use shoulder rests to reduce strain on the muscles of the neck, back, and shoulder, as well as to aid in supporting the weight of the instrument and to free the left hand for ease of **vibrato** and **shifting**. Many

Figure 126. A **shoulder rest**.

materials, sizes, and designs are available for shoulder rests. Modern players choose a model that provides the best support for their particular shoulder shape, neck length, and **chin rest** height. While use of a shoulder rest or **shoulder pad** is widely popular, many violinists and violists prefer to play without any supporting device.

See **shoulder pad** for information about sponges and other soft materials used to support instruments.

showpiece. A composition written specifically to display a performer's technical virtuosity and *bravura*. A showpiece is typically short and flashy with minimal or no accompaniment. Famous examples of string showpieces are Sarasate's *Carmen Fantasy* for **violin**, Tchaikovsky's *Variations on a Rococo Theme* for **cello**, and the popular "Orange Blossom Special" for **fiddle**.

shred. To play in a fast, highly **virtuosic** fashion.

shuffle. A rhythmic **bowing** pattern of long-short-short, long-short-short popular in **bluegrass** and **fiddle**. See also **double shuffle**, **Georgia shuffle**, and **Nashville shuffle**.

siciliano, siciliana, sicilienne. (It., Fr.) An instrumental dance of Sicilian origin in 6/8 or 12/8, featuring the

lilting *siciliano* rhythm of dotted eighth, sixteenth, eighth.

Figure 127. The *siciliano* rhythm in **Fritz Kreisler**'s *Sicilienne*, mm 1-3.

sight-reading. Playing music from written notation without having had prior opportunity to study or practice the part. Sight-reading is a skill highly prized by **orchestra** and **session** musicians who are required to perform large quantities of music with little or no preparation time.

sigudök. (Rus.) See **gudok**.

silent instrument. An instrument designed to make no **acoustic** sound. Silent instruments, also called practice instruments or mute instruments, were originally built without a **resonance chamber** in order to facilitate practicing without disturbing others. Modern silent instruments are also **electric instruments**, using the bodiless design to allow the player to generate and control their **tone** through an **amplifier** or synthesizer without any additional acoustic sound.

Figure 128. A bodiless **silent instrument**.

silent upright bass. See **electric upright bass**.

Simandl bow. See **German bow**.

Simandl, Franz (1840-1912). Viennese **double bass** player and **pedagogue** best known for his book *New Method for the Double Bass*, a position-by-position approach to **technique** first published in 1874 and still widely used today. As professor at the Vienna **Conservatory** from 1869 until 1910, Simandl's legacy of students includes Ludwig Manoly and Adolf Mišek. The **German bass bow** is sometimes referred to as the Simandl bow.

simile.
1. (It.) An instruction to continue playing the **articulation, bowstroke,** or **ornament** as before, without the need to have the markings continue.
2. (It.) A symbol of a single slash between two dots centered in the measure, representing an exact repeat of the entire previous measure. A *simile* symbol with two slashes placed across the barline indicates the exact repeat of the previous two measures.

Figure 129. A *simile* symbol indicating the exact repeat of the previous two measures, applied to the *continuo* line of Pachelbel's *Canon in D* mm 1-4.

sinfonia.
1. A **chamber orchestra.**
2. (It.) **Symphony** or instrumental movement within a choral work.

sinfonia concertante. (It.) A composition for soloist and **orchestra,** the most famous of which is Mozart's *Sinfonia Concertante* for violin and viola. See also **concerto.**

single shuffle. See **shuffle.**

size. String instruments of the **violin family** are built in a variety of sizes, using different measuring systems depending on which instrument is being measured.

On **violin,** full size is a standardized 14-inch body length, and almost all adult players use this size. Smaller size violins, intended to accommodate the hand size and arm length of a child, are given fractional labels with 4/4 being full size and 1/32 being a tiny child's violin. This fractional nomenclature seems somewhat arbitrary as it is unrelated to the actual dimensions of an instrument. A 1/2-sized violin measures 12 inches, clearly not half the length of the standard 14-inch full size. The fractional violins are designed so that a child will begin on a 1/32 size as a three-year-old, then progress through the sizes, growing into slightly bigger instruments, eventually reaching a full-size instrument by the mid-teen years. A few 7/8 violins, called "ladies size," have been built

to accommodate adults with small hands, but they are not generally popular as they have been found to have a smaller sound.

Cello sizing is similar though less standardized, with a typical 30-inch full-size body and smaller fractional sizes intended for a growing child. Some soloists prefer a smaller cello with a body of 29 inches or even 28 inches for ease of playability. Since the size of the cello has grown smaller through history, most older cellos built on a larger body model have been cut down to the smaller standard, even those made by Stradivarius.

The **viola** is made in a variety of sizes measured as inches of body length rather than fractional sizes. The most common full-size violas average 16 inches to 16.5 inches, though they are made as small as 15 inches and as large as 18 inches. Violas can also have varying widths and depths.

The **double bass** has the most variety of size and shape. Like violins, bass sizes are labeled by fractions that do not correspond to any actual size ratio. The most commonly used modern double bass is 3/4, measuring about 43.5 inches. Full-sized 4/4 basses, which measure around 45.7 inches, are rarely made or played because modern players find the finger spacing too large.

See these entries for other small string instruments, not intended for children: *pochette,* **violin piccolo, violoncello piccolo, chamber bass,** and **New Violin Family.**

slap bass. A percussive style of playing the **double bass** that combines plucking away from the instrument strongly enough that the **string** rebounds against the **fingerboard** with a loud snap, and slapping the strings against the fingerboard with the right hand. Slap bass is common in early **jazz** and is one of the main characteristics of **rockabilly bass** playing.

slap stroke. See *fouetté.*

slide.
1. The decorative piece covering the **horsehair** on the base of the **frog.** The slide is most often made of abalone. See **frog** for an illustration.
2. An expressive connection between two notes. See *portamento* and *glissando.*

slur. In music notation, a curved line over a succession of notes, indicating a *legato* connection between the notes. String players execute slurs by playing all the notes under the line in one stroke of the **bow.** The combination of a slur with dashes or dots (or both) over the notes may indicate one of many different bowstrokes. See **bowstroke** for a complete list of the possible interpretations of this notation. The slur should not be confused with the two other markings that look similar to the slur: the tie, a rhythm notation connecting two notes of the same pitch across a beat, and the **phrasing** mark, a line embracing all the notes that make up an entire phrase. A slur is also called *Bindung* in German, *chapeau* in French, and *legatura* in Italian.

See **Table 1: Bowstrokes** for a list of strokes and their notation.

slurred *staccato*. A series of short notes connected in the same **bow** with a stop between each, notated by the combination of a **slur** and **dots** over the notes. Slurred *staccato* is an **on the string bowstroke** that is easiest to execute on an **up-bow**, especially when played at a fast tempo. At its fastest, slurred *staccato* is executed with an uncontrolled tremble of the forearm. The slurred *staccato* bowstroke is also called **down-bow** *staccato*, firm *staccato*, or up-bow *staccato*, and it is generally more aggressive than the delicate *perlé* stroke. See also **flying *staccato*** stroke for the virtuosic **off the string** stroke and see **Table 1: Bowstrokes** for a list of strokes and their notation.

Figure 130. **Slurred staccato** from Saint-Saëns' *Introduction and Rondo Capriccioso*, op. 28, mm 87-88.

slurred tremolo. A trembling effect created by fluttering a finger against the **fingerboard** as quickly as possible while playing a lower note, either as an open string or a note stopped with another finger. Slurred tremolo, also called fingered tremolo, is notated by three bars drawn between two slurred notes, or by a combination of open note-heads with three bars. The notation for slurred tremolo can be similar or identical to notation for a measured 32nd note oscillation, occasionally leading to confusion. See also **tremolo** and **Table 1: Bowstrokes** for a list of strokes and their notation.

Figure 131. **Slurred tremolo** from the final movement of Elgar's *Enigma Variations*, **viola**, mm 114-116.

smorzando, smorzato. (It.) Fading away. Often abbreviated *smorz.*

snakewood. A tropical hardwood used to make the stick of a **baroque bow**, chosen for its strength, durability, and beauty.

snap *pizzicato*. See **Bartók *pizzicato*** and **slap bass**.

sol-fa. See *solfège*.

solfège, solfeggio. (Fr., It.) A **pedagogical** method of teaching sight-singing and aural skills by assigning a syllable to each diatonic **pitch**. Two different approaches to *solfège* are taught: fixed *do*, with the syllables always corresponding to a pitch class (*do* is always C), and moveable *do*, with the syllables always corresponding to a function within a key (*do* is always tonic).

soli. (It.) Plural of **solo**, usually indicating a passage in which an orchestral **section** plays alone.

solo. A piece or passage performed by a single player. A solo may be played completely alone, as in a **solo sonata**, or it may include an accompaniment part, as in a **concerto**. If a solo is called for in an **orchestra** work, the **section principal** is expected to play it. In the **genres** of **jazz** and **bluegrass**, a solo is the opportunity to play a featured **improvisation** while the other players of the band play **backup**.

solo break. The moment in **jazz** when the rhythm section creates a silence. The solo break is used either for a solo instrumentalist to lead into an **improvisation**, or for a member of the rhythm section to play a brief pick-up **solo**, bringing the band back in on the return of the **head**.

solo sonata. A significant work for an unaccompanied instrument.

solo tuning. A **double bass** tuning system of F# – B1 – E2 – A2, with each **string** a **whole-step** higher than standard **orchestral tuning**. Solo tuning is intended to produce a more penetrating **tone** by increasing the tension on the strings, and it requires a specific set of **light gauge strings** designed for this purpose. Sheet music for solo double bass indicates which tuning is called for, and some pieces, such as the **Koussevitsky Concerto**, are published in both a solo tuning and an **orchestral tuning** version. See also **double bass**, **five-string bass**, and **orchestral tuning**.

son filé. (Fr.) An even, singing **tone** sustained through lyrical passages by combining a slow **bow speed** with a close **contact point**.

sonata. A large-scale composition usually written as a **duet** for piano and one other instrument. The sonata is typically in three movements and is distinguished from an accompanied **solo** by the nature of the piano part, which is an equal or even dominant voice. Sonatas occasionally are written without piano, either as **solo sonatas** with only a single player, such as **J. S. Bach**'s sonatas for solo **violin**, or as a duet between two other instruments, such as Ravel's Sonata for Violin and Cello. Considered one of the greatest **genres** in Western **art music**, the sonata is the foundation of a string player's **recital** program. See also **chamber music, solo sonata,** *sonata da camera, sonata da chiesa,* and **trio sonata**.

sonata da camera. (It.) A type of Baroque **sonata** intended for performance in a chamber or private home. See also **chamber music, sonata,** and *sonata da chiesa*.

sonata da chiesa. (It.) A type of Baroque **sonata** intended for performance in a church. See also **chamber music, sonata,** and *sonata da camera*.

sonatina. (It.) A little **sonata**, usually short and relatively easy.

sonore. (It.) Sonorous, with **resonance**.

sordino. (It.) **Mute**.

sostenuto. (It.) Smooth, sustained.

sotto voce. (It.) With a soft **tone**, in a whispered or hushed voice.

sound wave. The pattern of vibrations moving through air or any other medium. Sound waves are created when an object vibrates, disturbing the surrounding air particles, causing them to vibrate as well. These particles then cause the particles next to them to vibrate, creating a wave of sound that travels in a manner similar to waves of water in the ocean. When the vibrating air particles reach the eardrum, it also vibrates, sending signals that the brain interprets as sound.

Although sound waves operate three-dimensionally, they are represented visually on a two-dimensional graph by sine curves called **waveforms**. A sound wave has four main elements: wavelength, **period, amplitude,** and **frequency**. The wavelength is the distance of one full cycle of the waveform. The period measures how much time is needed to complete each wavelength or cycle of a sound wave. Amplitude is the height of the sound wave, which determines volume. A taller waveform has a higher amplitude,

meaning more energy, and is therefore louder. Frequency indicates how quickly the sound wave moves, measured by how many cycles occur per second. The frequency of waveforms determines **pitch**, with the pitch rising as the frequency increases. A4 = 440 means the frequency of the sound wave is 440 cycles (periods) per second, producing our **standard tuning** A.

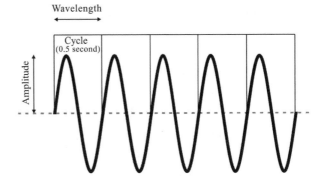

Figure 132. The visual representation of a **sound wave**.

sound-hole. An opening in the **top plate** of an instrument designed for enhancing sound radiation. Sound-holes reduce the stiffness of the wood under the **bridge**, allowing the vibrations to transfer more easily into the top plate of the instrument. Opening the **resonance chamber** of the instrument also amplifies the lowest octave of sound. Instruments of the **violin family** have a symmetrical pair of **f-holes** placed on either side of the bridge. **Viols** often have **c-holes** or may feature sound-holes carved in an ornate design.

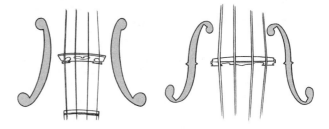

Figure 133. Two types of **sound holes: c-holes** on the left and **f-holes** on the right.

sound-table. See **top plate**.

soundbox. The body of an instrument. See **resonance chamber**.

sounding point. The exact place where the **bow** contacts the **string** in relation to the **bridge**. A close sounding point will be immediately adjacent to the bridge, while a far sounding point will be near or even over the **fingerboard**. Master **pedagogue Dorothy**

Delay taught a system of five sounding points with 1 being immediately against the bridge and 5 being just over the end of the fingerboard. **Shinichi Suzuki** used

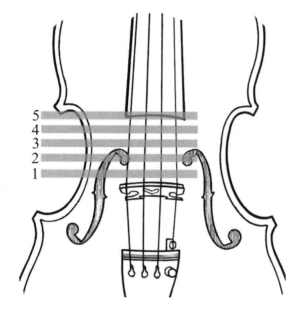

Figure 134. Dorothy Delay's five **sounding point** zones.

the image of "**Kreisler's** highway" with various lanes to convey this same concept. Delay's zones and Suzuki's lanes are parallel to the bridge, each about the width of the ribbon of **hair** on the bow. A contact point in zone 1, closest to the bridge, will produce the most intense, powerful sound, requiring tremendous control. As the bow moves away from the bridge, the sound gets warmer and gentler, as in zones 2 and 3, then softer and more transparent in zones 4 and 5. The sounding point is also called the **contact point**.

See also *sul tasto* and *sul ponticello*.

soundpost. A wooden dowel wedged between the top and back **plates** of an instrument, located near the treble foot of the **bridge** and visible through the right **f-hole**. The soundpost enhances the **acoustics** of the instrument by transferring vibrations from the bridge into the back plate of the instrument.

The soundpost should be positioned in line with the treble foot of the bridge, offset slightly towards the lower belly, and in symmetry with the **bass-bar** under the other foot of the bridge. The fit of the post against the top and back of the instrument, as well as its precise location, are significant factors in the **tone** of an instrument. Because minute adjustments in the placement and fit of the soundpost can create substantial changes in projection, richness, and tone color, finding the correct soundpost length and position are primary elements in a tonal **adjustment**.

The soundpost also serves as a pillar supporting the top plate under the weight of the bridge. If a soundpost falls, the tension on the **strings** should be loosened to prevent the top plate from being damaged by pressure on the bridge. A l**uthier** can easily reset the post using a **soundpost setter**.

Figure 135. The **soundpost** wedged between the top and back **plates** just below the treble foot of the **bridge**.

soundpost crack. A split in the wood of an instrument's top or back **plate** at the point of contact with the **soundpost**. A soundpost crack is a significant injury requiring major repairs, and usually results in a lower value for the instrument.

soundpost patch. A repair to the **top plate** of an instrument just under the treble foot of the **bridge** where the **soundpost** is wedged. A soundpost patch is a new piece of wood **inlaid** into the original top plate to replace wood damaged by repeated replacing and moving of the soundpost, or it may be part of a **soundpost crack** repair.

soundpost setter. A tool used to insert and adjust the **soundpost** through the **f-holes** of the instrument. The s-shaped soundpost setter has a sharpened point that is lodged in the post to hold it while inserting it through the f-hole and wedging it between the top and back **plates**. This procedure will leave a small notch on the post which should be visible through the right f-hole. Once the post is inside the instrument, the flared end of the setter is used to move the post to the optimal position. **Luthiers** may also use a scissors setter to grip the soundpost through the f-hole to facilitate positioning. Soundpost setters are sized small for **violin** or **viola**, and large for **cello** or **bass**. See **soundpost** for information about correct positioning.

Figure 136. An s-shaped **soundpost setter**.

sourdine. (Fr.) **Mute**. Often abbreviated *sourd.* and found in the phrases *mettez la sourd.*, to use the mute, and *ôtez la sourd.*, to remove the mute.

South, Eddie (1904-1962). American **jazz** violinist whose virtuosity pioneered a place for the **violin** as a lead jazz instrument. South was a prodigy whose studies at the Chicago College of Music, the Paris Conservatoire, and the Budapest **Conservatory** left him poised for a solo career, only to face the reality that in the 1920s racism barred black musicians from the classical music profession. Switching to jazz, South forged a brilliant career, performing with Lionel Hampton at Carnegie Hall, recording with Django Reinhardt and **Stéphane Grappelli** in Paris, and appearing almost daily on radio in New York during the 1940s.

spiccato. (It.) An **off-the-string bowstroke** with a controlled bounce. *Spiccato* can be indicated by **dots** over the note-heads or the word *saltando*, or it may simply be understood as appropriate to the style of the piece. See also **brush stroke**, **flying** *spiccato*, and **standing** *spiccato*, as well as **Table 1: Bowstrokes** for a list of strokes and their notation.

Spiessgeige. (Ger.) **Spike fiddle**.

spike. See **endpin**.

spike fiddle. A type of bowed **string instrument** characterized by a round **neck** that passes through the **resonance chamber** to protrude in a spike at the lower end. The **strings** attach to the spike, pass over a **bridge** on the face of the resonance chamber, and attach to **pegs** at the top end of the neck. Spike fiddles appear in countless varieties in many cultures, including the *huqin* from China, the *huur* from Mongolia, and the *rebab* from the Middle East. The spike fiddle is also called the *vièle à pique* (Fr.) and the *Spiessgeige* (Ger.).

Spitze. (Ger.) **Tip** of the **bow**. Often found in the phrase *an der Spitze*, or at the tip.

Spohr, Louis (1784-1859). German violinist, composer, and conductor known for his contributions to modern **violin** technique and orchestral conducting.

The child of musicians, Spohr had an early start and was already playing in the Duke of Brunswick's court **orchestra** by the age of fourteen. Spohr's performance career included tours of Europe performing with his harpist wife and **concerto** appearances, usually playing his own compositions. A star of the international stage, Spohr was considered the greatest German violinist of his generation.

As a **concertmaster**, first of the Gotha orchestra, then of the Theater an der Wien orchestra, Spohr was one of the first to lead an orchestra by directing with a baton, a tool he used only in rehearsals since the innovation was so new that in performances even his directing with his violin **bow** from the concertmaster seat was considered unusual. Spohr is also credited with being the first to put letters into the score and parts to aid in rehearsing. His role as a leading orchestra director grew throughout his career.

As a composer, Spohr was much celebrated during his lifetime, and he was considered a peer of Haydn, Mozart, and Beethoven. He wrote nine **symphonies**, ten operas, fifteen violin concertos, and many other works, all of which were very well received at the time, though none have held a place in the standard **repertoire**, with the exception of an occasional performance of his Violin Concerto no. 8, op. 47.

Spohr's lasting contributions are his invention of the **chin rest**, which facilitates much greater freedom of movement in the left hand, and an 1831 treatise *Violinschule* [Violin School or Grand Violin School], in which many of the latest advances in violin **technique** are explained, providing an invaluable reference to players interested in **historically informed performance**. Spohr taught throughout his career, training many great performers and composers including **Ferdinand David** and August Wilhelmj.

Springbogen. (Ger.) See *sautillé*.

springing arpeggio. An **arpeggio** played with the **flying spiccato bowstroke**, used most famously at the end of the **cadenza** in Mendelssohn's violin **concerto**.

springing bow. See *sautillé*.

spruce. A **tonewood** of the Picea genus, most often chosen for making the **top plate** of instruments in the **modern string family** because it is both stiff and lightweight, the ideal combination for transmitting sound.

staccato. (It.) A detached, **on the string bowstroke** with clearly articulated notes. *Staccato* is usually notated with **dots** over the note-heads and can be played either on separate bows or hooked into the same bow with a clean stop after each note. See also *martelé*, **flying** *staccato*, **slurred** *staccato*, and **up-bow** *staccato*, as well as **Table 1: Bowstrokes** for a list of strokes and their notation.

staccato à ricochet. (It.) See **flying** *staccato*.

staccato volante. (It.) See **flying** *staccato*.

Stainer, Jacob (1617-1683). Austrian **luthier** whose instruments produce what many consider the epitome of beautiful sound. Stainer studied **lutherie** in Cremona, where it is thought he studied with a German maker, as his violin style was based on a German design. After a few years of traveling to sell his instruments, Stainer set up shop in Austria where he become so well known that he received commissions from across Europe. Stainer made **violins**, *viole da braccio*, bass **viols**, **cellos**, and **double basses**. His first known instrument is dated 1638, and his last violin is marked 1682.

Stainer's violins are characterized by a highly arched body, delicate **f-holes**, excellent **varnish**, and fine craftsmanship comparable to that of **Stradivari**. Stainer violins have a **tone** often described as silvery, a quality that was most desirable until Stradivari created his new violin model with a more powerful, golden tone.

Stamitz, Carl Phillip (1745-1801). German composer and violinist, violist, and *viola d'amore* player who toured Europe performing as a **virtuoso** on these instruments. Stamitz promoted the **viola** and enriched the **repertoire** for both the viola and *viola d'amore* by composing numerous **solo** works, many of which include daring techniques such as **triple stops**, **left-hand** *pizzicato*, and **harmonics**.

stand.
1. A device for holding sheet music in place. See **music stand**.
2. The musicians reading from a single orchestral **part** placed on a **music stand** or **desk** between them. The front stand refers to the **principal** players. See also **principal** and **conventions of orchestral playing**.
3. A device for holding an instrument when it is not being played.

stand extensions. A device that widens the **desk** area of a **music stand** to accommodate an oversize part or to eliminate page turns. Stand extensions are usually plastic pieces that work best when attached to a standard metal music stand.

stand light. A light that attaches to the top of a **music stand** to illuminate the sheet music beneath it, useful in any low-light performance situation. Stand lights containing an electric bulb are bright but require an electrical connection, while those with a battery powered LED light are dimmer but more versatile and portable.

stand partners. Musicians who read from the same sheet music placed on a shared **stand**, particularly in **orchestra**. See **conventions of orchestral playing**.

stand-up bass. See **double bass**.

standard pitch. The international standard frequency for determining pitch. Modern standard pitch is based on A4 = 440 Hz. See also **concert pitch** and **baroque pitch**.

standard tuning. The common system of setting the pitch of each **open string**, also called *accordatura*. Standard tuning for the **modern string** family is:
violin G3 – D4 – A4 – E5
viola C3 – G3 – D4 – A4
cello C2 – G2 – D3 – A3
double bass E1 – A1 – D2 – G2 (**orchestral tuning**)
These tunings are based on the fixed reference of A4 = 440 Hz. See also *scordatura*, **solo tuning**, *and* **standard pitch**.

standing *spiccato*. A bouncing **bowstroke** in which the **bow** repeatedly hits the **string** in exactly the same place along the hair. See **Table 1: Bowstrokes** for a list of strokes and their notation.

stark. (Ger.) Strong. *Stark* is found in music as an expressive direction or may be used to designate a **heavy gauge string**.

steel strings. Strings with a core of spiraled steel. Many steel strings are encased in a winding of another metal, such as aluminum, silver, nickel, tungsten, or titanium, giving them a more sophisticated sound. Steel strings offer a clear, direct, responsive **tone** that is much more stable and durable than **gut strings**, making them a popular choice of **double bass** players, and many country, folk, **fiddle**, and **jazz** musicians. Student instruments that are small and inexpensive also do well with steel strings. See also **strings, synthetic strings,** and **gut strings**.

Steg. (Ger.) **Bridge**. The phrase *am Steg* or *auf dem Steg* mean to play on the bridge, or *ponticello*.

stick. The wooden rod of the **bow**. See **bow, pernambuco**, and **snakewood**.

stick bass. See **electric upright bass**.

Stimme. (Ger.) **Part** or voice.

stool. A high seat used by **double bass** players. Many stools are geared to the specific needs of the double bassist, including adjustable seat height, attached foot rest or back rest, and **ergonomic** designs.

stop. To change the **pitch** by pressing the string against the fingerboard, changing the vibrating length of the string. Playing two strings at once creates a **double stop**, three strings a **triple stop**, etc.

stopped harmonics. See **artificial harmonics**.

Stradivari, Antonio (1644-1737). Italian **luthier** whose **violin** making set a standard that has been followed for more than 250 years. As a young man, Stradivari apprenticed under **Amati**. In 1666 Stradivari began marking instruments with his own **label**, marked by a double circle enclosing a Maltese cross and the initials A. S. He used geometry to rework the proportions of the violin, giving it a longer, shallower body that produced a more powerful, penetrating **tone**. Every detail of his instruments was personally crafted, including the **pegs, fingerboard, tailpiece**, and **inlay** patterns. Stradivari's choice of **bridge** design remains the modern form. He even made **bows** and **cases** for his instruments.

The years 1700-1720 are considered a golden period for Stradivari during which he produced his most magnificent instruments, including **violas** and **cellos**. Many believe the secret to the rich tone of these instruments is in the **varnish**, a recipe which has been the subject of much debate since the exact formula has never been discovered.

Stradivari made his last violin at the age of ninety-two, and it has been calculated that he made more than 1,100 instruments including violins, violas, cellos, **lutes**, guitars, harps, and **mandolins**. Of these about 650 survive today, including 63 cellos and 13 violas.

Many of these instruments are given sobriquets, or nicknames, for their famous owners: the 1673 "**du Pré**'" cello, the 1690 "**Auer**" violin, the 1698 "**Joachim**" violin, the 1710 "**Vieuxtemps**" violin, the 1720 "**Piatti**" cello, and the 1724 "**Sarasate**" violin.

The instruments of Stradivari have gained tremendous value as they age, and they are primarily owned by museums or private estates, which lend them out to famous players. In 2011, the mint condition 1721 "Lady Blunt" violin sold at auction for $15.8 million.

Throughout the 19th century, many thousands of violins were made in factories and workshops all bearing a Stradivari label. These inexpensive copies were not intended to deceive buyers but rather to give an indication of the model around which the instrument was built.

strappato. (It.) Sharply accented, torn. For example, *strappato* was used by **Vivaldi** in "Spring" of the *Four Seasons*, directing the **viola** player to imitate a barking dog.

Streicher. (Ger.) **Strings**, string **section**, **string instrument** players.

Streichquartett. (Ger.) **String quartet**.

stretto. (It.) Hasty, rushing.

Strich. (Ger.) **Bowstroke**, commonly found in the phrases: *mit breitem Strich*: with broad strokes; *Strich für Strich*: change bow on every note; *grosser Strich*: with whole bows. See **Table 1: Bowstrokes** for a list of strokes and their notation.

Strichart. (Ger.) **Bowstroke**.

string bass. See **double bass**.

string bending. See **bent note**.

string crossing. Moving the **bow** from one **string** to another. Coordinating string crossings with fingering can be one of the most challenging techniques of playing a **string instrument**, particularly when the crossings are rapid and irregularly placed. String crossings are most easily executed at the **balance point** of the bow, when the weight on either end of the stick is equal. See also *bariolage* and **double shuffle**.

string gauge. The indicator of the thickness and tension of a string. String gauges are not standardized, so measurements and labeling varies by brand. In general, many **steel strings** and **synthetic strings** are available in tensions of heavy, medium, and light, while **gut strings** are indicated by a number measuring the diameter rather than tension. **Medium gauge strings** are the choice of most players as they provide a balance of clarity, volume, and playability. A **light gauge string** will respond quickly and speak with clarity but may create a small, thin **tone**. A **heavy**

gauge string offers a stronger tone but may give a slower response.

Every instrument responds differently to string types and gauges, so finding the best string gauge depends on discovering what works well with a specific instrument in the hands of an individual player. The genre and style of music being played is also a factor in choosing a string gauge. A cellist playing a Baroque period instrument may choose a heavy gauge to help the gut strings project, while a rock musician playing electric cello may choose a light gauge steel string for brilliant tone, counting on amplification to provide enough projection. See also strings.

string height. The distance between the strings and the fingerboard. See also action and adjustment.

string instrument, stringed instrument. An instrument that makes sound through vibrations of strings. The term is commonly used to indicate the bowed instruments of the violin family and viol family, though technically the category also includes plucked string instruments such as the guitar, lute, and harp, and struck string instruments such as the piano and hammered dulcimer. A string instrument is also called a chordophone. See also modern string family.

string length. The measure of string stretched between the nut and the bridge, also called mensur, or vibrating length.

string orchestra. An ensemble comprised only of sections of violin, viola, cello, and double bass.

string trio. A chamber music ensemble comprised of violin, viola, and cello. See also chamber music.

string tube. A plastic container for holding spare strings included in some instrument cases. Tubes protect new strings and provide storage without the need for bending.

stringendo. (It.) Hurrying, speeding up, rushing ahead.

strings. The stretched cords on an instrument that vibrate to create sound. There are three basic types of strings for the modern string instrument family of violin, viola, cello, and double bass: gut strings, steel strings, and synthetic strings.

Gut strings are made from a cord of stretched animal intestines that is wound with aluminum or silver. These strings offer a warm, complex tone but are very susceptible to changes in temperature and humidity. While most modern string players use synthetic or steel strings, gut strings are still popular,

particularly on baroque instruments and in historically informed performance.

Steel strings have a core of spiraled steel usually encased in a winding of another metal such as aluminum, silver, nickel, tungsten, or titanium. These strings offer a clear, direct, responsive tone that is much more stable and durable than gut strings, making them a popular choice of double bass players, and many country, folk, fiddle, and jazz musicians. Student instruments that are small and inexpensive also do well with steel strings.

Synthetic strings have a core of nylon or a similar synthetic material wound in metal such as aluminum, chrome, silver, or gold. Designed to combine the stability and brilliance of steel strings with the warmth and depth of gut strings, synthetic strings are the most popular choice, especially for classical players.

The string gauge indicates the thickness and tension of a string. String gauges are not standardized, so measurements and labeling vary by brand. See string gauge for details about the gauge measurements for various string types.

Musicians have an extensive array of string brands, materials, and gauges from which to choose. Every instrument has a unique response to different types of strings and each player will have specific considerations to fit their personal playing and the style of music. The only way to find the best strings for a particular player and instrument is to experiment.

As strings are played and stretched, they gradually lose their brilliance and clarity. A string that is "sour" or no longer has integrity will be impossible to tune and the pitch will sag at the end of each note. Active players put a fresh set of strings on their instrument every three to six months, depending on the type of strings and how much playing is done each day. Because new strings take a few days to stretch and settle in, it is common to keep a set of lightly used strings to replace a broken string at the last minute.

Many instrument cases are fitted with a string tube, meant to keep new strings from getting kinked or bent.

String players who experience corrosion of their strings due to the moisture and acidity of their skin should use strings with windings of silver or gold.

stroh viol. A hybrid string instrument invented by Augustus Stroh in 1899, designed to amplify sound for gramophone recordings. The stroh viol is the fingerboard of a standard violin, viola, cello, or double bass attached to a solid wooden body with the bridge sitting upon a tympanum, which transmits sound into a large metal horn. Often the instrument has a second, smaller horn directed towards the player. Stroh instruments quickly went out of use with the advent of improved electric recording technology in the late

1920s. The stroh viol is also called phono fiddle, violinophone, cornet violin, horn violin, stroh fiddle, stroh violin, or stroh cello.

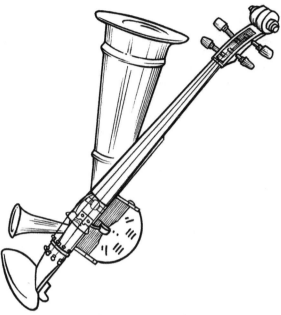

Figure 137. A **stroh viol**.

stroke.
1. The movement of the **bow** pulling the **string**, often used as a shortened term for **bowstroke**.
2. An **articulation** mark indicating *staccato*.

strum. Play *pizzicato* **chords** in the style of a guitar. **Violin**, **viola**, and even occasionally **cello** players will hold the instrument like a guitar to strum with the thumb of the right hand.

style galant. See **galant**.

subito. (It.) Suddenly, immediately. Often found in the phrases *attaco subito*, to continue at once, *subito forte*, to suddenly play loudly, and *volti subito* (abbreviated V. S.), to turn the page immediately.

suite.
1. Any set of instrumental pieces intended to be performed together, such as movements from an opera or ballet, e.g.. the suite from Bizet's *Carmen* or the suite from Tchaikovsky's *Nutcracker*.
2. A set of five or six instrumental dances intended to be performed together, also called a dance suite or *partita*. The suite was popular in the Baroque era, with a standardized order of **allemande, courante, sarabande,** and **gigue**, with the occasional inclusion of other dances such as **gavotte** or **boureé**, or the addition of a non-dance prelude.

The six suites for solo **cello** and the three **partitas** for solo **violin** by **J. S. Bach** are the foundation of the **string instrument repertoire**. *Dance and the Music of J.S. Bach* by Meredith Little and Natale Jenne (Indiana University Press, 2009) offers an excellent resource for understanding the dance aspects of Bach's music.

sul, sull', sulla. (It.) "On the," usually found in the phrases *sul G*, on the G **string**, *sul ponticello,* on the **bridge**, or *sulla tastiera*, on the **fingerboard**.

sul ponticello. (It.) Play with the **bow** on the **bridge**, creating a raspy, metallic **tone**. See also **contact point**.

sul tasto, sulla tastiera. (It.) Play with the **bow** over the **fingerboard**, creating a feathery, translucent **tone**. See also **contact point**.

super soloist. **Concertmaster**, used primarily in Europe.

supination. The rotational movement of the forearm from the elbow that turns the palm of the hand inward. For **string instrument** players, the term supination is usually used to describe rotating the forearm of the **bow** arm away from the player. Supination is a way to operate the **lever** of the **bow** by shifting the weight away from the index finger and onto the little finger in order to lift the bow away from the **string**. Supination can also refer to the approach of the left hand to the **fingerboard**, in which a rotation of the forearm turns the hand towards the little finger, facilitating an extended reach. See also **hand frame** and **pronation**.

sur. (Fr.) On or over, usually found in the phrases *sur une corde*, on a single **string**, *sur le chevalet,* on the **bridge**, or *sur la touche*, over the **fingerboard**.

sur la touche. (Fr.) Play with the **bow** over the **fingerboard**, creating a feathery, translucent **tone**.

sur le chevalet. (Fr.) Play with the **bow** on top of the **bridge**, creating a raspy, metallic **tone**.

sur une corde. (Fr.) Play on a single **string**.

suspension case. A case designed to hold an instrument by the top and bottom **blocks** and **neck**, placing no weight on the delicate back or **bridge**.

Suzuki method. An early-childhood approach to education based on the belief that with a supportive environment young children can learn music in the same way as they learn their mother tongue. See **Suzuki, Shin'ichi**.

Suzuki, Shin'ichi (1898-1998). Japanese **pedagogue**, humanist, and founder of the **Suzuki method**, whose early-childhood approach to talent education revolutionized how music is taught.

Although he was the son of a **violin** factory owner, Suzuki did not learn to play music until age seventeen, when he taught himself the violin by listening to records. As a young man, Suzuki traveled to Berlin where he studied with Klingler, a student of **Joachim**, and befriended amateur violinist Albert Einstein. It was in this environment that Suzuki had the revelation that if music was a language, then children could learn to play at a very early age just as they learn to speak their mother tongue. Defying the convention of starting violin lessons around the age of ten, Suzuki began teaching children as young as two to play by ear, producing astonishing results.

At the heart of Suzuki's method is his humanist principal of "character first." Suzuki believed that by being exposed to music and learning to play at a very young age in an environment of love and support, children would become kind, compassionate human beings who could bring understanding and peace to the world. Suzuki also challenged the notion that only children perceived as talented could become accomplished musicians, teaching that with early exposure to music in a loving, supportive environment, any child could learn "talent."

The Suzuki method combines individual private lessons with weekly group lessons with parents taking a very active role. To supplement his philosophy, Suzuki created a graded set of ten violin books that take students from the starting song of "Twinkle" through a largely baroque **repertoire** to conclude with two **concertos** by Mozart. As the Suzuki method has grown to include the **viola**, **cello**, **double bass**, flute, piano, and many other instruments, equivalent books have since been created for each instrument.

Although the Suzuki method remains controversial, it has become an internationally embraced approach to learning music. The first generation of great performers who got their start at a very young age through Suzuki training include violinists Hilary Hahn, Rachel Barton Pine, Leila Josefowicz, Sarah Chang, and Nicola Benedetti, as well as **jazz** violinist Regina Carter and cellist Wendy Warner.

sweet spot. The precise placement of a microphone in relation to an **acoustic** instrument that captures the best sound.

swing.
1. A quality of approach to playing that is the defining characteristic of the **jazz** swing style. Elusive and hard to define, swing is the combination of a driving rhythmic approach and cohesive **ensemble** work that results in energized, visceral dance music.
2. A long-short treatment of moving notes, called swung notes, that is instrumental in filling music with the rhythmic drive and irresistible energy characteristic to the jazz swing style. For string players, swing is accomplished by playing a lazy, elongated first note, followed by a jerked, short second note, most easily achieved above the middle of the **bow** with a very relaxed upper arm. Although swing is commonly explained to classically trained players as turning common time into 12/8, with a triplet feeling for all eighth notes rather than a strict dotted-eighth rhythm, this belies the subtlety of the swing rhythm, which has a natural elasticity that escapes any strictly proportional rhythmic notation.
3. A jazz style that evolved in the 1930s, epitomized by the big bands of Duke Ellington, Count Basie, and Benny Goodman. Swing is characterized by an energetic pulse, tight **ensemble**, and a swung note treatment of rhythm. Swing jazz is intended for a dancing audience and tends to be more structured than other more improvisatory styles of jazz.

swung note. Any note given the long-short treatment of **swing** rhythm used to create the drive and energy characteristic of the **jazz** swing style. Most often swung notes are notated as straight eighth notes with the uneven execution implied by the style of the music. See **swing** for more information.

sympathetic resonance, sympathetic vibration. An **acoustic** phenomenon in which a **string** of an instrument responds to the external vibrations of a sound with the same frequency. A sympathetic vibration will be activated by any pitch on the harmonic series of that string, with the strongest response from a vibration of the same pitch class as the affected string. Sympathetic vibration is a key component in the rich and complex **tone** of **string instruments**. The more sympathetic vibrations a composition evokes, the more **resonant** the sound, inspiring many composers to choose the keys of G, D, and A when writing for string instruments. One of the best ways to hone good **intonation** on a string instrument is by placing notes so that they activate the sympathetic vibrations of the other strings. Some instruments, such as the **baryton**, the *nyckelharpa*, and the **Hardanger fiddle** have **sympathetic strings** designed with the sole purpose of vibrating sympathetically.

sympathetic strings. Strings which are not played with the **bow** but rather resonate sympathetically when the instrument is played. Sympathetic strings, sometimes called resonating strings, usually pass through rather than over the **bridge** and are placed beside or behind the **fingerboard**. Instruments with sympathetic strings include the **Hardanger fiddle**, baryton, *viola d'amore*, **gadulka**, and **nyckelharpa**.

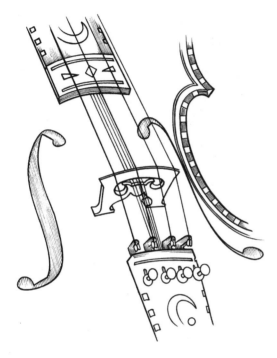

Figure 138. **Sympathetic strings** passing through the **bridge** and under the **fingerboard** of a **Hardanger fiddle**.

symphony.
1. A large **ensemble** made up of **string instruments**, woodwinds, brass instruments, and percussion. A symphony is also called a full **orchestra** or philharmonic.
2. A large-scale composition for orchestra, usually with four movements.

synthetic strings. Strings with a core of nylon or a similar synthetic material. Synthetic strings are made with a type of nylon called perlon or similar composite core wound in metal such as aluminum, chrome, silver, or gold. Designed to combine the stability and brilliance of steel strings with the warmth and depth of **gut strings**, synthetic strings are the most popular choice, especially for classical players. See also **strings**, **steel strings**, and **gut strings**.

~ T ~

tablature, tabs. A system of writing music by indicating the placement of fingers on **strings** rather than using standard notation. Tabs for string players usually consist of a horizontal space representing each string marked with finger numbers representing each note. Tablature uses the same basic **bowing** markings, and rhythm indications as standard notation.

Figure 139. **Fiddle tablature** for *Amazing Grace* with standard notation shown below.

table. The **top plate** of an instrument, also called the belly, sound-table, or sound plate.

tacet. A direction for the player to remain silent for the entire movement. Tacet *al fine* indicates that there is no further music for that particular **part** for the remainder of the piece.

tag. A short rhythmic **lick** that signals the end of a **fiddle** tune.

tail peg. See **button**.

tailgut. The cord that attaches the **tailpiece** to the instrument. The tailgut is a loop of gut, nylon, or wire that runs over the **saddle** and around the end **button**, with both ends anchored to the tailpiece. Because the tailgut allows the tailpiece to be suspended above the **top plate**, it is central to the **resonance** of the instrument. Changing the material, length, and stiffness of the tailgut is one component of an instrument **adjustment**.

tailpiece. The piece anchoring the end of the **strings** beyond the **bridge**. The tailpiece is usually made of **ebony**, **rosewood**, or **boxwood** to match the other **fittings** of the instrument, though modern tailpieces can also be made of metal, plastic, or **carbon fiber**. The tailpiece has a raised **nut** or **saddle** over which the strings pass and slotted holes into which the **ball end** of the string is fitted. Some tailpieces have **fine tuners** fitted into the string holes or integrated fine tuners in place of string holes. The tailpiece is secured by the **tailgut**, which passes over the saddle and loops around the end **button** or **endpin**.

Figure 140. A French **tailpiece**.

Tailpieces are made in one of three standard shapes: English or Hill, with a peaked ridge, French with a rounded arch, or tulip, with a wineglass shape. A special tailpiece design with a curved end uses varied **afterlength** to eliminate **wolf tones**.

The choice of material and design of a tailpiece, as well as its placement in relation to the saddle, has a significant effect on the sound of the instrument. The density of the particular wood influences the way vibrations are transmitted through the instrument. Light tailpieces, such as those made of boxwood or aluminum, can free the sound, but they may also add to wolf tones. Heavier tailpieces of ebony can warm the **tone** but may dampen overall **resonance**. Changing the material, design, size, or placement of the tailpiece is one component of instrument **adjustment**.

tailpin. See **button** and **endpin**.

tallone. (It.) **Frog**.

talon. (Fr.) **Frog**. The phrase *au talon* means to play near the frog.

tap. An **ornament** common in **Irish fiddle** music. A tap is a **grace note** placed during a note in a melody, played by releasing the main note to briefly play a lower note, then quickly returning to the main note. See also **cut** and **double cut**.

tap tuning. A technique of improving the **tone** of a **string instrument** by measuring frequencies of the tones produced by tapping the **plates** of the instrument, then carving the plates until the tap tones are balanced and symmetrical. Tap tuning is also called plate tuning.

Tartini, Guiseppe (1692-1770). Italian violinist, **pedagogue**, composer, and theorist who was one of the founding fathers of string technique.

Tartini pursued a career in music in defiance of his parents' desire for him to become a priest. After years performing in church **orchestras**, opera houses, and touring across Italy, Tartini opened his own **violin** school in Padua around 1730, which was to become the first famous violin training ground to attract students from all over Europe.

As a pedagogue, Tartini focused on **bow** mastery, comparing the breathing of a singer to the movements of the bow, and redesigning the bow to be longer in order to give the player more "breath." His set of fifty variations on a theme by Corelli, titled *L'arte dell arco* [The art of bowing], serves as one of the primary tools for mastering **baroque bow** technique.

Tartini's compositions are primarily solo violin **concertos** with string accompaniment and violin **sonatas**, of which one work remains in the **canon** of literature: the "Devil's Trill" Sonata, op. 1 no. 4. According to Tartini, he dreamed that he lost a violin showdown with the devil, and upon waking he immediately notated the devil's pyrotechnic music, filled with **double trills** that are fiendishly difficult even by modern standards.

Tartini also worked extensively on **music theory** and **acoustics**, producing several treatises on his ideas, most of which were not well received at the time. From these, his exploration of the acoustic phenomenon of combination tones, known today as **Tartini tones**, has developed into a string player's primary tool for **tuning** an instrument and perfecting the **intonation** of **double stops**.

Tartini tones. The acoustic phenomenon caused when two **sound waves** bump into each other, producing a pulsing sound. Tartini tones occur when two notes are played steadily and with intensity, creating a third tone that vibrates at the difference between the two original notes. Listening for Tartini tones can help with tuning a **string instrument**. As two **strings** become closer in tune, the pulse will slow, eventually disappearing altogether when exact tuning is reached. Named for **Guiseppe Tartini** who first documented the phenomenon in 1714, Tartini tones are also called beats, differential tones, or difference tones. See also **sound waves**.

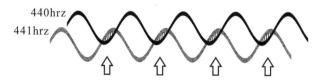

Figure 141. A visual representation of two slightly different **sound waves** colliding to produce a **Tartini tone**.

tastiera. (It.) **Fingerboard**. *Sulla tastiera* means to play with the **bow** over the fingerboard.

tasto. (It.) **Fingerboard**. *Sul tasto* means to play with the **bow** over the fingerboard.

technique. The physical skills of playing an instrument.

Teil, teilen. (Ger.) **Part**, division. *Teilen* means to play *divisi*, and *nicht teilen* means non *divisi*.

temperament. An adjusted **tuning** that allows for the entire span of a keyboard or other fixed-pitch instrument to sound in tune in every key. A wide variety of temperament systems have been developed and employed throughout history, including **Pythagorean intonation**, **mean-tone temperament**, and **equal temperament**. See also **just intonation** and **tempered tuning**.

tempered tuning. The technique of altering the tuning of pitches from their natural **overtone series** in order to facilitate playing in tune over a wide *tessitura* and in many keys. Tempered tuning systems include the most common modern tuning of **equal temperament**, as well as historical tunings of **mean-tone temperament** and **Pythagorean intonation**. Tempered tuning is used by pianos, guitars, and other fixed-pitch instruments. String players and vocalists often use untempered **just intonation** for its natural consonance.

tempo rubato. (It.) Expressive timing suspended over the pulse of the music. Derived from the Italian word for "robbed," *tempo rubato* is a lengthening of important notes by stealing time from the surrounding notes, allowing the performer to play freely on top of the underlying pulse. See also **agogic accent** and **phrasing**.

tendonitis. An injury commonly suffered by string players. Tendonitis is an inflammation and swelling of the tendons, caused by repetitive motion and overuse. Tendonitis in the wrist or elbow is the most common performance-related injury suffered by string players, and it should be taken seriously. Icing and anti-inflammatory drugs can help in the short term, but the best solution is to learn to play in a relaxed, **ergonomic**, healthy way that avoids injury altogether. Playing without injury has been the subject of many recent developments, and special equipment and training courses are available to musicians experiencing tendonitis or other performance-related injuries. See also **Alexander Technique, carpal tunnel syndrome, ergonomics, ergonomic instrument**, and **Feldenkrais Method.**

tenor viola. The largest-size **viola** with a body measuring as long as nineteen inches. Most tenor violas have been cut down to smaller dimensions, leaving very few in original condition. An extant tenor viola example is a 1664 **Guarneri** with wings added to the **plates** at the **bouts** to expand the width and a body length measuring nineteen inches. Other makers of tenor violas include **Amati, Stainer**, and **Stradivari**. The tenor viola is a member of the **violin family** and should not be confused with the tenor **viol**. See also *Altgeige*, **contralto viola**, *viola pomposa*, *viola da spalla*, **Tertis viola**, and **vertical viola**.

tension.
1. Physical strain or stress while playing. Tension is one of the greatest obstacles in mastering a **string instrument** and may lead to performance-related injuries such as **tendonitis** and **carpal tunnel syndrome**. Pedagogical methods and special equipment are designed to aid musicians in playing free of tension. See also **Alexander Technique, carpal tunnel syndrome, ergonomics, ergonomic instrument**, and **Feldenkrais Method.**
2. The tightness of the **horsehair** as it is stretched between the **frog** and the **tip** of the **bow**. The hair should have enough tension so that the stick does not drag on the **string** but not so much that the bow loses its **cambre**, or concave curve. Finding the correct hair tension is an important component in producing a rich **tone** and executing **off the string bowstrokes**. The tension should be released when the bow is not in use.
3. The tightness of the strings as they are stretched between the **nut** and the **tailpiece**. Adjusting the string tension by turning the tuning **pegs** changes the **pitch** of an **open string**. Tension is one of the variables in different types of strings. See **strings** for detailed information.

tenuto. (It.) Held. *Tenuto* is an indication to sustain the note for its full value or even stretch it beyond that value. *Tenuto* is indicated by a horizontal dash above the note-head of the affected note or the word *tenuto* or *ten*. As an articulation mark, the dash or *tenuto* line over a note-head may have several somewhat contradictory meanings. For example, the dash may indicate that the note should be played *legato*, that is, smoothly connected to the note that follows. Depending on the context, the dash may even mean that the note should be played with an **agogic accent**, lasting slightly longer than its portion of the rhythm. Contrarily, the dash may also indicate that the note should be played *portato*, with a leaning into the note and a slight detachment from the note that follows. When combined with a **slur**, the dash means to make a slight, pulsed separation between notes without changing **bow**. See also **articulation**.

terminal vibrato. A technique of beginning a sustained note without **vibrato** and gradually increasing the width and intensity of the vibrato to the end of the note.

Tertis, Lionel (1876-1975). English **viola** player celebrated for being one of the first musicians to bring the viola, which he called the "Cinderella of **string instruments**," to international fame.

Like many great violists, Tertis trained on **violin**, studying at the Leipzig Hochschule für Musik and the Royal Academy of Music in London, where he switched to viola. Tertis became a well-known soloist touring Europe and America.

Determined to expand the scant viola **repertoire**, Tertis **transcribed** many works for the viola, including Elgar's **cello concerto** and Mozart's clarinet concerto, and he commissioned and inspired many new compositions for the instrument from such composers as Bax, Bridge, Walton, and Vaughan Williams.

As a performer, Tertis was known for his large, deep **tone**, which he cultivated to the point of designing a large model of viola capable of producing cello-like **resonance** in the lower range (see **Tertis viola**).

An active writer about his instrument, Tertis authored a number of articles and books including *Cinderella No More* and *My Viola and I*.

Tertis viola. A design for the **viola** developed by viola soloist **Lionel Tertis** and **luthier** Arthur Richardson. The Tertis viola measures 16 ¾ with dimensions large enough to produce a rich tone combined with a light-weight **scroll** and angled **fingerboard** to facilitate ease of playability in the high register. Richardson made 178 Tertis violas with the label Richardson-Tertis. Some modern luthiers make violas called "Tertis model" with larger lower and middle bouts

and narrow upper bouts based on the Richardson-Tertis design.

Terzgeige. (Ger.) A *violino piccolo* tuned a third higher than a standard **violin**.

The Art of Bowing. See *L'arte del arco*.

thematic index. A list of works, usually of one composer. The works in a thematic index or thematic catalog may be arranged in chronological order or may be organized based on medium of performance, type of work, or key. Unlike **opus** numbers, which are assigned by the composer, a thematic index is created by a scholar who is able to systematically account for the entire compositional output of a composer's life. Thematic index systems commonly used in music for **string instruments** include **BWV (J. S. Bach)**, Deutsch (Schubert), **Hoboken** (Haydn), **Köchel** (W. A. Mozart), and Ryom (Vivaldi). The Library of Congress and many university library websites offer excellent comprehensive guides to thematic indexes.

theory. See **music theory**.

thorough-bass. See *basso continuo*.

thrown bowstroke. Any **bowstroke** that is begun by throwing the bow at the string from above. A thrown bow is usually used to provide the impetus for a bouncing, **off the string** bowstroke, with the exception of the *fouetté* stroke, which is a thrown bow that remains **on the string**. Thrown bows generate ample energy for rebounding but provide much less control than notes begun **from the string**. Thrown strokes include *battuto*, **drum stroke**, *jeté*, and *ricochet*. See **Table 1: Bowstrokes** for a list of strokes and their notation.

thumb position. The technique of placing the side of the left thumb on the **string** to facilitate playing in high registers on the **cello** and **double bass**. In thumb position, the player moves the left thumb out from behind the **neck** and places it adjacent to the other fingers on the **fingerboard**. By stopping the string with the side of the thumb, the player creates a sort of moveable **nut**, allowing for passagework spanning two octaves or more to be played without **shifting**. Thumb position is usually begun at the half-string **harmonic** and can be placed anywhere along the upper portion of the fingerboard.

Thumb position is first mentioned in Michel Corrette's 1741 treatise *Méthode pour apprendre le violoncelle*, though it is believed that cellists were using thumb position earlier, when the technique of holding the instrument between the calves rather than balanced on the floor freed the left hand to move easliy in the upper registers.

See also **finger pattern**.

Figure 142. **Thumb position** shown on the **double bass**.

tilt-block. A wooden piece built around the **endpin button** of a **double bass** to provide an anchor for a tilted endpin without the need of drilling a hole into the lower **block** of the instrument. The Seaton saddle is a tilt-block design with several endpin holes, each at a different angle. See also **endpin, Laborie endpin**, and **egg pin**.

timbre. **Tone-color**, the quality of sound that makes an instrument unique.

tin fiddle. A metal **violin** popular in early 20th-century Ireland. Tin fiddles were made and sold by traveling tinsmiths who combined the metal body with a wood **neck** usually salvaged from a broken **fiddle**, making a cheap, durable instrument.

tip.
1. The pointed top end of the **bow**, usually a hatchet-shaped piece of wood carved from the same block as the **stick**. The tip holds the **horsehair** away from the stick, allowing **tension** to be put on the hair. The point of the tip is protected by a plate of ivory, metal,

or other material. See also **baroque bow, bow, French bow, German bow**, and **Tourte bow**.
2. An indication in printed music instructing the musician to play in the uppermost portion of the **bow**, near the tip.

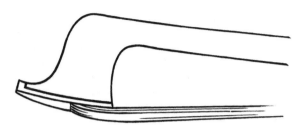

Figure 143. The **tip** of a modern **Tourte bow**.

tiré. (Fr.) **Down-bow**.

tonal adjustment. See **adjustment**.

tonalization. An exercise designed to improve the production of a beautiful, even **tone**.

tone.
1. The quality of sound. String players strive to produce a resonant, rich, complex tone.
2. A general term for a musical sound.

tone-color. The quality of a sound that differentiates it from the same **pitch** played on a different instrument, by a different musician, or in a different manner. Tone-color on **string instruments** is created by varying the speed, **contact point**, and weight of the **bow-stroke** in combination with changing intensity of **vibrato** and weight of the left hand. An accomplished player will have an extensive palette of tone-colors ready to create a particular mood or character in the music.

tonewood. Any wood chosen for its **acoustic** properties to be used for the construction of musical instruments. Tonewoods most commonly used in the **modern string instrument family** are **spruce** and **maple**.

Tonleiter. (Ger.) **Scale**.

top block. See **block**.

top hat pegs. See **hat pegs**.

top plate. The thin piece of carved wood that is the top of the instrument. The top plate, alternately called the table, the face, or the belly, is hand carved from two **bookmatched** slabs of spruce, joined in the center. The top plate is shaped into an arch to bear the pressure from the **bridge**, with two **f-holes** carved into it to release the sound, and a **bass-bar** glued to the underside to help transmit vibrations. The precise shape and thickness of the top and back plates determine the sound of an instrument. See also **back plate** and **plate** for an illustration.

Tortelier, Paul (1914-1990). French cellist, conductor, and composer who began his career as an **orchestra** musician, gaining international recognition for his performances of Richard Strauss' *Don Quixote.*

Tortelier studied with Gérard Hekking at the Paris Conservatoire, where he won the *premier prix* playing the Elgar concerto. Tortelier went on to build an international reputation for being one of the finest soloists of his time. His playing was characterized by an athletic enthusiasm combined with an expressive tenderness. His orchestral work included playing principal and soloist with the Boston Symphony under Koussevitzky.

Tortelier was an influential **pedagogue**, serving on the faculty of the Paris Conservatoire, the Folkwang Hochschule in Essen, and the Nice Conservatoire, and teaching **masterclasses** on a BBC television show. He produced a **cello** method, *How I Play, How I Teach,* and composed a number of pieces, most of which are for cello. Tortelier also invented the bent **endpin**, called the **Tortelier endpin**, which allows the cello to be positioned more horizontally while playing.

Tortelier endpin. A **cello endpin** that is curved to allow the instrument to be positioned more horizontally while playing. See **endpin**.

touche. (Fr.) **Fingerboard.**

Tourte bow. The modern **bow** as standardized by **François Xavier Tourte** around 1786. The Tourte bow is characterized by a concave **stick**, a tall hatchet-shaped **head**, a screw mechanism to adjust **horse hair tension**, and a metal **ferrule** to achieve a wide ribbon of hair. Most modern players use this model of bow, with the exception of double bassists who play with a **German bass bow**. Tourte was the first to use **pernambuco** wood, which he bent into a concave curve using heat rather than carving the stick. See also **bow**.

Tourte, François Xavier (1747-1835). French **bow** maker who standardized the modern bow. The son of **luthier** and bowmaker Nicolas Pierre Tourte, François Xavier Tourte established himself as the preeminent bowmaker in Paris. Around 1786, after years of making various **transitional bows**, Tourte arrived on the design that has become the standard modern violin bow. The Tourte bow, as it has come to be called, is characterized by a concave **stick** that tapers to the **tip**, a tall hatchet-shaped **head**, a screw mechanism to adjust **horsehair tension**, and a metal **ferrule** to achieve a wide ribbon of hair. Tourte was the first to use **pernambuco** wood, which he shaped into a concave **cambre** by heating rather than carving the stick. See also **Tourte bow**.

Tourte mute. A rubber mute that attaches to the **strings** for ease of sliding on and off the **bridge**, preferred by orchestral players for its convenience. See also **mute**.

Figure 145. A rubber **Tourte mute** positioned on the **bridge**.

tous. (Fr.) All, everyone.

transcription.

1. The adaptation of a composition for an instrument other than the one for which it was intended. A transcription seeks to remain as true to the original as possible. For example, the transcription of **J. S. Bach**'s Cello Suites up an octave and into **alto clef** enables the pieces to be played on the **viola**.

Figure 144. The modern **Tourte bow** design for **violin** or **viola**.

2. The writing down of a previously unnotated piece of music. For example, transcriptions of jazz violinist **Stéphane Grappelli's** most famous **improvisations**, published as sheet music for other musicians to study.

transitional bow. Any of the many bow designs from the Classical era as bow making evolved from the **Baroque bow** to the modern **Tourte bow.** Transitional bows are characterized by a stick that is longer and straighter than the Baroque bow yet not as concave as the Tourte bow. A greater space between the stick and hair was created by the development of the hatchet-shaped **tip** of the bow, and the **frog** is reinforced by the addition of the **shoe,** furthering development of the adjustable frog. With no standardization, bows from this era vary widely in length, weight, materials, and balance. In particular, makers experimented with a wide variety of shapes and sizes of the tip. See **bow** for an illustration of a transistional bow as compared to a modern bow and a baroque bow.

transpose. To raise or lower all the pitches in a piece by the same interval in order to play them in a different key, in a different octave, or on a different instrument.

transposing instrument. An instrument using standard musical notation to designate a physical location rather than an actual sounding pitch. The only regularly transposing **string instrument** is the **double bass,** which has a **concert pitch** one octave lower than is indicated by printed music. Other string instruments may become transposing instruments on the rare occasion that a part is written with *scordatura* string **tunings** but is notated as if the **strings** were tuned normally, producing a sounding pitch that is different from what is written on the page. Examples of these transposing works include the "fiddle" **solo** from the second movement of Mahler's fourth **symphony** and the solo **viola** part from Mozart's *Sinfonia Concertante.* See also **concert pitch,** *scordatura,* and **standard pitch.**

travel bass. A **double bass** designed with a removable **neck** and **fingerboard** that allows a full-sized instrument to be folded into a compact **case** for ease of traveling.

tremblement. (Fr.) **Trill.**

tremolo. (It.) A rapid, trembling **bowstroke.** *Tremolo* is played with tiny, unmeasured bows, and is notated by

three or more slashes through the stem of the note. See also **slurred** *tremolo.* See **Table 1: Bowstrokes** for a list of strokes and their notation.

Figure 146. A *tremolo* passage from Debussy's *La mer no. 1 De laube à midi sur la mer,* **double bass,** mm 12-15.

trick fiddling. Showmanship on the **violin** which includes physical stunts integrated into a piece of music. Trick fiddling can include playing the instrument behind the back, playing while lying down, flipping the **fiddle,** tossing the **bow** into the air, or doing gymnastics, all while playing accurately and in rhythm.

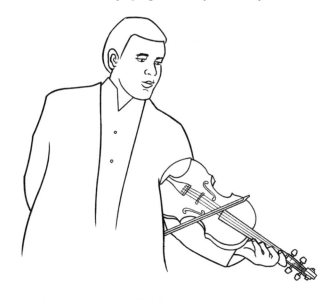

Figure 147. **Bowing** behind the back as part of a **trick fiddling** routine.

trill. An **ornament** produced by a rapid alternation between a notated pitch and the next higher note. **String instruments** trill by setting a finger on the main pitch and quickly tapping the higher pitch. In some instances, particularly in a high register or when using an extended hand position, a trill may be executed by using a **vibrato** movement to raise and lower the trilling finger.

In modern practice, the trill is begun from the main notated pitch. This is considered stylistically appropriate for music from the Romantic era and later. In music from the Baroque and Classical eras, the trill is begun from the higher, ornamental note, and may be leaned on to create an *appoggiatura*. Trills may be finished with the additional ornament of a *Nachschlag*.

Trills are notated by *tr* over the ornamented note, sometimes followed by a wavy horizontal line, which may indicate the duration of the trill.

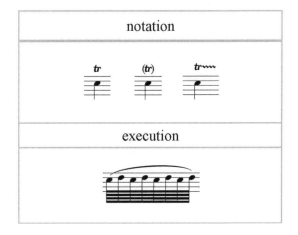

Figure 148a. Three types of **trill** notation and their execution.

The pitch of the upper note of a trill is determined by the key signature unless a tiny **accidental** is indicated next to the trill notation.

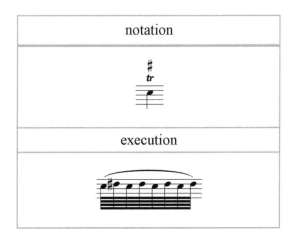

Figure 148b. A **trill** with an **accidental** and its execution.

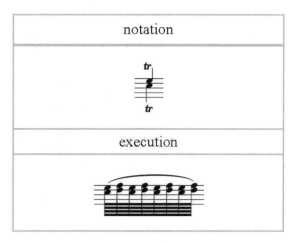

Figure 148c. A **double trill** and its execution.

trio.
1. An **ensemble** of three players. The most common trios that include **string instruments** are the string trio, with **violin, viola**, and **cello**, and the piano trio, with violin, piano, and cello.
2. The music composed for an **ensemble** of three players. See also **chamber music, piano trio**, and **string trio**.

trio sonata. One of the most popular instrumental **genres** in the Baroque era, with two or three melody instruments and a **continuo** part alongside the keyboard part. See also **chamber music, solo sonata, *sonata da camera, sonata da chiesa***, and **sonata**.

triple concerto. A large-scale orchestral work featuring three soloists, such as the **concerto** for **violin, piano**, and **cello** by Beethoven.

triple stop. Three notes sounding simultaneously. On **string instruments** it is possible to play three notes simultaneously for a brief time by using a fast **bow-stroke** and flat **bow tilt** with a **contact point** close to the **fingerboard**. Most often a triple stop is either **rolled** or **broken**, depending on the character and style of the piece.

tromba marina. (It.) See **trumpet marine**.

true legato. Notes connected as smoothly as possible. See **legato**.

Trummscheit. (Ger.) See **trumpet marine**.

trumpet marine. A bowed **string instrument** primarily played in Medieval and Renaissance Europe. The trumpet marine, or *tromba marina*, has a single **string** stretched over a triangular or cone-shaped body four to seven feet long that is open at the base. The string passes over a vibrating **bridge** on the top **plate** near the lower end of the body. With one foot glued to the instrument and the other foot loose to vibrate against the **soundboard**, the bridge creates a buzzing **timbre** similar to that of a trumpet.

The string is generally tuned to D1 three octaves below middle C, and is not stopped but rather plays only **harmonics** touched lightly at the **nodes** by the thumb or finger of the left hand. The nodes for these harmonics are labeled A, D, F, A, D, F, G, A, B, C, D on bits of paper glued beneath the string. Some marine trumpets include additional **sympathetic strings**.

The marine trumpet is played while standing, with the top of the **neck** leaning against the player's left shoulder and the open base of the body resting on the ground. It is bowed between the hand and the **nut** at the highest end of the string.

Figure 149. Playing the **trumpet marine**.

The shape of the instrument combined with the distinct timbre of the vibrating bridge and the production of a natural harmonic series is similar to a natural trumpet, thus its name. Because it was used by nuns as a substitute for the trumpet, which women were not permitted to play, the trumpet marine is also known as the nun's **violin**, the nun's **fiddle**, or the *Nonnengeige*. Other names for the instrument include *trompette marine* (Fr.), *Trummscheit, Trumscheit, Marien Trompet, Trompetengeige* (Ger.), and *tromba marina* (It.).

Tubbs family. English family of bowmakers considered among the best. The Tubbs line of **bows** was begun in the early 19th century by three brothers: William, Henry, and Thomas, who most likely trained in the workshop of the elder Edward **Dodd**.

The most important of these three was Thomas (1790-1863), whose bows were the first English examples to have modern **mountings** including a **Parisian eye**, tortoiseshell **frog**, and metal **shoe**. His sticks were short, oval, and fixed with an angled frog. William Tubbs (1814-1878), son of Thomas, took over the business in 1851. William developed his father's bow design to have a smaller, more delicate stick with a fully mounted frog, similar to the French style. He also worked refitting the open frog on older bows with modern frogs.

James Tubbs (1835-1921), son of William, was the most important bowmaker in the Tubbs family. After learning from his father and uncle, James began producing particularly fine bows with an individual style characterized by a broad **head**, a narrow **chamfer**, and a round stick. He fitted them with **mountings** of gold, ivory, and tortoiseshell, and stamped them JAS TUBBS. Many of James Tubbs' bows bear the stamp W. E. HILL, as he worked for the Hill shop for much of his career. It is estimated that James Tubbs, with the help of his son Alfred, produced about five thousand bows for **violin**, **viola** and **cello**. These bows are prized for their responsive grip on the string.

tune.
1. To adjust the **pitch** of an instrument. **String instruments** are tuned by changing the amount of **tension** on each string using tuning **pegs**.
2. To adjust the **intonation** of a note. On unfretted string instruments, individual notes can be tuned by making minute changes in the placement of a finger while stopping the **string**.
3. A melody or song, commonly used in the popular **genres** of **bluegrass**, **fiddle**, folk, and **jazz**. "Calling a tune" means choosing the next song to be performed and counting off to get the band started together.

tuner. An electronic device used to aid in tuning an instrument. Tuners may generate a tone that the player matches, or may use a microphone to detect the **pitch** acoustically and guide the player with a digital display. Some tuners are designed to clip to the instrument, taking input directly from the vibrations of the instrument, making it possible to tune in a noisy environment.

Figure 150. An electronic clip-on **tuner**.

Basic digital tuners register and generate only the pitches needed for a specific instrument, while **chromatic** tuners can recognize and produce any pitch. **Electric instruments** may have built-in tuner displays that read the pitch from the electric signal of the **pickup**. Tuners can also be found online and in smart-phone applications.

Tuners can be valuable tools for developing good **intonation**. The most useful electronic tuners for training intonation should be fully chromatic, have a finely calibrated input display, be able to generate any pitch, and include an adjustable pitch setting ranging from 438 to 445 Hz, as well as a choice of tuning systems including **just intonation**, **equal temperament**, and **mean-tone temperament**. In addition, many tuners include a **metronome** function.

The term "tuner" can also refer to **fine tuners** or adjusters on the **tailpiece** of the instrument.

tuning.
1. The process of adjusting the **pitch** of an instrument. **Standard tuning** is based on the fixed reference of A4 = 440 Hz, with some performers, particularly those in the **historically informed performance** field, preferring a slightly different reference pitch.

For **string instruments**, tuning is accomplished through adjusting the **tension** of each **string** by turning the **pegs** or **fine tuners** until the correct pitch is reached. The A string is tuned first, usually using a **tuning fork**, **tuner**, or other instrument as a reference point, then the other strings are tuned to each other.

In an **ensemble**, if a fixed-pitch instrument, such as a piano or harpsichord is used, that instrument will provide the reference pitch. **String quartets** often tune to the cellist's; **string orchestras** tune to the **concertmaster's** A; and **full orchestras** take the tuning pitch from the oboe.

Precision in tuning is accomplished by listening for the **beats** produced by the interaction between the **sound waves** of the string and the reference pitch. All the tuning intervals used by string players are perfect, with the reference pitch at a unison and the strings at a fourth or fifth, so the tone will be pure, clear, and free of beats when correct tuning is reached. This is done by turning the pegs so that any beats slow in pulse until they eventually disappear altogether.

Cello and **double bass** may also use **harmonics** to check the tuning between strings. For example, when the harmonic produced at the 1/2 string **node** of one string exactly matches the harmonic produced at the 1/3 string note on the next lower string, the strings are in tune with each other.

Standard tuning for the modern string family is:
violin: G3 – D4 – A4 – E5
viola: C3 – G3 – D4 – A4
cello: C2 – G2 – D3 – A3
double bass: E1 – A1 – D2 – G2 (**orchestral tuning**)

Using a tuning other than standard is known as *scordatura*. Tuning usually refers only to setting the pitches of **open strings**. Playing in tune by stopping each note in the precisely correct location on the **fingerboard** is called **intonation**. See also *accordatura*, **fine tuner**, *scordatura*, **tuner**, **intonation**, **pegs**, and **standard tuning**.
2. The system of adjusting intervals in relation to each other. String players most often use the untempered tuning system of **just intonation** for its natural consonance. When playing with piano or another fixed-pitch instrument, string players need to adjust their tuning method accordingly. See **just intonation**, **equal temperament**, and **mean-tone temperament**.

tuning fork. A two-pronged metal implement that produces a fixed **pitch** when struck, used as a reference for **tuning**. Invented in 1711 by John Shore, the tuning fork is designed to produce a perfect sine **waveform** resulting in a particularly pure **tone**. While tuning forks can be made to sound any pitch, they are most commonly set at the modern **standard tuning** of A4 = 440 Hz.

Figure 151. A **tuning fork**.

Turetzky, Joseph (b. 1933). American **double bass** player, **pedagogue**, and composer, known for championing the double bass as a **solo** instrument by cultivating over three hundred new pieces for the **repertoire** and expanding bass **technique** to include innovative use of *glissando*, **harmonics**, **bowstrokes**, and percussive effects using the body of the instrument. At home in both **art music** and **jazz**, Turetzky has appeared as a soloist around the world. He is the most recorded solo double bassist, and the author of *The Contemporary Contrabass*.

turn. An **ornament** which begins on the note above the main printed note, moves to the main note, then the note below, and returns to the main note. An inverted turn reverses the order, beginning with the note below the printed pitch, and then rising.

The turn is notated by ∾ either above the ornamented note or between it and the following note. The pitches in the turn are determined by the key signature unless tiny **accidentals** are shown next to the turn symbol.

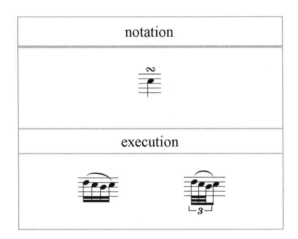

Figure 152a. A **turn** symbol placed above the note and two possible executions.

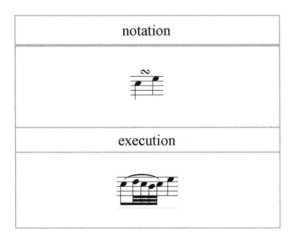

Figure 152b. A **turn** symbol placed after the note and one possible execution.

Like most ornaments, the timing and exact placement of a turn is an artistic choice of the performer

that can vary widely based on style, tempo, and context.

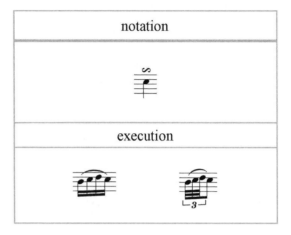

Figure 152c. An inverted **turn** symbol placed above the note and two possible executions.

tutti. (It.) All, everyone. *Tutti* is used in contrast to a **solo** marking, to indicate that the entire **section** should play.

two-finger vibrato. See **close shake** and **vibrato trill**.

tzigane. (Fr.) Gypsy.

~ U ~

über. (Ger.) Over, above.

Übung. (Ger.) Exercise or **etude**.

ukelin. See **bowed psaltery**.

una corda. (It.) One string. Often found in the phrase *sul una corda*, meaning to play the passage entirely on one **string** to create a particular **tone color** or character.

underslide. See **shoe**.

unison. Together. Usually found after a *divisi* passage, indicating that all players in the **section** should return to the same **part**.

up-bow. A **bowstroke** that is pushed away from the **tip** and towards the **frog**, indicated by the symbol ∨ placed above the note. Because up-bow is generally considered a weaker movement than **down-bow**, it is conventionally chosen for notes played on upbeats and weak beats. Up-bow is also called *Aufstrich* in German, *arcata in su*, in Italian, and *poussé*, or "push," in French.

See also **rule of down bow** and **Table 1: Bow-strokes** for a list of strokes and their notation.

upper mordent. See **mordent**.

upper saddle. See **nut**.

upright bass. See **double bass**.

ütögardon. A Hungarian folk instrument used in traditional dance music, also called the "beaten cello." Carved from wood and shaped similar to a **cello**, the *ütögardon* has four **strings**, three of which are tuned in unison D and hammered with a stick, and the fourth of which is tuned an octave higher and plucked to snap against the **fingerboard**. The *ütögardon* uses only open strings.

~ V ~

V. S. (It.) *Volti subito*, meaning turn the page immediately.

vamp. A short pattern that is repeated until the entrance of a soloist.

Vardi, Emanuel. (1917-2011). American **viola** player whose virtuosity helped redefine the role of the viola in the 20th century. Vardi began studies on **violin** with his father and then studied at Juilliard with Constance Seeger and Edward Dethier. Switching to viola, he studied with Primrose and played in the NBC Symphony. Vardi was the first violist to give a full recital in New York's Town Hall, a performance which earned him the "Recitalist of the Year" award from New York music critics, and he was one of the first violists to perform a **solo** recital in Carnegie Hall. Vardi was also a pioneer in bringing the viola to the **genre** of **jazz** by performing, recording, and touring with jazz greats such as Louis Armstrong, B. B. King, and Jaco Pastorius.

varnish. The clear coating that colors and protects the wood of an instrument. Varnish is crucial to the **tone** and value of a **string instrument**, and various recipes for varnish are protected secrets subject to study and controversy. Oil and friction from a player's hands will wear away the varnish, particularly on the right **shoulder** of an instrument, which can be retouched by a **luthier** and protected with tape. Varnish can be damaged by exposure to sunlight or heat, and applying **polish**, especially **French polish** or **shellac**, will permanently alter the quality of an instrument's varnish.

Vega Bach bow. See **Bach bow**.

Venuti, Joe. (1903-1978). American violinist considered the most important pioneer of the **violin** as a **solo** instrument in early **jazz**. Venuti brought a **Paganini**-inspired classical **virtuosity** to his style of jazz, incorporating four-octave **runs**, **left-hand** *pizzicato*, *glissandi*, and a **bravura** persona that became known as the "hot" playing style characteristic of jazz soloists in 1920s' swing. Venuti's work and his long-standing partnership with guitarist Eddie Lang have left a legacy that has been highly influential for generations of artists including Django Reinhardt and **Stéphane Grappelli**.

vertical viola. A variation on the **viola** designed by Carleen Hutchins as part of the **new violin family**. The vertical viola is 2.5 inches longer than a standard viola and is held vertically to be played like a **cello**. Also called an alto **violin**, the vertical viola became the most successful of Hutchins' eight violin sizes when Yo-Yo Ma used one to perform and record Bartók's viola **concerto**.

vibrato. Undulation in **pitch** that enriches **tone**, creates expressivity, and aids in sound projection. On **string instruments**, vibrato is achieved by rolling the fingertip along the **string** when stopping a note.

There are three main techniques of vibrato for **violin** and **viola**, each using a different pivot point for initiating the movement. **Arm vibrato** is created from the elbow, which opens and closes to rock the entire forearm and hand. **Hand vibrato**, also called wrist vibrato, is initiated at the wrist, with only the hand rocking back and forth. **Finger vibrato** is the smallest and used only in special circumstances, with the movement originating at the base knuckle where an individual finger meets the hand. Every violinist or violist has a preferred vibrato, usually the type that was learned first, and an accomplished player will be able to do all three vibrato techniques, allowing a choice of the one appropriate to the character and technical demands of the passage at hand.

For **cello** and **double bass,** only one vibrato technique is used: an arm movement initiated from the elbow that rocks the forearm and hand, rolling the fingertip up and down the line of the string.

The pulse of vibrato should be controlled and measured, requiring a relaxed **posture** and careful training. The roll of vibrato can be widened or narrowed, and the speed of the undulation increased, decreased, or even brought to a stop in any combination. Vibrato needs to be adjusted according to the string, finger, style of playing, character of music, etc. A fast, wide vibrato produces the energetic, vigorous tone central to **bravura** playing, while a fast, narrow vibrato creates a delicate, shimmery effect more suitable for pale **tone colors**. The width or intensity of vibrato can be developed through a phrase, even on a single sustained note, as a powerful tool of expressivity.

Although historically there has been much debate over when and how much vibrato to use, beginning in the 20th century a continuous vibrato has been the norm for string players and is considered an important aspect of a player's signature sound. The absence of vibrato is a special tone color, indicated by the marking *non vibrato*.

See also **vibrato trill, two-finger vibrato, measured vibrato,** and **terminal vibrato**.

vibrato trill. A trill created by using the wrist or arm movement of **vibrato** rather than tapping the trill finger from the base joint. The vibrato trill is used mainly in the extreme upper register where pitches lie very close together.

vièle à pique. (Fr.) **Spike fiddle**.

vielle. Medieval name for a **fiddle** or **hurdy-gurdy**.

vielle à roue. (Fr.) See **hurdy-gurdy**.

Viennese tuning. A five-string **double bass** tuning system of F1 – A1 – D2 – F#2 – A2 used during the Classical era in Vienna and implied in the scores of **Mozart** and Haydn. This triad-based tuning facilitates playing with **open strings** and **harmonics**, particularly in D major and closely related keys, but proves very challenging when playing in other keys. Although most literature written with Viennese tuning has been modernized for **orchestral tuning,** the **historically informed performance** movement has brought renewed interest in reviving the Viennese system.

Vieux, Maurice (1884-1951). French violist and **pedagogue** whose work played a key role in the development of the **viola** in Europe. Vieux studied at the Paris Conservatoire with Laforge and Leport, winning

the *premier prix* in 1902. He joined the Paris Opéra **orchestra**, becoming **principal** in 1908 and remaining until 1947. As a soloist he premiered many new works written for him, including Bruch's *Romance,* and as a chamber musician he gave first performances of works by French composers including Saint-Saëns, Fauré, Debussy, and Milhaud.

A dedicated teacher, Vieux filled **Théophile Laforge's** viola faculty position at the Paris Conservatoire in 1918 and taught there for the next thirty years, writing several pedagogical *étude* collections and leaving a legacy of successful students.

Vieuxtemps, Henry. (1820-1881). Belgian violinist, composer, and **pedagogue** who founded the **violin** school at the St. Petersburg **Conservatory** and furthered the development of the **Franco-Belgian school of violin playing**.

Vieuxtemps studied violin with Bériot and then made his debut in Paris, launching a career as a touring **virtuoso**.

As a soloist, Vieuxtemps had tremendous success in Europe and was one of the first musicians to tour extensively in the United States. Always programming masterworks of Bach, Mozart, Haydn, and Beethoven alongside more contemporary works, Vieuxtemps revived interest in many older works, particularly Beethoven's violin **concerto**. Also a **viola** player and active performer of **chamber music**, Vieuxtemps championed the late string quartets of Beethoven.

In the tradition of **Paganini**, Vieuxtemps wrote **showpieces** to display his virtuosity, often aimed at delighting specific audiences along his tours, such as his *Souvenir d'Amerique* (Variations on Yankee Doodle), op. 17, written for his tours of America. Unlike Paganini, Vieuxtemps gave the orchestra a more significant role in his five violin concertos, which place the soloist in a texture of a rich symphonic backdrop. Of Vieuxtemps' fifty-nine published compositions, almost all of which are for violin, the fourth concerto and a few showpieces remain in the standard repertoire.

A dedicated **pedagogue**, Vieuxtemps made significant contributions to the development of violin playing in Russia. As soloist to the tsar and founder of the violin school at the St. Petersburg Conservatory, Vieuxtemps initiated the formation of the **Russian school of violin playing**. In his later work as professor of violin at the Brussels Conservatory, Vieuxtemps was a dedicated proponent of the Franco-Belgian school and trained many fine performers, most notably **Ysaÿe**.

vihuela de arco. (Sp.) A bowed **string instrument** similar to a guitar characterized by a flat back and guitar-shaped **C bouts**. The *vihuela de arco* has between five and seven **strings**, is built in an assortment of sizes with various **tunings**, and is considered the precursor to the **viol**. The *vihuela de arco* usually has **gut frets** and is played either horizontally against the chest or vertically while balanced on the knee. Popular in Spain from the 15th through the 17th century, the *vihuela de arco* is used today in **historically informed performances** of Spanish Renaissance music.

The *vihuela de pendola* is the same instrument but plucked with a quill rather than bowed, and the unqualified term *vihuela* usually refers to the finger-plucked *vihuela de mano*.

viol family. Bowed **string instruments** popular during the Renaissance and Baroque eras, characterized by a **fretted fingerboard**, six **strings**, a flat back, and sloping shoulders.

Viols are played vertically, either balanced on the lap or held between the knees. The instruments use **gut strings** usually tuned in fourths with a major third in the middle, similar to the modern guitar, and have moveable gut **frets** that can be adjusted to suit a particular key.

The arched viol **bow** is held underhand on the stick near the **balance point**. The open **frog** design of the bow allows the musician to press on the **hair** with two fingers while playing, effecting changes in **articulation** and **dynamics**.

Figure 153. Instruments from the **viol family**.

Historically, viols were made in a variety of sizes and shapes, eventually becoming a standardized family of six sizes: *pardessus de viole*, treble viol, alto viol, tenor viol, bass viol, and contrabass viol, also known as a *violone*. A chamber **ensemble** of various sizes of viols is called a **consort.**

The viol is also commonly called a *viola da gamba*, or "leg viol," because of how it is held. Other names for the instrument include *viola cum arculo*, and *vihuela* or *vihuela de arco*. Closely related instruments include the **baryton** and the *viola d'amore*. It should be noted that the *viola da braccio*, or "arm viola," is not a member of the viol family, but is related to the modern **violin**.

Although the viol family was eventually replaced by the louder, more brilliant **violin family**, the growing popularity of early music and **historically informed performance** in the late 20th century has brought a revival of the instruments and their **repertoire**.

viola. The middle instrument in the **modern string family**, which also includes the **violin, cello**, and **double bass**. The viola is held horizontally on the left shoulder, balanced underneath the jawbone, and is played with a **horsehair bow**. The viola is slightly larger than the violin, and is tuned C3 – G3 – D4 – A4, a fifth lower than a violin and an octave higher than a cello.

Developed in the early 16th century along with the violin and cello, the modern viola design grew from the *viola da braccio*. The viola has traditionally been an **ensemble** instrument, playing the inner harmonies in the **string quartet** and the **symphony orchestra**, which typically includes a **section** of six to fourteen violists. Only in the 20th century, through the championing of musicians like **Paul Hindemith** and **William Primrose**, has the viola begun to emerge as a **solo** instrument.

The viola is constructed of a top and back **plate**, each hand carved into a convex arch to support the weight from the **bridge**. The **ribs** form the sides of the instrument, made from six thin strips of **maple** that have been bent using heat and water to match the shape of the plates. The ribs and plates are held together with **hide glue** and reinforced at the joints by **linings** and **blocks**. Inside the body, the **soundpost** and **bass-bar** sit beneath the bridge, supporting the structure of the instrument against the tension of the **strings** and helping to transfer **sound waves** across the surfaces of the plates. **F-holes** cut into the top plate are shaped to maximize the **acoustic resonance** of the **sounding chamber**. The **fingerboard**, usually made of **ebony** for its smooth texture, is glued to a **neck** of maple, which is carved in a single piece from the **heel** to the **scroll**. The four strings are stretched

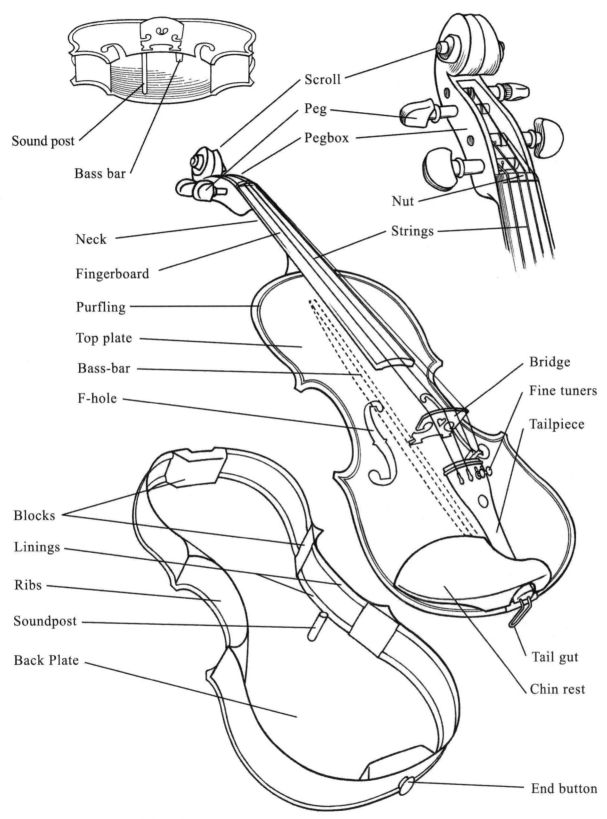

Sound post

Bass bar

Scroll

Peg

Pegbox

Nut

Neck

Strings

Fingerboard

Purfling

Top plate

Bass-bar

F-hole

Bridge

Fine tuners

Tailpiece

Blocks

Linings

Ribs

Soundpost

Back Plate

Tail gut

Chin rest

End button

Figure 154. The **viola**.

taut between a **tailpiece** tied to the **end button** on the **lower bouts**, and the **pegs** wedged into holes in the **pegbox** on the instrument's **head**. The strings pass over a thin bridge, carved from a wedge of maple, which transfers the vibrations of the strings to the **resonance chamber** of the body. The strings are held slightly above the surface of the fingerboard by the raised ebony **nut** at the top of the fingerboard. A wooden **chin rest** is usually clamped to the lower bout to aid the player in holding the viola without damping the sound.

Unlike the violin, the **size** of the viola has not been standardized. Violas have an average body length of 16 to 16.5 inches, though they are made as small as 15 inches and as large as 18 inches. In order to match the **acoustic** qualities of the violin, the viola would need dimensions based on a 20-inch length—much too large to be played horizontally. Many experimental designs address this challenge, from instruments made with particularly lightweight materials, to violas with startling and unconventional body shapes. For more on these designs, see **Tertis viola**, *viola alta*, **vertical viola**, **Rivinus design**, **cutaway instrument**, and **ergonomic instrument**. See also *Altgeige*, **tenor viola**, *viola pomposa*, *viola da spalla*, and *violetta*.

viola alta. (It.) A **viola** design made to be a proportionally exact enlargement of a **violin**, measuring 18.9 inches. The *viola alta* was conceived of by violist Hermann Ritter (1849-1926) in an attempt to create a viola with the same **acoustic** properties as a violin. Richard Wagner used *viola altas* in some of his Bayreuth opera **orchestras**, though the instrument was deemed too large to be practical. Even after Ritter reduced the size slightly and added a fifth **string** tuned to the violin's E, the instrument never caught on. See also **Tertis viola** and **vertical viola**.

viola bastarda.
1. A small bass **viol** of the 16th and 17th centuries.
2. A virtuosic style of composition for viol that is highly ornamented and improvisatory in effect, involving dramatic changes of register.

viola d'amore. (It.) A bowed **string instrument** popular in Europe during the Baroque and Classical eras. The *viola d'amore* has the shape of a **viol**, with sloping shoulders and a flat back. Unlike a viol, the *viola d'amore* is unfretted and played horizontally on the shoulder like a **violin** or **viola**. The instrument is often characterized by "flaming sword" **sound holes** and an elongated **pegbox** ending in a blindfolded cupid **scroll**.

The *viola d'amore* has two sets of **strings**: seven playing strings that lie over the **bridge** and seven **sympathetic strings** that pass through the bridge and

Figure 155. A *viola d'amore*.

under the **fingerboard**. While the instrument historically used variable tunings, the modern **tuning** for the *viola d'amore* is A2 – D3 – A3 – D4 – F#4 – A4 – D5 with the sympathetic strings tuned identically to the playing strings. Notation for *viola d'amore* music is often written *scordatura*, allowing for greater ease of reading by a violinist.

viola da braccio. (It.) A term for any member of the **violin family**, used in the 16th and 17th centuries to distinguish it from a *viola da gamba*, or member of the **viol family**. The name is derived from how the instruments are held: *da braccio* meaning "on the arm" and *da gamba* meaning "on the leg." See also **violin family**.

viola da gamba. (It.) A term for any member of the **viol family**, used in the 16th and 17th centuries to distinguish it from a *viola da braccio*, or member of the **violin family**. The name is derived from how the instruments are held: *da braccio* meaning "on the arm" and *da gamba* meaning "on the leg." See also **viol family**.

viola da spalla. (It.) A bowed **string instrument** from the 18th century similar to a small **cello** but held horizontally across the chest using a shoulder strap. The *viola da spalla*, also called the *violoncello da spalla*, uses standard cello **tuning** of C2 – G2 – D3 – A3 and plays the bass line in an **ensemble**.

viola di fagotto. (It.) A bowed **string instrument** with the tuning and range of a **cello**, but played horizontally like a **viola**. The *viola di fagotto* uses **strings** wound with copper that **buzz** against the **fingerboard**, creating a bassoon-like **timbre**. The *viola di fagotto* is also called *Fagottgeige* (Ger.).

viola pomposa. (It.) A type of **viola** with five **strings** used during the 18th century. The *viola pomposa* is tuned either as a standard viola with the **violin's** E string on top: C3 – G3 – D4 – A4 – E5; or possibly D3 – G3 – D4 – G4 – C5. The *viola pomposa* is larger than the standard viola but smaller than a **cello**. It is held with the aid of a strap and played horizontally across the chest. Musicologists believe it is possible that some or all of **J. S. Bach's suites** for **solo** cello were written for this instrument. See also **cello**, *viola da spalla*, and *violoncello piccolo*.

violalin. A five-string hybrid between a **violin** and a **viola**, tuned C3 – G3 – D4 – A4 – E5.

Violano Virtuoso. A mechanical player **violin** designed by Henry Sandell in 1905. The Violano Virtuoso is a real violin with metal pins acting as fingers suspended over each note and a rosined roll spinning against the **strings** to replicate the **bow**. The machine is operated by perforated rolls of paper. Originally the Violano Virtuoso was only an electric self-playing violin in a cabinet, though eventually it was modified to include a player piano for accompaniment. See also **violina**.

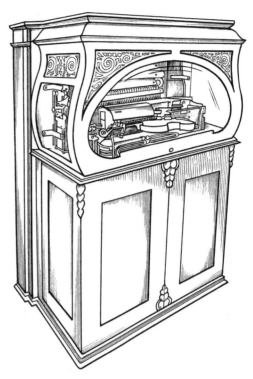

Figure 156. The **Violano Virtuoso** with a player piano.

violectra. An electric **violin** designed by Barcus-Berry with a **tuning** of G2 – D3 – A3 – E4, one octave lower than **standard tuning**. The violectra is one of the instruments used by **Jean-Luc Ponty** to forge a place for the violin in modern **jazz** and rock.

violetta.
1. A term used variously to mean any **string instrument** from **violin**, to **viola**, **cello**, or even **viol**.
2. A type of viola that is tuned G2 – D3 – A3 – E4 one octave lower than the standard violin. One of many attempts to fix the **acoustic** challenges of the viola, the *violetta* was designed by German violinist, mathematician, and physicist Dr. Alfred Stelzner (1852-1906). **Luthiers** Richard Wiedemann and Augustus Paulus made the instrument based on Stelzner's ideas of elliptical curves and elongated **sound holes**. Stelzner's *violetta* garnered some attention from great violinists, but ultimately it never caught on. See also *cellone*.

violetta marina. (It.) A bowed **string instrument** used by Handel about which little is known, other than it had **sympathetic strings** and was compared to the *viola d'amore*.

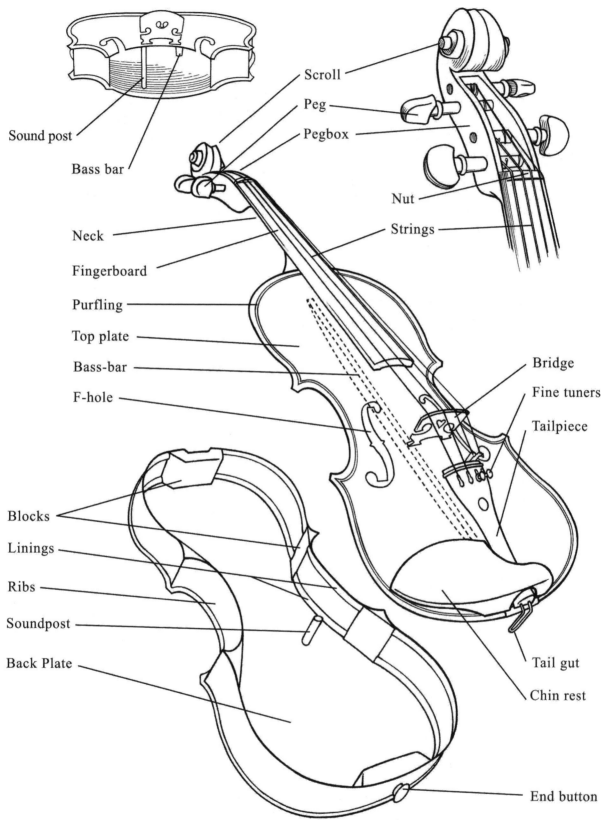

Sound post

Bass bar

Scroll

Peg

Pegbox

Nut

Neck

Strings

Fingerboard

Purfling

Top plate

Bass-bar

F-hole

Bridge

Fine tuners

Tailpiece

Blocks

Linings

Ribs

Soundpost

Back Plate

Tail gut

Chin rest

End button

Figure 157. The **violin**.

violetta piccola. (It.) A term for the **violin**.

violin. The smallest, highest-pitched instrument in the **modern string family**, which also includes the **viola**, **cello**, and **double bass**.

The violin is held horizontally on the left shoulder, balanced beneath the jawbone, and is played with a horsehair bow. The four **strings** of the violin are standardly tuned G3 – D4 – A4 – E5.

The violin was developed along with the viola and cello in the early 16th century, emerging from the *viola da braccio*, or "arm viol." The oldest surviving violin is the "Charles XI" **Amati**, made in 1560.

The violin has traditionally been a **solo** instrument and the dominant melodic member of string **chamber music ensembles** and **orchestras**. Two violins form the high voices of the **string quartet**; the violinist is a member of the **piano trio**; and the modern orchestra includes ten to twenty-eight violinists in two **sections**. The violin, often called a **fiddle**, is a lead instrument in many **genres** of music, including **art music, bluegrass**, Indian classical, Celtic, zydeco, country, folk, and **gypsy jazz**.

The violin is constructed of a top and back **plate**, each hand carved into a convex arch to support the weight from the **bridge**. The **ribs** form the sides of the instrument, made from six thin strips of **maple** that have been bent using heat and water to match the shape of the plates. The ribs and plates are held together with **hide glue** and reinforced at the joints by **linings** and **blocks**. Inside the body, the **soundpost** and **bass-bar** sit beneath the bridge, supporting the structure of the instrument against the tension of the strings and helping to transfer **sound wave** vibrations across the surfaces of the plates. **F-holes** cut into the top plate are shaped to maximize the **acoustic resonance** of the **sounding chamber**. The **fingerboard**, usually made of **ebony** for its smooth texture, is glued to a **neck** of maple, which is carved in a single piece from the **heel** to the **scroll**. The four strings are stretched taut between a **tailpiece** tied to the **end button** on the lower **bouts**, and the **pegs** wedged into holes in the **pegbox** on the instrument's **head**. The strings pass over a thin bridge, carved from a wedge of maple, which transfers the vibrations of the string to the **resonance chamber** of the body. The strings are held slightly above the surface of the fingerboard by the raised ebony **nut** at the top of the fingerboard. A **chin rest** is usually clamped to the lower bout to aid the player in holding the violin without damping the sound.

violin family. Bowed **string instruments** of a design developed in Italy in the 16th century. The violin family includes the **modern string family** of **violin**, **viola**, **cello**, and **double bass** and encompasses violin ancestors such as the *vielle*, *rebec*, and *viola da braccio* as well as **baroque instruments** and variants including the **Hardanger fiddle**, *basse de violon*, and *violino piccolo*. See also **modern string family** and **viol family**.

violin zither. See **bowed psaltery**.

violina. An automated mechanical **violin** and piano combination designed by Ludwig Hupfeld around 1911. The violina has three real violins, each with a row of mechanical fingers positioned above each note along the stings. The violins are played by a circular, rotating **horsehair bow**, and can be controlled for volume and **vibrato** by the use of suction created by bellows. The violins and the attached player piano are operated by a perforated paper roll. The violina is also called the Hupfeld Phonoliszt Violina. See also **Violano Virtuoso**.

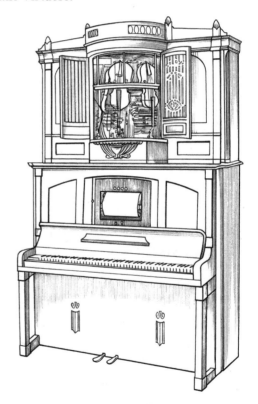

Figure 158. An automated **violina** player piano with three **violins**.

violino piccolo. (It.) A small **violin** tuned a third, fourth, or fifth higher than the standard violin, that was used from the 16th century through the mid-18th century to play parts written in high registers. With the development of **shifting** technique, the need for a *violino piccolo* diminished, and the instrument is now mostly obsolete. Recently the *violino piccolo* has enjoyed a revival through the **historically informed**

performance movement, particularly in performances of **J. S. Bach's** first Brandenburg concerto BWV 1046.

violino principale. (It.) Principal **violin**, usually indicating a **solo** violin **part** in an **orchestra** work.

violinophone. See **stroh viol**.

Violoncellguitarre. (Ger.) See **arpeggione**.

violoncello. The formal name for a cello. See **cello**.

violoncello da spalla. (It.) See *viola da spalla*.

violoncello piccolo. (It.) A small **cello** from the Baroque era used to play in high registers. Although **J. S. Bach** wrote cantatas with an *obbligato* part labeled *violoncello piccolo*, and his sixth **suite** for **solo** cello indicates an instrument with five **strings**, there is no documentation establishing exactly how the instrument was constructed or played. It has been argued that the *violoncello piccolo* mentioned by Bach was actually a *viola pomposa*, a small cello held horizontally across the chest. Modern **luthiers** have been making *violoncello piccolo* instruments at the request of baroque cellists. These cellos are roughly 7/8 **size** and include a fifth upper string with the tuning C2 – G2 – D3 – A3 – E4. See also **cello**, *viola da spalla*, and *viola pomposa*.

violoncino. (It.) **Cello** or small **bass violin**.

violone. (It.) In modern terms, a contrabass **viol**. Historically the term has been used variously to mean any member of the **viol family**, or any low **string instrument**, including bass viol, **cello**, or **double bass**.

violone basso. (It.) **Cello**.

violone da brazzo. (It.) **Cello**.

Viotti bowing. See *saccadé*.

Viotti, Giovanni Battista (1755-1824). Italian violinist, composer, and founder of the **French school of violin playing**. Recognized as a young talent, Viotti studied with Pugnani in Turin and gave a highly successful **solo** debut at a 1782 Concert Spirituel in Paris. In spite of a career as a top violinist, Viotti stopped concertizing in 1791 to become administrator of a new opera house, a post he had to abandon a year later when he fled to London to escape the revolution. Although Viotti continued to perform for a few years, he eventually retired from the concert stage entirely in 1798.

Viotti performed in public for less than ten years, yet he left a legacy so influential that he is considered a great luminary and stands as the central figure of the **violin** family tree, the root from whom all great performers since can trace their heritage. Like many violinist composers, Viott's works are dominated by his instrument. He wrote twenty-nine violin **concertos**, of which only a few remain in the **repertoire**, used primarily as student pieces.

virtuoso. A performer of extraordinary technical skill.

Vivaldi, Antonio (1678-1741). Italian violinist and composer who is one of the founding fathers of the **violin** as a **virtuoso** instrument. As master of violin at the Ospedale della Pietà in Venice, Vivaldi taught music to and composed for orphaned girls, who performed critically acclaimed concerts from behind a screen to raise money for the orphanage. Vivaldi composed over five hundred **concertos** to feature the musicians in the Ospedale della Pietà, including works for **solo** violin, two violins, four violins, **cello**, *viola d'amore*, **lute**, **mandolin**, and wind instruments. The most famous of these are the *Four Seasons* violin concertos, op. 8, which remain today the most performed and recorded works from the Baroque era. As a virtuoso on the violin, Vivaldi commanded a brilliant **technique** and was known for his flashy **improvisations**. His teaching legacy is at the root of the violinist family tree, and all great masters of the instrument can trace their **pedagogical** lineage back to Vivaldi in some way.

voice leading. Techniques in the performance of **polyphonic** music which guide the listener's ear along the melodic line. Voice leading may include balancing a two-voice part with more **bow** weight on the melodic line, giving a distinct **tone color** to the important voice, or tapering a **chord** in such a way that only the melodic voice remains at the end.

volti subito. (It.) Turn the page immediately, often abbreviated V.S.

volute. The flared curl of an instrument's **scroll**.

Vorschlag. (Ger.) See *appoggiatura*.

Vuillaume, Jean-Baptiste (1798-1875). French **luthier** whose **violin** shop dominated Europe trade and who was admired for his mastery of techniques of the old Italian school. The son of a family of luthiers, Vuillaume trained with his father then worked with François Chanot in Paris. In 1823 Vuillaume began to sign his own instruments, and in 1827 he opened his own workshop.

In the 1830s, noticing the higher value placed on old Italian instruments over new ones, Vuillaume began making imitations of instruments by **Stradivari**, Nicolò **Amati**, and **Maggini**, including several copies of **Paganini's Guarneri** "del Gesù" violin. This endeavor met with great success, making Vuillaume the pioneer of fine-instrument imitation, a skill at which he remains practically unrivaled. By closely examining so many master instruments for his copies, Vuillaume was able to incorporate many of their finest features into his own instruments.

Vuillaume created many innovations for **string instruments**, including the enormous three-string **octobass**, the large **contralto viola**, a hollow steel **bow**, and a bow that any player could easily **rehair**. By the end of his career, Vuillaume had produced around three thousand instruments and built the most successful luthier shop of the 19th century, one that trained an entire generation of fine instrument and bow makers.

vuota. (It.) Open, used in the phrases *corda vuota*, meaning to play an **open string**, and *misura vuota*, meaning an empty bar or G.P.

~ W ~

walking bass. A **double bass** part of regular notes moving along a **scale** to fill in between the roots of **chords**. The walking bass is most commonly found in baroque music and **jazz**.

Larghetto

Figure 159. A **walking bass** line from Handel's *Messiah* Part I, scene 12, "The people that walked in darkness have seen a great light," **continuo** part, mm 1-2.

walkup. See **bass walkup**.

walnut oil. Oil extracted from walnuts used as one of the principal ingredients in **string instrument varnish**.

warm-up. Exercises designed to loosen the joints, promote blood circulation in the muscles, focus the mind, and generally prepare for playing.

waveform. The visual representation of sound. A waveform is a series of curves mapped on a graph with changes in sound amplitude on the vertical axis and time on the horizontal axis. The number of waveforms is determined by vibrations per second. Each instrument produces a distinctive waveform shape and size. Most audio recording programs display waveforms to provide visual information about the sound that has been recorded.

Violin:

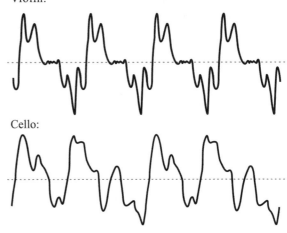

Cello:

Figure 160. The **waveforms** created by a **violin** and a **cello**.

waves. See **sound waves**.

wedge. The small piece of wood, usually **maple**, used to secure the **horsehair** into the **frog** and **tip** of the **bow**.

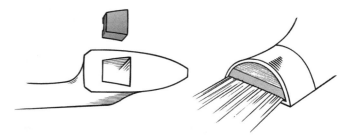

Figure 161. The **wedges** used to secure the **horsehair** into the **tip** and **frog** of the **bow**.

weg. (Ger.) Away, off, found in the phrase *Dämpfer weg*, directing the players to take off the **mutes**.

weich. (Ger.) Weak, soft, delicate. *Weich* is used to designate a **light gauge string** or may be found as an expressive indication in music.

weight. The degree to which the natural heaviness of the body is directed into the instrument. Weight is the force exerted from below, created by gravity, as opposed to **pressure**, which is force exerted from above, created by muscle effort. For **string instruments**, weight is most often used referring to the **bow**, indicating the degree of arm weight that is transferred through the **stick** of the bow onto the **string**, using the **lever** of the **bow hold**. Whether a musician should use pressure, weight, or a combination of the two is one of the fundamental components in different schools of **bow hold**. Weight can also be used to help the fingers of the left hand **stop** the strings against the **fingerboard**, helping keep the hand relaxed to facilitate **shifting**, **vibrato**, **intonation**, and speed of fingering. See also **bow hold**, **German bow hold**, **French bow hold**, **Franco-Belgian bow hold**, **Russian bow hold**, **tension**, and **lever**.

whipped bow. See *fouetté*.

whistle, whistle tone, whistling E. The high pitched, piercing sound occasionally produced by the **open string** E on a **violin**, caused when the string vibrates in a twisting motion rather than a sideways motion. A whistling E can be unpredictable and difficult to fix, making it one of the most infuriating problems to plague violin players. Many factors can contribute to the creation of the whistle tone. A string that has aged and tarnished, or has too much **rosin** buildup is much more likely to whistle, so putting on a fresh string may solve the problem. The instrument **set-up** may be faulty, with a **nut** that is too low, a **tailpiece** that is incorrectly placed, a poorly fitted **soundpost**, or a mismatched **bridge** contributing to the whistle. Taking the violin to a **luthier** for an **adjustment** will take care of any of these issues. Playing **technique** is the other common cause of a whistling string. Beginning the open string note with a poor choice of **contact point**, **bow tilt**, **bow angle**, or **pressure** can cause the string to whistle. In addition, the slightest touch of the E string by a finger or even the side of the hand will interrupt the normal vibration pattern of the string. There is a string made by Kaplan called a non-whistling E, designed to reduce the occurrence of the whistle tone by including a damping **winding**, though at the cost of beauty of **tone**.

whole consort. A consort made entirely of instruments from the same family. See **consort**. See **historically informed performance** and **viol family**.

whole shift. An archaic term indicating a **shift** the distance of a third.

whole-step.
1. The distance of a major second between two notes.
2. The standard spacing between consecutive fingers. For the violin, viola, and cello, the whole-step is an important element of **finger patterns** and **fingerboard mapping**. The whole-step measurement can be linear, as between two notes of a **scale** a whole tone apart, or cross-string with the distance of a major sixth or perfect fourth being created by the same spacing of consecutive fingers. Double bass is the exception, not only because it is usually tuned in fourths, but also because the **fingerboard** spacing is so large that whole-steps are usually played with nonconsecutive fingers. See **finger pattern** for illustrations.

Wieniawski, Henryk (1835-1880). Polish violinist and composer who developed the **Russian bow hold**. The son of a professional pianist, Wieniawski was eight when he entered the Paris Conservatoire to study with Massart and at age eleven won the *premiere prix* in the **violin**. Wieniawski began his career as a traveling **virtuoso** when he has thirteen, playing with his pianist brother.

After extensive touring throughout Europe, Wieniawski became violin soloist to the tsar in St. Petersburg, where he led both the **orchestra** and the **string quartet** of the Russian Musical Society, and served as professor at the newly formed **conservatory**, where he had great influence on the formation of the **Russian school of violin playing**.

In 1872 he embarked on a tour of the United States with pianist Anton Rubenstein, giving 215 performances in 239 days performing a program that included Beethoven's "**Kreutzer**" sonata. Exhausted by relentless concertizing, Wieniawski accepted the offer in 1875 to replace **Vieuxtemps** as professor of the violin at the Brussels Conservatory.

As a composer, Wieniawski applied the technical virtuosity of Paganini with Romantic notions of expressivity. Like the other violinist-composers of his era, Wieniawski wrote primarily violin works for his own performance. His Polish nationalism is evident in his mazurkas and polonaises, and several of his works, in particular the elegant and flashy Second **Concerto**, op. 22, have joined the standard repertoire.

A violinist held in the very highest regard, Wieniawski was known for his richly expressive interpretations and intense **vibrato**. His unconventional style of bowing with a relatively high elbow that leaned heavily onto his index finger offered a particularly powerful **bow technique**. As a result of his years teaching at the St. Petersburg Conservatory and his broad influence in Russia, Wieniawski's bow hold was adopted by the Russian school of violin playing and is now known as the Russian bow hold.

winding.

1. A protective covering around the **stick** of the **bow** near the **frog**. The winding, which is used to prevent wear and tear from the fingers on the stick, is traditionally whalebone **lapping**, though modern bows more often use plastic or metal threads instead. At the base of the winding is the **grip**, a piece of leather glued around the stick to cushion and protect the contact point between the thumb and frog. The replacing of a worn winding and grip is part of regular bow maintenance.

2. An encasing outer layer on **strings**, used to protect and strengthen the core. **Steel strings** usually have a winding of another metal such as aluminum, silver, nickel, tungsten, or titanium. **Synthetic strings** are wound in metal such as aluminum, chrome, silver, or gold. **Gut strings** most often have a winding of aluminum or silver. String players who experience corrosion of their strings due to the moisture and acidity of their skin should use strings with windings of silver or gold.

wolf, wolf note, wolf tone. A rough, choking sound produced when the **pitch** being played matches the natural resonating **frequency** of the instrument's body, creating an artificial **overtone** that **beats** against the original pitch. Wolf tones are present on every **string instrument** and occur most often on the lowest, heaviest **string**. There are many approaches to fixing a wolf tone. A player may be able to temporarily avoid the wolf while playing by using a particularly wide **vibrato**, pulling the string slightly to the side when stopping that note, or (for cellists) squeezing the lower **bouts** with the knees. Repositioning or refitting the **soundpost**, recarving or replacing the **bridge**, or changing the position of the **tailpiece** may minimize or move the wolf. A good instrument **adjustment** by a **luthier** will address all of these potential solutions. Finally, the use of a **wolf eliminator** device attached to the instrument can be effective in countering the wolf tone. See **wolf eliminator, wolf resonator**, and **wolf suppressor**.

wolf eliminator. A device designed to counteract the **wolf tone acoustic** phenomenon. There are two types of wolf eliminators: a wolf suppressor and a wolf resonator. The wolf suppressor clamps onto the **afterlength** of the string, with its placement adjusted in relation to the **bridge** to fit the exact spot to best cancel the **frequency** of the wolf tone. The wolf resonator is a spring-mounted metal weight that vibrates sympathetically at the specific **pitch** of the instrument's wolf tone, canceling the wolf tone. It sits di-

rectly on the top **plate** or inside of the instrument's table, held in place by putty. Both types of wolf eliminator are made in a variety of weights and sizes.

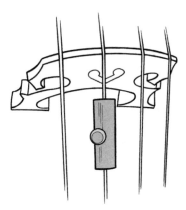

Figure 162. A **wolf eliminator** attached to the **afterlength** of a **string**.

wolf resonator. A type of **wolf eliminator** that is a spring-mounted metal weight that vibrates sympathetically at the specific **pitch** of the instrument's **wolf tone**, canceling the wolf tone. It sits directly on the top **plate** or inside of the instrument's table, is held in place by putty, and is made in a variety of weights and sizes.

wolf suppressor. A type of **wolf eliminator** that clamps onto the **afterlength** of the **string**, with its placement adjusted in relation to the **bridge** to fit the exact spot to best cancel the **frequency** of the **wolf tone**. Wolf eliminators are made in a variety of weights and sizes.

worm gear. The most common design for **mechanical pegs**, particularly those used on the **double bass**. The **string** is tightened or loosened by turning the knob end of the worm, or screw-shaped gear, which rotates the gear end of the capstan around which the string is

Figure 163. The **worm gear** mechanism of a **mechanical tuner**.

wound. The design of a worm gear reduces the rotational speed of the gear, allowing for precise tuning. A worm gear is also called worm drive, worm wheel, or machine head.

wound string. A **string** encased in a layer of metal. See **winding**.

wrist shake. See **hand vibrato**.

wrist vibrato. See **hand vibrato**.

~ X ~

xänorphika. A bowed keyboard instrument.

~ Y ~

Ysaÿe, Eugène (1858-1931). Belgian violinist, conductor, and composer who was central to the modernization of **violin** playing into the 20th century.

Ysaÿe began violin lessons at age five with his father, eventually studying with **Wieniawski** in Brussels and **Vieuxtemps** in Paris. By 1882, with help from Anton Rubenstein, Ysaÿe began touring Europe as a soloist and working with the leading composers in France. Called "The King of Violin," Ysaÿe garnered international fame and enjoyed a long career performing across Europe and in America.

Ysaÿe dedicated himself to the cultivation and promotion of modern music, inspiring many new works to be written for him including Chausson's *Poème*, **Kreisler's** *Recitativo and Scherzo*, Saint-Saëns' first **string quartet**, Fauré's second violin **sonata** and piano **quintet**, and Debussy's string quartet. Frank wrote his famous violin sonata for Ysaÿe, presenting it to him as a wedding gift.

As a conductor, Ysaÿe found further outlets for championing modern composers. He founded the Concerts Ysaÿe, where he conducted a large **orchestra** in concerts mainly of modern music, and he spent four years as music director of the Cincinnati Orchestra.

Unlike many virtuoso-composers, Ysaÿe rarely performed his own works. Of his many compositions, those that stand firmly in the standard **repertoire** are

his Six Sonatas for **Solo** Violin, op. 27, which represent the pinnacle of violin technique, and his Sonata for Solo Cello, op. 28.

A legend during his lifetime, Ysaÿe was revered for combining flawless **technique** with a powerhouse sound and tremendous expressive freedom. In Ysaÿe, virtuosity was not just a gratuitous show of skill, but rather a means to create more profound, deeply moving music. This new, modern way of playing was the basis of his work as a professor at the Brussels Conservatoire, where he refined the **Franco-Belgian school of violin playing** and produced a generation of exceptional musicians including Gingold, Brodsky, and **Primrose**.

~ Z ~

zarabanda. (Sp.) See *sarabande*.

złóbcoki. (Pol.) A small **fiddle** from Poland, similar to a *pochette*.

About Table 1: Bowstrokes

The numerous terms and techniques for the myriad variety of string instrument bowstrokes is probably the most complex and difficult-to-explain aspect of string playing. Terms naming individual bowstrokes are most often in French and have generally agreed-upon meanings, though specific definitions and the technique of exactly how to achieve each stroke varies depending on bow hold, era, and the legacy of teaching lineage. The issue of bowstrokes is further complicated by the fact that while the Western notation system has symbols for articulations and bowings, there are no symbols to represent bowstrokes. In modern conventions, bowstrokes are an artistic choice of the individual player, reached by interpreting a combination of bowing and articulation marks in the context of style, era, and genre. It is important to understand that this table makes no attempt to definitively codify bowstroke notation, but rather offers merely the notation most commonly interpreted as a particular bowstroke. Many bowstrokes share identical notations and some have no notation at all. Anyone truly wanting to understand or communicate a particular bowstroke should consult directly with an expert string player.

Table 1: Bowstrokes

general bowing terms		
term	notation	description
down-bow *Abstrich* (Ger.) *arcata in giù* (It.) *tire* (Fr.)	⊓	A **bowstroke** that is pulled away from the **frog** and towards the **tip**.
up-bow *Aufstrich* (Ger.) *arcata in su* (It.) *poussé* (Fr.)	V	A **bowstroke** that is pushed away from the **tip** and towards the **frog**.
slur *Bindung* (Ger.) *chapeau* (Fr.) *legatura* (It.)		A *legato* connection between notes. String players execute slurs by playing all the notes under the slur line in one stroke of the bow.
free bowing		Play without preset bowings. The term is used most often in orchestral settings to indicate that the standard **conventions** of unified bowings do not apply. Instead, each performer is to choose bowings independently, often as they are felt in the moment.
on the string *à la corda* (Fr.) *alla corda* (It.)		Any **bowstroke** that is executed with the bow **hair** remaining in contact with the **string**.
off the string *saltando* (It.) *springender Bogen* (Ger.)		Any **bowstroke** in which the **bow** bounces so that the **hair** loses contact with the **string**. Off the string strokes may be **thrown** from above the string or initiated from the string.
from the string		Any **bowstroke** begun with the **horsehair** in full contact with the **string**, usually used to control the start of an **off the string** passage.
thrown stroke *gettato* (It.)		Any **bowstroke** that is begun by throwing the **bow** at the **string** from above. Thrown strokes include *battuto*, **drum stroke**, *jeté*, and *ricochet*.

off the string bowstrokes		
term	notation	description
battuto (It.)		An entirely vertical, **thrown** stroke in which the **string** is beaten with the **bow**. *Col legno battuto* beats the string with the wood of the **stick**.
brush stroke on-ish off-ish		A gentle *spiccato* **bowstroke** in which the **bow** approaches the string with long, horizontal movements, creating a softer **articulation** than regular *spiccato*. The brush stroke may be an interpretation of **dots**, lines, the combination of lines and dots, or may simply be stylistically understood.
drum stroke feather bowing		A **thrown**, *ricochet* **bowstroke** with two rapidly bounced notes per **bow** on alternating bows. The drum stroke is notated by the combination of **slurs** and **dots** over consecutive pairs of notes.
jeté (Fr.) *picchettato* (It.)		An **off the string bowstroke** in which the **bow** is **thrown** onto the **string**, bounces several times in the same direction, then is lifted off again. *Jeté* is slower and more controlled than *ricochet* or **flying** *spiccato*.
piqué (Fr.) *pikieren* (Ger.)		A small, biting **bowstroke** with a quick release that may leave the **string**. *Piqué* is the basic stroke used in the **shoe shine** bowing.
ricochet (Fr.)		A **thrown bowstroke** in which the **stick** rebounds several times in the same direction. *Ricochet* is notated by a combination of **dots** and **slurs** over the notes.
shoe-shine		A **bowstroke** used for dotted rhythms with the long note played **up-bow** and the short note played **down-bow**, all near the **frog**. The feel of the stroke is similar to that of shining a shoe.
spiccato (It.)		An **off the string bowstroke** with a controlled bounce. *Spiccato* can be indicated by **dots** over the note-heads, the word *saltando*, or may simply be understood as appropriate to the style of the piece.
standing *spiccato*		A bouncing **bowstroke** in which the **bow** repeatedly hits the **string** in exactly the same place along the **hair**.
flying *spiccato*		A **thrown**, **off the string bowstroke** in which many notes are bounced with the bow moving in the same direction. Flying *spiccato* is notated by the combination of a **slur** and **dots** over the notes.
flying *staccato* *staccato à ricochet* (Fr.) *staccato volante* (It.)		A **bowstroke** with a stopped **articulation** between notes bowed in the same direction with the **bow** springing away from the **string** slightly between notes. Flying *staccato* is initiated **from the string**, resulting in much less bounce than the thrown **flying** *spiccato* bowstroke.

on the string bowstrokes		
term	notation	description
collé (Fr.)		A **bow** technique executed entirely with the fingers. *Collé* can be used in a **legato** stroke to smooth the moment of a change in direction, or it can be used to create a biting *staccato* stroke near the **frog** in which the bow pinches the **string**, then is picked off by pulling the fingers sharply into the hand.
detaché (Fr.) saw stroke (fiddle)		The basic one-note-per-bow separated **bowstroke**. In general, all notes written with no **articulation** markings or **slurs** are considered *détaché*.
detaché lance (Fr.)		Sharply accented, **legato** *détaché*.
detaché porté (Fr.)		*Détaché* in which the beginning of each note is leaned on for emphasis.
flautando (It.)		A light, fast **bowstroke**, creating a translucent, flute-like **tone**.
fouetté (Fr.) slap stroke		A whipped **bowstroke** executed by slapping the **bow** onto the **string** at the **tip**, creating a biting **accent**. In *fouetté* the bow does not bounce, but remains in firm contact with the string.
hooked bow		Two notes played on the same **bow** with a stop between them. Hooked bows are used to manage **bow distribution**, especially in rhythms with uneven note values.
louré (Fr.) *portato* (It.)		A slightly detached, pulsing **bowstroke**, notated by the combination of **slurs** and dashes.
martelé (Fr.) *gehämmert* (Ger.) hammered *martellato* (It.)		A vigorous, detached **bowstroke** created by a heavy, biting start released into a fast, floated **bow** which reaches a complete stop before beginning the next stroke. *Martelé* is notated by wedges or **accents** above the notes.
perlé (Fr.)		A series of articulated notes in a single **bow**, notated by the combination of a **slur** and **dots** over the notes. *Perlé* is generally more delicate than the closely related **slurred staccato** stroke.

on the string bowstrokes		
term	notation	description
saccade (Fr.) Viotti bowing		A jerked **bowstroke** that **accents** the second, third, or fourth note under a **slur**. *Saccadé is* notated with *sf* under the accented note.
sautillé (Fr.)		A rapid, bouncing **bowstroke**. Although generally considered an **off the string** stroke, in a great *sautillé* the **stick** bounces but the **hair** does not actually leave the **string**. *Sautillé* can be indicated by **dots**, by the word **saltando**, or may simply be understood as appropriate to the style of the piece.
staccato (It.) *abstossen* (Ger.) *brisé* (Fr.)		A detached, **on the string bowstroke** with clearly articulated notes. *Staccato* is usually notated with **dots** over the note-heads and can be played either on separate **bows** or **hooked** into the same bow with a clean stop after each note.
slurred *staccato* firm *staccato* up-bow *staccato*		A series of short notes connected in the same **bow** with a stop between each, notated by the combination of a **slur** and **dots** over the notes. Slurred *staccato* is an **on the string** bowstroke that is easiest to execute on an **up-bow**, especially when played at a fast tempo.
tremolo (It.) *balancement* (Fr.) *bebend* (Ger.)		A rapid, trembling **bowstroke**. *Tremolo* is played with tiny, unmeasured **bows**, and is notated by three slashes through the stem of the note.
slurred *tremolo* fingered *tremolo*		A trembling effect between two notes. Slurred *tremolo*, also called fingered *tremolo*, is notated by three bars drawn between two slurred notes, or by a combination of open note-heads with three bars.

Further Reading

General

Berman, Joel, Barbara G. Jackson, and Kenneth Sarch. *Dictionary of Bowing and Pizzicato Terms* (Bloomington: ASTA Publications, 2010).

Bruser, Madeline. *The Art of Practicing: A Guide to Making Music from the Heart* (New York: Three Rivers Press, 1999).

Cremer, Lothar. *Physics of the Violin* (Cambridge: MIT Press, 1984).

Dubal, David. *The Essential Canon of Classical Music* (New York: North Point Press, 2001).

Fuld, James. *The Book of World-Famous Music: Classical, Popular, and Folk* (New York: Dover Publications, 2000).

Green, Barry. *The Inner Game of Music* (Garden City, NJ: Doubleday, 1986).

James, Jan. *Practical Acoustics of Instruments of the Violin Family: Bridging Science and Art* (Aumsville, OR: Strobel, 2002).

Klickstein, Gerald. *The Musician's Way: A Guide to Practice, Performance, and Wellness* (Oxford: Oxford University Press, 2009).

Latham, Alison, ed. *The Oxford Companion to Music* (Oxford: Oxford University Press, 2002).

Rossing, Thomas D. *The Science of String Instruments* (New York: Springer Press, 2010).

Sadie, Stanley, ed. *The Violin Family* (London: Macmillan Press, 1980).

Sadie, Stanley, and John Tyrrell, eds. *The New Grove Dictionary of Music and Musicians* (Oxford: Oxford University Press, 2004) and online at www.oxfordmusiconline.com.

Violin

Beament, James. *The Violin Explained: Components, Mechanism, and Sound* (Oxford: Oxford University Press, 2001).

Boyden, David. *The History of Violin Playing from Its Origins to 1761 and Its Relationship to the Violin and Violin Music* (London: Oxford University Press, 1965).

Farga, Franz. *Violins and Violinists* (London: Camelot Press, 1940).

Katz, Mark. *The Violin: A Research and Information Guide* (New York: Routledge, 2006).

Kolneder, Walter. *The Amadeus Book of the Violin* (Portland: Amadeus Press, 1972).

Martens, Frederick H., ed. *Violin Mastery: Interviews with Heifetz, Auer, Kreisler, and Others* (Mineola: Dover, 2006).

Menuhin, Yehudi, and William Primrose. *Violin & Viola* (London: Macdonald and Jane's, 1976).

Menuhin, Yehudi. *The Violin: An Illustrated History* (Paris: Flammarion, 2009).

Nelson, Shiela M. *The Violin and Viola: History, Structure, Techniques* (Mineola: Dover Publications, 1972).

Sandys, William, and Simon Andrew Foster. *History of the Violin* (Mineola: Dover, 2006).

Schoenbaum, David. *The Violin: A Social History of the World's Most Versatile Instrument* (New York: Norton, 2012).

Silvela, Zdenko. *A New History of Violin Playing* (Universal Publishers, 2001).

Stowell, Robin, ed. *The Cambridge Companion to the Violin* (Cambridge: Cambridge University Press, 1992).

Viola

Barrett, Henry. *The Viola: Complete Guide for Teachers and Students* (Tuscaloosa: University of Alabama Press, 1972).

Menuhin, Yehudi, and William Primrose. *Violin & Viola* (London: Macdonald and Jane's, 1976).

Nelson, Shiela M. *The Violin and Viola: History, Structure, Techniques* (Mineola: Dover Publications, 1972).

Reiley, Maurice. *The History of the Viola* (Ann Arbor: Braun-Brumfield, c.1991).

Cello

Cowling, Elizabeth. *The Cello* (New York: Scribner, 1984).

Markevitch, Dimitry. *Cello Story* (Miami: Summy-Birchard, 1984).

Pleeth, William. *Cello* (London: Kahn & Averill, 2001).

Stowell, Robin, ed. *The Cambridge Companion to the Cello* (Cambridge: Cambridge University Press, 1999).

Double Bass

Benfield, Warren, and James Seay Dean. *The Art of Double Bass Playing* (Miami: Summy-Birchard, 1973).

Brun, Paul. *A New History of the Double Bass* (Villeneuve d'Ascq: P. Brun Productions, 2000).

Goldsby, John. *The Jazz Bass Book - Technique and Tradition* (San Francisco: Backbeat Books, 2002).

Mooter, Greg. *The Bass Player's Handbook* (Boston: Berklee Press, 2002).

Turetzky, Bertram. *The Contemporary Contrabass* (Berkeley: University of California Press, 1974).

West, Chris. *A Guide to Double Bass Harmonics* (Amazon Kindle, 2012).

Historically Informed Performance

Boyden, David. *The History of Violin Playing from Its Origins to 1761 and Its Relationship to the Violin and Violin Music* (London: Oxford University Press, 1965).

Brown, Clive. *Classical and Romantic Performing Practice 1750-1900* (Oxford: Oxford University Press, 1999).

Butt, John. *Playing with History: The Historical Approach to Musical Performance* (Cambridge: Cambridge University Press, 2002).

Carter, Stewart, and Jeffret Kite-Powell. *A Performer's Guide to Seventeenth-Century Music, Second Edition* (Bloomington: Indiana University Press, 2012).

Crum, Alison. *Play the Viol: The Complete Guide to Playing the Treble, Tenor, and Bass Viol* (Oxford: Oxford University Press, 1992).

Cyr, Mary. *Style and Performance for Bowed String Instruments in French Baroque Music* (Burlington: Ashgate Publishing, 2012).

Donnington, Robert. *Baroque Music, Style and Performance: A Handbook* (New York: Norton, 1982).

———. *The Interpretation of Early Music, New Revised Edition* (New York: W. W. Norton & Company, 1992).

Kite-Powell, Jeffrey, ed. *A Performer's Guide to Renaissance Music, Second Edition* (Bloomington: Indiana University Press, 2007).

Laird, Paul. *The Baroque Cello Revival: An Oral History* (Lanham: Scarecrow Press, 2004)

Lawson, Colin, and Robin Stowell. *The Historical Performance of Music: An Introduction* (Cambridge: Cambridge Univerity Press, 1999).

Mather, Betty Bang. *Dance Rhythms of the French Baroque: A Handbook for Performance* (Bloomington: Indiana University Press, 1988).

Milsom, David. *Theory and Practice in Late Nineteenth-Century Violin Performance: An Examination of Style in Performance, 1850-1900* (Burlington: Ashgate Publishing, 2003).

Monical, William L. *Shapes of the Baroque: The Historical Development of Bowed String Instruments* (New York: The American Federation of Violin & Bow Makers, 1989).

Musgrave, Michael, and Bernard D. Sherman. *Performing Brahms: Early Evidence of Performance Style* (Cambridge: Cambridge University Press, 2003).

Neumann, Frederick. *Ornamentation in Baroque and Post-Baroque Music, with Special Emphasis on J.S. Bach* (Princeton: Princeton University Press, 1983).

Planyavsky, Alfred. *The Baroque Double Bass Violone* (Lanham: Scarecrow Press, 1998).

Ritchie, Stanley. *Before the Chinrest: A Violinist's Guide to the Mysteries of Pre-Chinrest Technique and Style* (Bloomington: Indiana University Press, 2012).

Schröder, Jaap. *Bach's Solo Violin Works: A Performer's Guide* (New Haven: Yale University Press, 2007).

Stowell, Robin. *The Early Violin and Viola: A Practical Guide* (Cambridge: Cambridge University Press, 2001).

——. *Violin Technique and Performance Practice in the Late Eighteenth and Early Nineteenth Centuries* (Cambridge: Cambridge University Press, 1985).

Vielhan, Jean-Claude. *The Rules of Musical Interpretation in the Baroque Era* (Paris: Alphonse Leduc, 1977).

Wainwright, Jonathan, and Peter Holman. *From Renaissance To Baroque: Change In Instruments And Instrumental Music In The Seveteenth Century* (Burlington: Ashgate, 2005).

Walden, Valerie. *One Hundred Years of Violoncello: A History of Technique and Performance Practice, 1740-1840* (Cambridge: Cambridge University Press, 2004).

Woodfield, Ian. *The Early History of the Viol* (Cambridge: Cambridge University Press, 1988).

Pedagogical Treatises

Alexanian, Diran. *Complete Cello Technique: The Classic Treatise on Cello Theory and Practice*, 1922 (repr. Mineola: Dover, 2003).

Auer, Leopold. *Violin Playing as I Teach It*, 1921 (repr. Mineola: Dover, 1980).

——. *Violin Master Works and Their Interpretation*, 1925 (repr. Mineola: Dover, 2012).

Baillot, Pierre Marie. *The Art of the Violin*, 1835 (repr. Evanston: Northwestern University Press, 1991).

Courvoisier, Karl. *The Technique of Violin Playing: The Joachim Method* (New York: Schirmer, 1897).

Flesch, Carl. *The Art of Violin Playing*, 1923 (repr. New York: Fischer, 2000).

Geminiani, Francesco.*The Art of Playing on the Violin. [Facsimile of 1751 edition]* (London: Oxford University Press, 1951?).

Mantel, Gerhard, and Barbara Haimberger Thiem. *Cello Technique: Principles and Forms of Movement*, 1975 (repr. Bloomington: Indiana University Press, 1995).

Mozart, Leopold. *A Treatise on the Fundamental Principles of Violin Playing*, 1756 (repr. Oxford: Oxford University Press, 1985).

Pettiford, Oscar, and Erik Moseholm. *Jazz Bass Facing*, 1962 (repr. Winona, MN: Music Sales America, 1993).

Primrose, William. *Technique is Memory* (Oxford: Oxford University Press, 1960).

Simandl, Franz. *New Method for the Double Bass Books 1 & 2*, 1904 (repr. New York: Carl Fischer, 1987).

Suzuki, Shinichi. *Nurtured by Love: The Classic Approach to Talent Education*, 1969 (repr. Miami: Warner Brothers Publication, 1983).

——. *Ability Development from Age Zero*, 1981 (repr. Miami: Warner Brothers, 1999).

Zimmermann, Frederick. *Contemporary Concept of Bowing Technique for the Double Bass*, 1956 (repr. Milwaukee: Hal Leonard, 1966).

Biographies and Autobiographies

Agus, Ayke. *Heifetz as I Knew Him* (Portland: Amadeus Press, 2001).

Allsop, Peter. *Arcangelo Corelli: "New Orpheus of Our Times"* (Oxford: Oxford University Press, 1999).

Auer, Leopold. *My Long Life in Music* (London: Duckworth, 1924).

Axelrod, Herbert R., and Leslie Sheppard. *Paganini* (Neptune City: Paganiniana Publications, 1979).

Axelrod, Herbert R., ed. *Heifetz* (Neptune City: Paganiniana Publications, 1976).

Biancolli, Amy. *Fritz Kreisler: Love's Sorrow, Love's Joy* (Portland: Amadeus Press, 1998).

Blum, David. *Casals and the Art of Interpretation* (Berkeley: University of California Press, 1980).

Booth, John. *Vivaldi* (London: Omnibus Press, 1989).

Brown, Clive. *Louis Spohr: A Critical Biography* (New York: Cambridge University Press, 2006).

Burton, Humpfrey. *Menuhin: A Life* (London: Faber and Faber, 2000).

Campbell, Margaret. *The Great Violinists* (London: Anova, 1980).

——. *The Great Cellists* (London: Gollancz, 1988).

Coleman, Janet, and Al Young. *Mingus/Mingus: Two Memoirs* (Berkeley: Creative Arts Book Co., 1989).

Dalton, David. *Playing the Viola: Conversations with William Primrose* (Oxford: Oxford University Press, 1990).

De'ak, Stephen. *David Popper* (Neptune City: Paganiniana Press, 1982).

Duleba, Wladyslaw. *Wieniawski* (Neptune City: Paganiniana Press, 1984).

Easton, Carol. *Jacqueline du Pré: A Biography* (Cambridge: DaCapo Press, 2000).

Eisler, Edith. *21st Century String Quartets* (San Anselmo: String Letter Publishing, 2000).

Ginsburg, Lev. *Vieuxtemps: His Life and Times* (Neptune City: Paganiniana Publications, 1984).

——. *Tartini: His Life and Times* (Neptune City: Paganiniana, 1981).

Grabkowski, Edmund. *Henryk Wieniawski* (Warsaw: Interpress, 1986).

Heller, Karl. *Antonio Vivaldi: The Red Priest of Venice* (Portland: Amadeus Press, 2003).

Hunt, David. *Jazz Bass Artists of the 1950s* (Dearborn Hights, MI: Cranston, 2009).

Jabłoński, Maciej, and Danuta Jasińska, eds. *Henryk Wieniawski: Composer and Virtuoso in the Musical Culture of the XIX and XX Centuries* (Poznań: Rhytmos, 2001).

Kahn, Albert E. *Joys and Sorrows: Reflections by Pablo Casals* (New York: Simon & Schuster, 1970).

Kenneson, Claude. *Musical Prodigies - Perilous Journeys, Remarkable Lives* (Portland: Amadeus Press, 2003).

King, Terry. *Gregor Piatigorsky: The Life and Career of the Virtuoso Cellist* (Jefferson, NC: McFarland, 2010).

Kloss, Sherry. *Jascha Heifetz Through My Eyes* (Muncie, IN: Kloss Classics, 2000).

Landon, H. C. Robbins. *Vivaldi: Voice of the Baroque* (Chicago: University of Chicago Press, 1996).

Liane, Curtis, ed. *A Rebecca Clarke Reader* (Bloomington: Indiana University Press, 2004).

Lister, Warwick. *Amico: The Life of Giovanni Battista Viotti* (Oxford: Oxford University Press, 2009).

Lynn, Stacey, ed. *21st Century Cellists* (San Anselmo, CA: String Letter Press, 2001).

Macleod, Joseph. *The Sisters d'Aranyi* (London: Wilmer Brothers, 1969).

Menuhin, Yehudi. *Unfinished Journey* (New York: Knopf, 1976).

——. *The Compleat Violinist: Thoughts, Exercises, Reflections of an Itinerant Violinist* (New York: Summit Books, 1986).

Mingus, Charles. *Charles Mingus - More Than a Fake Book* (New York: Hal Leonard, 1991).

——. *Beneath the Underdog: His World as Composed by Mingus* (New York: Knopf, 1971).

Palmer, Fiona *Domenico Dragonetti in England (1794-1846): The Career of a Double Bass Virtuoso* (London: Oxford University Press, 1997).

Piatigorsky, Gregor. *Cellist* (Cambridge: DaCapo, 1976).

Priestley, Brian. *Mingus: A Critical Biography* (Cambridge: DaCapo, 1984).

Primrose, William. *Walk on the North Side: Memoirs of a Violist* (Provo: Brigham Young University Press, 1978).

Pulver, Jeffrey. *Paganini: The Romantic Virtuoso* (New York: DaCapo Press, 1936).

Roth, Henry. *Violin Virtuosos from Paganini to the 21st Century* (Los Angeles: California Classics, 1997).

Sachs, Harvey. *Virtuoso: The Life and Art of Niccolo Paganini, Franz Liszt, Anton Rubinstein, Ignace Jan Paderewski, Fritz Kreisler, Pablo Casals, Wanda Landowska, Vladimir Horowitz, Glenn Gould* (London: Thames & Hudson, 1982).

Schonberg, Harold. *The Virtuosi: Classical Music's Legendary Performers from Paganini to Pavarotti* (New York: Vintage Books, 1988).

Schueneman, Bruce R. *The French Violin School: Viotti, Rode, Kreutzer, Baillot, and Their Contemporaries* (Kingsville: Lyre of Orpheus Press, 2002).

Schwarz, Boris. *Great Masters of the Violin* (New York: Simon & Schuster, 1983).

Starker, Janos. *The World of Music According to Starker* (Bloomington: Indiana University Press, 2004).

Sugden, John. *Paganini* (London: Omnibus Press, 1980).

Tertis, Lionel. *My Viola and I* (London: Elek, 1974).

Tortelier, Paul. *How I Play, How I Teach* (London: Chester Music, 1993).

VanClay, Mary, and Stacey Linn, eds. *Violin Virtuosos* (San Anselmo: String Letter Publishing, 2000).

VanClay, Mary, ed. *21st Century Violinists, Volume 1* (San Anselmo: String Letter Publishing, 1999).

White, John. *Lionel Tertis: The First Great Virtuoso of the Viola* (Rochester, NY: Boydell, 2006).

Williams, Amédée. *Lillian Fuchs: First Lady of the Viola* (Lewiston: E. Mellen Press, 2004).

Wilson, Elizabeth. *Rostropovich: The Musical Life of the Great Cellist, Teacher, and Legend* (Chicago: Ivan R. Dee, 2007).

———. *Jacqueline du Pré: Her Life, Her Music, Her Legend* (New York: Arcade Publishing, 1999).

Wolff, Christoph. *Johann Sebastian Bach: The Learned Musician* (New York: Norton, 2001).

Ysaÿe, Antoine. *Ysaÿe: His Life, Work and Influence* (London: Heinemann, 1947).

Ergonomics and Healthy Playing

Alcantara, Pedro de. *Indirect Procedures: A Musician's Guide to the Alexander Technique* (Oxford: Oxford University Press, 2007).

Conable, Barbara, and Benjamin Conable. *What Every Musician Needs to Know About the Body: The Application of Body Mapping to Music* (Portland: Andover Press, 2000).

Green, Barry. *The Inner Game of Music* (Garden City, NJ: Doubleday, 1986).

Horvath, Janet. *Playing Less Hurt: An Injury Prevention Guide for Musicians* (Minneapolis, MN: J. Horvath, 2004).

Johnson, Jennifer. *What Every Violinist Needs To Know About the Body* (Chicago: GIA Publications, 2009).

Kempter, Susan. *How Muscles Learn: Teaching Violin With The Body In Mind* (Miami: Warner Brothers, 2003).

Kind, Ethan. *An Alexander Technique Approach to Double Bass Technique* (Amazon Kindle, 2011).

———. *An Alexander Technique Approach to Cello Technique* (Amazon Kindle, 2011).

———. *An Alexander Technique Approach to Viola Technique* (Amazon Kindle, 2011).

———. *An Alexander Technique Approach to Violin Technique* (Amazon Kindle, 2010).

Klickstein, Gerald. *The Musician's Way: A Guide to Practice, Performance, and Wellness* (Oxford: Oxford University Press, 2009).

Llobet, Jaume Rosset I. *The Musician's Body* (Burlington: Ashgate, 2007).

Mackie, Vivian. *Just Play Naturally: An Account of Her Study with Pablo Casals in the 1950s and Her Discovery of the Resonance Between His Teaching and the Principles of the Alexander Technique* (London: Duende Editions, 2002).

Paull, Barbara, and Christine Harrison. *The Athletic Musician: A Guide to Playing Without Pain* (Lanham: Scarecrow Press, 1999).

Watson, Alan H. D. *The Biology of Musical Performance and Performance-Related Injury* (Lanham: Scarecrow Press, 2009).

Orchestral and Ensemble Playing

Baron, John H. *Chamber Music: A Research and Information Guide* (New York: Routledge, 2002).

Berger, Melvin. *Guide to Chamber Music* (Mineola: Dover, 1985).

——. *Guide to Sonatas: Music for One or Two Instruments* (New York: Doubleday, 1991).

Daniels, David. *Orchestral Music: A Handbook* (Lanham: Scarecrow Press, 2005).

Eisler, Edith. *21st Century String Quartets* (San Anselmo: String Letter Publishing, 2000).

Grave, Floyd and Margaret Grave. *The String Quartets of Joseph Haydn* (Oxford: Oxford University Press, 2008).

Green, Elizabeth. *Orchestral Bowings and Routines* (Ann Arbor: Edwards Letter Shop, c.1949).

Griffiths, Paul. *The String Quartet: A History* (London: Thames & Hudson, 1985).

Hefling, Stephen E. *Nineteenth-Century Chamber Music* (New York: Routledge, 2004).

Kjelland, James. *Orchestral Bowing: Style and Function* (Van Nuys, CA: Alfred, 2004).

Lawson, Colin. *The Cambridge Companion to the Orchestra* (Cambridge: Cambridge University Press, 2003).

Peyser, Joan. *Orchestra: Origins and Transformations* (New York: Watson-Guptil, 1986).

Radice, Mark A. *Chamber Music: An Essential History* (Ann Arbor: University of Michigan Press, 2012).

Stowell, Robin, ed. *The Cambridge Companion to the String Quartet* (Cambridge: Cambridge University Press, 2003).

Repertoire

Beisswenger, Drew. *North American Fiddle Music: A Research and Information Guide* (New York: Routledge, 2011).

Berger, Melvin. *Guide to Chamber Music* (Mineola: Dover, 1985).

——. *Guide to Sonatas: Music for One or Two Instruments* (New York: Doubleday, 1991).

Boyd, Malcolm. *Bach: The Brandenburg Concertos* (Cambridge: Cambridge University Press, 1993).

Brahms, Johannes. *Concerto for Violin Op. 77: A Facsimile of the Holograph Score* (Washington: Library of Congress/Harvard University Press, 1979).

Carrington, Jerome. *Trills in the Bach Cello Suites: A Handbook for Performers* (Norman: University of Oklahoma Press, 2009).

Eiche, Jon F., ed. *The Bach Chaconne for Solo Violin: A Collection of Views* (Urbana: American String Teachers Association, 1985).

Everett, Paul. *Vivaldi: The Four Seasons and Other Concertos, op. 8* (Cambridge: Cambridge University Press, 1996).

Feves, Michael, and Henk Laamboij. *A Cellist's Companion: A Comprehensive Catalogue of Cello Literature* (Lulu.com, 2007).

Grave, Floyd, and Margaret Grave. *The String Quartets of Joseph Haydn* (Oxford: Oxford University Press, 2008).

Hill, Ralph. *The Concerto* (Baltimore: Penguin Books, 1952).

Irving, John. *Mozart: The 'Haydn' Quartets* (Cambridge: Cambridge University Press, 1998).

Johnson, Rose-Marie. *Violin Music by Women Composers: A Bio-bibliographical Guide* (New York: Greenwood Press, 1989).

Keef, Simon P., ed. *The Cambridge Companion to the Concerto* (Cambridge: Cambridge University Press, 2005).

Ledbetter, David. *Unaccompanied Bach: Performing the Solo Works* (New Haven: Yale University Press, 2009).

Lester, Joel. *Bach's Works for Solo Violin: Style, Structure, Performance* (Oxford: Oxford University Press, 1999).

Lindeman, Stephan D. *The Concerto: A Research and Information Guide* (New York: Routledge, 2006).

Little, Meredith, and Natalie Jenne. *Dance and the Music of J. S. Bach* (Bloomington: Indiana University Press, 2001).

Lockwood, Lewis, and Mark Kroll, eds. *The Beethoven Violin Sonatas: History, Criticism, Performance* (Urbana: University of Illinois Press, 2004).

Lockwood, Lewis, Joel Smirnoff, Ronald Copes, Samuel Rhodes, and Joel Krosnick. *Inside Beethoven's Quartets: History, Performance, Interpretation* (Cambridge: Harvard University Press, 2008).

Loft, Abraham. *Violin and Keyboard: The Duo Repertoire* (New York: Grossman Publishers, 1973).

Markevitch, Dimitry. *The Solo Cello: A Bibliography of the Unaccompanied Violoncello Literature* (Berkley: Fallen Leaf Press, 1989).

Maurice, Donald. *Bartok's Viola Concerto: The Remarkable Story of His Swansong* (Oxford: Oxford University Press, 2004).

Musgrave, Michael, and Bernard D. Sherman. *Performing Brahms: Early Evidence of Performance Style* (Cambridge: Cambridge University Press, 2003).

Nardolillo, Jo. *The Canon of Violin Literature: A Performer's Resource* (Lanham: Scarecrow Press, 2012).

Neumann, Frederick. *Ornamentation in Baroque and Post-Baroque Music, with Special Emphasis on J.S. Bach* (Princeton: Princeton University Press, 1983).

Pople, Anthony. *Berg: Violin Concerto* (Cambridge: Cambridge University Press, 1991).

Roeder, Michael Thomas. *A History of the Concerto* (Portland: Amadeus Press, 1994).

Rostal, Max. *Beethoven: The Sonatas for Piano and Violin* (London: Toccata Press, 1985).

Salmenhaara, Erkki. *Jean Sibelius: Violin Concerto* (Wilhelmshaven: Heinrichshofen-Bücher, 1996).

Schmidt-Beste, Thomas. *The Sonata* (Cambridge: Cambridge University Press, 2011).

Schröder, Jaap. *Bach's Solo Violin Works: A Performer's Guide* (New Haven: Yale University Press, 2007).

Siblin, Eric. *The Cello Suites: J. S. Bach, Pablo Casals, and the Search for a Baroque Masterpiece* (New York: Atlantic Monthly Press, 2009).

Smaczny, Jan. *Dvorák: Cello Concerto* (Cambridge: Cambridge University Press, 1999).

Stegemann, Michael. *Camille Saint-Saëns and the French Solo Concerto from 1850 to 1920* (Portland: Amadeus Press, 1991).

Steinberg, Michael. *The Concerto: a Listener's Guide* (Oxford: Oxford University Press, 1998).

Stowell, Robin. *Beethoven: Violin Concerto* (Cambridge: Cambridge University Press, 1998).

Sutcliffe, W. Dean. *Haydn: String Quartets op. 50* (Cambridge: Cambridge University Press, 1992).

Szigeti, Jospeh. *The Ten Beethoven Sonatas* (Bloomington: American String Teachers Association, 1965).

White, Chappell. *From Vivaldi to Viotti: A History of the Early Classical Violin Concerto* (London: Gordon and Breach, 1992).

Winold, Allen. *Bach's Cello Suites: Analyses and Explorations* (Bloomington: Indiana University Press, 2007).

Winter, Robert. *The Beethoven Quartet Companion* (Berkeley: University of California Press, 1995).

Ysaÿe, Antoine. *Historical Account of the Six Sonatas for Unaccompanied Violin op. 27 of Eugène Ysaÿe:And Chronological Summary of the Major Events in the Master's Life and Career Followed by a Catalogue of His Compositions and a Discography* (Brussels: Editions Ysaÿe, 1968).

Instruments, Luthiers, and Maintenance

Apel, William. *Italian Violin Music of the Seventeenth Century* (Bloomington: Indiana University Press, 1990).

Doring, Earnest N. *The Guadagnini Family of Violin Makers* (Mineola: Dover, 2012).

Faber, Toby. *Stradivari's Genius: Five Violins, One Cello, and Three Centuries of Enduring Perfection* (New York: Random House, 2006).

Hill, W. Henry, Arthur F. Hill, and Alfred E. Hill. *Antonio Stradivari: His Life and Work (1644-1737)* (Mineola: Dover, 1963).

Hill, W. Henry. *The Violin-Makers of the Guarneri Family (1626-1762)* (Mineola: Dover, 1989).

McKean, James N. *Commonsense Instrument Care: How to Look After Your Violin, Viola or Cello, and Bow* (San Anselmo: String Letter Publishing, 1988).

Traeger, Chuck. *Setup and Repair of the Double Bass for Optimum Sound: A Manual for Players, Makers, and Repairers* (Aumsville, OR: H. Strobel, 2004).

———. *Coda to the Setup & Repair of the Double Bass for Optimum Sound* (Aumsville, OR: H. Strobel, 2009).

Westberg, Megan. *Your Dream Instrument: An Insider's Guide to Buying Violins, Violas, Cellos, Basses & Bows* (San Anselmo, CA: String Letter Publishing, 2008).

Periodicals

American String Teacher Journal
Fiddle On Magazine
Fiddler Magazine
Journal of the American Viola Society
Strings Magazine
Teen Strings
The Strad
Violin Society of America Journal

Websites

The American Viola Society
    www.americanviolasociety.org
Bass Musician
    www.bassmusicianmagazine.com
Bowed Electricity
    www.bowedelectricity.com
CelloBello
    www.cellobello.com
Fiddle Hangout
    www.fiddlehangout.com
Grove Music Online
    www.oxfordmusiconline.com
IMSLP/Petrucci Music Library
    imslp.org
Internet Cello Society
    www.cello.org
Mimi Zweig String Pedagogy
    www.stringpedagoy.com
Online Journal of Bass Research
    www.ojbr.com
String Visions
    stringvisions.ovationpress.com
Strings Magazine Online
    www.allthingsstrings.com
Violin Masterclass
    www.violinmasterclass.com
Violinist.com
    www.violinist.com

About the Author and the Illustrator

Author, violinist, and violist **Jo Nardolillo** performs as a concerto soloist, recitalist, concertmaster, chamber musician, and orchestra member throughout the United States and in Europe. As a champion of music by living American composers, she has commissioned, recorded, and given the world premieres of many new works. She has been heard around the country on radio and television broadcasts, and she has performed with many of the world's leading musicians.

Nardolillo's performance highlights include the world premiere of Thomas Pasatieri's Viola Concerto, which was written for Nardolillo, the Berg Violin Concerto with the St. Petersburg State Symphony in Russia; recital tours of the United States, Ireland, and Russia; and live radio and television broadcast concerts in New York, Kentucky, and the Pacific Northwest. Nardolillo is the founding member of the innovative new-music ensemble TangleTown Trio and the gypsy jazz band Touché.

Dr. Nardolillo has also served as concertmaster of Seattle's 5th Avenue Theatre, the Metropolitan Symphony Orchestra, and the Skagit Opera; acting associate concertmaster and principal second violin of the New Hampshire Music Festival Orchestra, associate concertmaster of the Maryland Symphony and the Fort Collins Symphony; principal second violin of the Boulder Philharmonic; visiting concertmaster of the Bangor and Waterloo Symphonies; and assistant principal second of the Annapolis Symphony. She has also been a member of the Alabama Symphony, the Youngstown Symphony, and the Tuscaloosa Symphony, and she has performed with the New World Symphony and served as principal second at the National Orchestral Institute. She has done session work recording movie and video-game soundtracks for Seattle Music and Skywalker Ranch.

Dr. Nardolillo earned a bachelor's degree in music from the Cleveland Institute of Music, a master's degree in music from Rice University, and a Doctorate of Musical Arts degree from the Eastman School of Music where she was awarded a certificate in pedagogy from the Institute for Music Leadership and was Mikhail Kopelman's teaching assistant. Nardolillo has taught at the Eastman School of Music, where she received the prestigious TA Award for excellence in teaching, as well as Rice University, the Cleveland Institute of Music, the University of Rochester, Asbury University, the University of Puget Sound, the Hochstein School of Music, the Levine School of Music, and the Gadsden Center for the Arts. She served as assistant professor of music at Mercer University, where she was named outstanding faculty of the year for 2007-2008.

Nardolillo's first book, *The Canon of Violin Literature*, was published in 2011 by Scarecrow Press as part of its Music Finders Series.

When she performs, Dr. Nardolillo plays a 1791 Johannes Cuypers violin, a 1991 John Newton viola, and a 2009 Brad Higgins fiddle.

Illustrator **T. M. Larsen** is a professional double bass player active in the Pacific Northwest. As an orchestra musician, he has performed with the Seattle Symphony, the Seattle Opera, the Pacific Northwest Ballet, the Seattle Baroque Orchestra, the Northwest Chamber Orchestra, and the Northwest Sinfonietta, where he serves as principal bass. As a jazz bassist, Mr. Larsen has been a member of the Jim Baker Band and the Northwest Sinfonietta Jazz Quintet.

Mr. Larsen has created illustrations for Orchestra2001 (Philadelphia), International Opus, Labyrinth Books, the Northwest Sinfonietta, Liberty Winds, the Spoleto Music Festival, the American Composer's Forum, and the Philadelphia Ballet Orchestra.